"In this volume, Moneim A. Fadali, M.D., has taken a complex and difficult issue, and rendered it comprehensible. He examines animal experimentation, not only from an ethical standpoint, but also from an eminently practical view of the problems it has caused for both doctors and patients. More than that, Dr. Fadali has shown us what to do about it, including how research can be conducted in much better ways without animals."

Neal D. Barnard, M.D., President,
Physicians Committee for Responsible Medicine
Washington, D.C.

"The reality of damage to humans is stressed and documented in the first four chapters, but it pervades the whole book. Fadali is a man of immense culture, and that not only medical. However, don't be put off! He also has an immense capacity to make himself understood, to adapt himself to the knowledge level of the average reader. This is the endowment of a true and mature culture and a further act and proof of love. Fadali ends with this exhortation: 'Stop vivisection. NOW. Persevere upright!'—and with an assertion which resonates with promise: 'The task is not impossible.'"

Pietro Croce, M.D., Pathologist
Professor Emeritus, Pathology, University of
Milano, Italy
Member of American College of Pathologists
Hon. President, Doctors in Britain Against
Animal Experiments

"In appreciation and admiration of those who have the knowledge to fight, the wisdom to learn, and the courage to change."

Bill & Giselle Abernathy
Attorneys at Law
Toluca Lake, California

"Moneim Fadali's book, entitled **Animal Experimentation: A Harvest of Shame** *is a rare work in the sense that it represents a serious challenge to orthodox medicine by one of its most distinguished and highly qualified disciples. Moneim Fadali painstakingly demonstrates that animal experimentation not only hurts animals, but it hurts people as well, because 'conclusions drawn from animal research, when applied to human disease, are likely to delay progress, mislead and do harm to the patient.' Hopefully, this book will pave the way for other, equally outspoken, medical specialists to contribute works in their field of expertise."*

Andre Menache B.Sc. (Hons), B.V.Sc., MRCVS.
President, Doctors and Lawyers for Responsible
Medicine, United Kingdom

"This book is an important contribution to the growing English language stock of medical science criticism. Doctor Fadali has drawn on deep insights and long experience from his training and practice as a specialist and consultant in thoracic and cardio-vascular surgery to produce a text that is passionate, informative and original as well as highly readable. Thoughtful people who have not before considered this issue will find their intellectual curiosity completely satisfied. Those already committed to modernization of medical science through abandonment of animal experimentation will find here a fresh new approach and wealth of new historical information."

Dr. Peter Mansfield, M.D., M.B.,
B. Chir., F.P. Cert., Cert. G.A.M.
Past President
Doctors in Britain Against Animal Experiments

"It takes a surgeon/scientist of Doctor Fadali's stature, clarity and courage to de-bunk the dogma of the 'indispensability of animal research.' In this remarkable book, he illuminates the dark dungeons of animal experimentation with the bright lights of reason and compassion. I commend Doctor Fadali and highly recommend his **Animal Experimentation: A Harvest of Shame.***"*

Michael Klaper, M.D.
Physician, Author
Vegan Nutrition: Pure and Simple

"Doctor Fadali's **Animal Experimentation:**
A Harvest of Shame *is a significant and important
contribution to the growing weight of published
evidence which reveals the sham of vivisection. It is
long past time that we closed the book on vivisection and turned our minds and our research talents
to the tasks of halting the apparently relentless increase in illness and of promoting good health. If we
don't, the outlook for our children and grandchildren
is not good. I found the book most readable,
stimulating and refreshing. It has the added
weight of its author being an experienced surgeon."*

> Dr. Eddie Moore, O. St. J., M.D., Ch. B.,
> M.F. Hom., M.F., G.M.
> Consultant in Public Health
> Dundee, Great Britain
> Founder Vice-President
> Doctors in Britain Against Animal Experiments

*"In rhythmic, almost Shakespearian, prose, surgeon
Moneim Fadali walks us through 2,000 years of
medical history to show that sacrificing animals
at the altar of medical science has done nothing to
advance, and much to retard, the growth of modern
medical procedures and knowledge. He interweaves
his own experience of medicine—including vivi-
section-facilitated surgical disasters—in a way that
is at once personal and highly credible. This book
deserves the widest possible readership."*

> Brandon P. Reines, D.V.M., President
> The Center for Health Science Policy
> Washington, D.C.

OTHER BOOKS BY DR. FADALI

1. *COPING AND BEYOND*

On ending sorrow Dr. Fadali has written this formidable book. A partial listing of its contents tells what it is all about:

RIGHT SEEING; EACH MAKES HIS OWN WORLD; THOUGHT AND FEELING: Are They Incompatible?; DESIRE, LUST, AND THE BLUES!; THE EGO: Is It for Real?; SORROW AND THE END OF SORROW; INNOCENCE AND KNOWLEDGE: Can We Have Both?; THE MEADOWS ARE CALLING; THE ETHICS AND ARTISTRY OF WALKING; OUR SURVIVAL AND OUR INTERNAL ENVIRONMENT; CONTROLLING OUR WANDERING THOUGHTS; BIOENERGY; EVEN THOUGH YOU TIE A HUNDRED KNOTS: The String Remains One; ART AND LIBERATION; THE KEYNOTE OF NATURE; ENDING THE FEAR OF AGING AND DEATH; INFLUENCE OF ATTITUDE, INTERNAL ENVIRONMENT, NUTRITION AND EXERCISE ON THE AGING PROCESS; COPING WITH STRESS, HANDICAPS AND DISEASE.

According to Dr. Fadali, "We all have the ingredients to make it." *Coping and Beyond* proffers the key to the bountiful, renewable treasury each and every one have. Rearrange yourself. Find the missing parts. *Coping and Beyond*: Indispensable.

2. *LOVE, PASSION & SOLITUDE*

A master weaver, Dr. Fadali's poetry adorns the underdog, canoes the drifter, wayfares the wanderer, assuages ache and rekindles momentum. Doves, sea gulls, crows, lions, coyotes, snails, spiders, mountains bearing witness, caverns in contemplation, talking rocks, pebbles pressed into the soil, dust suspended beneath the clouds, elusive neutrinos dancing and flashing, children laughing, the haunting rhapsody of the desesparados, leap and poise bequeathed on the sincere dancer, the chapter of flowers and a covenant recused, re-edified, rivers praying for rain, oceans subject to time and tide, a labyrinth deciphering the voice of silence.

On the page and between the lines you encounter the high and the low, the loathsome and the awesome, cappers and dappers, the famed and the shamed, newsmongers and warmongers.

When asked, "Why do you keep making the verse?" Dr. Fadali replied, "I am only answering the lark."

ANIMAL EXPERIMENTATION
A HARVEST OF SHAME

ANIMAL EXPERIMENTATION
A HARVEST OF SHAME

Moneim A. Fadali, M.D.,
M.Ch., F.A.C.S., F.R.C.S. (C), F.A.C.C., F.A.C.C.P.
Diplomate of the American Board of Thoracic Surgery
Diplomate of the American Board of Surgery
Fellow of the Royal College of Surgeons, Canada in
Thoracic and Cardiovascular Surgery
Fellow of the American College of Surgeons
Fellow of the American College of Cardiology
Fellow of the American College of Chest Physicians
Member, California Medical Association
Member, Los Angeles County Medical Association
Commissioner, Medical State Board of California

Hidden Springs Press
Los Angeles, California

For information, write:

Hidden Springs Press
P.O. Box 29613
Los Angeles, CA 90029

Or call: (213) 664-0007
    FAX: (213) 664-6782

If this book is unavailable from your local bookseller, it may be obtained directly from the publisher.
Call toll-free 1-800-848-5505 (orders only).

ISBN 1-885113-55-2

Printed in the United States of America

TO CARMEN

AND

To Lisa who understood Carmen's wish,
a survival wish to which I had to concede.

Contents

is human experimentation because the first leads
to the second; therefore, the first and second are
one and the same.

Chapter Four:
The argument that clinical research involving
humans is unethical and inaccurate is misleading.
It has the veneer of morality, yet ignorant and
naive. Animal experimentation is merely a
prelude covering up and legitimizing human
experimentation.

Chapter Five:
The claim that we owe most of our advances and
breakthroughs in medicine to vivisection is false.
Held sacrosanct by many, the fictitious notion
should be laid to rest. Discarded.

Chapter Six:
Alternatives to animal experimentation are many,
versatile, available, ethical, reliable, and scientific,
not pseudoscientific like vivisection is. Vivisection
has no reason to be.

Chapter Seven:
Learning surgical technique by practicing on live
animals is a sham, unnecessary, imprudent and
cruel. It has never produced a great surgeon.
There are decent means to acquire surgical
skill and dexterity.

Acknowledgments

Special thanks to Bill and Giselle Abernathy, my legal advisors, for their legal advice and counsel in bringing this book to where it is now. And, to Arthur Vergara, Poet and Editor, DeVorss and Company, Publishers, Marina del Rey, California, who helped set form and format and effect tone, tenor and inflection. Last, but not least, to my fellow creatures, all creations, all species, animal and plant, who share ambience and abode. They made me realize the essence of my humanity and see clearly what it is all about.

The indispensables: Air, Water and Soil together with the splendid assembly of the inanimate nurtured the double helix: Love and Compassion.

Foreword

by

Neal D. Barnard, M.D.
President,
Physicians Committee for Responsible Medicine

In this volume, Moneim A. Fadali, M.D., has taken a complex and difficult issue, and rendered it comprehensible. He examines animal experimentation, not only from an ethical standpoint, but also from an eminently practical view of the problems it has caused for both doctors and patients. More than that, Dr. Fadali has shown us what to do about it, including how research can be conducted in much better ways without animals.

Scientists have long known of serious problems with animal experimentation. In the early 1960s, as the risks of smoking were debated, animals were forced to inhale tobacco smoke, often with contraptions that were as crude as they were cruel. But the animals consistently refused to get lung cancer. In the *New England Journal of Medicine*, Dr. Clarence Little went to bat for the tobacco industry. He wrote, "... the lungs of animals have been exposed for long periods to whole tobacco smoke—which is the accused material —without the production of any malignant tumors. There have been many experiments here and abroad, and none have been able to produce carcinoma of the lungs in animals." The anti-tobacco forces argued that when tobacco tar is concentrated and painted on animals' skin, animals did get cancer, but others countered that this hardly mirrored how tobacco is used by smokers.

Policy-makers were left scratching their heads. If animals did not get cancer after inhaling smoke, perhaps smoking was not so dangerous after all. Maybe there was no justification for putting warnings on cigarette packs. One doctor wrote in a prominent journal that smokers who do not have a chronic cough probably run very little risk.

The truth was revealed by ignoring the animal tests and turning instead to studies of human populations. There was no question about it—smokers had a much higher lung cancer risk.

Likewise for heart disease. Studies of human populations have clearly shown that heart attacks occur more commonly in people with high cholesterol levels, high blood pressure, or sedentary lifestyle, or who smoke. Those findings allowed researchers to go one step further. They designed safe human experiments to lower the cholesterol levels in individuals and see whether their heart disease risk dropped. Indeed, that is exactly what happened.

Of course, there have been researchers who have felt compelled to feed butter to monkeys and conduct other animal experiments, but it is impossible to argue that such studies were essential to medical progress, even in the most generous assessment. If anything, they wasted time and money that could have been much better spent. In his surgical practice, Dr. Fadali has had to treat the heart and vascular diseases that would be much less common if researchers and the public had embraced the findings of human population studies much earlier and taken more far-reaching steps to prevent heart disease.

An editorial in the journal *Stroke* lamented the wastefulness of animal experiments. Rodent experiments led to 25 new drug treatments for stroke. But when these drugs were tested in humans, all 25 proved to be failures. The time, money, and research attention that went to such experiments were wasted. Instead, the editorial suggested more study of human stroke patients using modern brain imaging techniques. In the early 1970s, we did not have computerized tomography, positron emission tomography, or magnetic resonance imaging. We have them now, and they tell us much more about the brain than crude animal experiments ever could.

Even more telling are statistics on drug tests. The U.S. General Accounting Office found that of the 198 new drugs that entered the market between 1976 and 1985, more than half (52%, to be exact) were more dangerous than the premarket tests had predicted, so much so that they had to be relabeled with new warnings or, in some cases, pulled off the market. These drugs had all been animal-tested. But animal tests simply do not make drugs safe for people.

Dr. Fadali seeks to return compassion to the research enterprise. Doing so demands eliminating experiments on animals, who are not able to consent or even to resist for very long the manipulations, surgical procedures, and ultimate fatality that awaits them. When science is ethical, it will also be more effective because we will have turned away from surrogate subjects and will concentrate our efforts on the study of human tissues and human beings, using safe, state-of-the-art methods.

Foreword

by

Michael Giannelli, Ph.D.
Executive Director,
The Ark Trust Inc.

The central thesis of Dr. Moneim Fadali's new book is well contained in its title: *Animal Experimentation: A Harvest of Shame*. He forcefully contends that the living legacy of vivisection is an ignominious trail of misdirected science, misguided medicine, ethics gone astray and, of course, enormous suffering to both humans and nonhumans alike. These are profoundly serious charges which might not be taken seriously were it not that Moneim Fadali carries extremely impressive credentials as a practicing cardiovascular and thoracic surgeon. For that reason alone, this book cannot be ignored by those truly seeking knowledge of this bitterly controversial subject and who are unafraid to re-examine their cherished basic assumptions.

But Moneim Fadali is much more than a highly trained and very successful physician. He is equally a scholar, a poet/philosopher and an activist. His scholarship is manifest in the comprehensive research and detailed examination which this book provides into the history of medicine. Again and again, he presents credible evidence that the greatest advances in medical science owe little if anything to the animal laboratory. Indeed, he provided innumerable illustrations where vivisection has delayed medical progress for people because results from the animal lab were misleading, inconclusive, or duplicative of information already known. As poet/philosopher, he frequently punctuates his treatise with striking images and insightful metaphors, personally challenges the reader to stir the sleeping moral conscience inside, and often envelops his prose in an aura of deep emotion. As activist, he does not shy away from confrontation; indeed on virtually every page he throws down the gauntlet of challenge to those who would defend the status quo. Some might fault him for intermixing measured chains of logic with periodic bursts of indignation and even condemnation. But agree with him or not, no one will ever be in doubt about his perspective nor the reasons for it.

For obvious reasons, the primary focus of the book is the use—and misuse—of animals sacrificed in the name of science. In addition to critiquing the empirical record of the field in terms of practical benefits to medicine and human health, the author endeavors to disclose other major flaws in the professional practice of vivisection which collectively result in so much suffering to animals: legal and regulatory omissions; professional privilege; psychological and political motivations; etc. He does not wince from citing many documented examples of grossly inhumane testing and experimentation. For those presently convinced that only "humane" research is allowed, these sections will be a disturbing revelation. Equally valuable is his summary exposition of the practical alternatives to animal vivisections, from clinical research to the latest developments in computer modeling.

One of the most interesting and ultimately valuable aspects of this book is that it also seeks to put the animal experimentation debate into a more meaningful and much broader context. In this sense, vivisection per se is seen as a microcosm of the worst in human nature: arrogance, aggressiveness and selfishness. The author's premise is that vivisection is a major example, but only one example, of animal exploitation which is pervasive, cross-cultural, and traditionally entrenched. Other examples are all too readily found in the worlds of sport, of fashion, of entertainment, and most dramatically of all, in the world of food. The latter subject merits special notice, not only because the number of animals sacrificed for human consumption dwarfs that in any other area, but also because as a physician deeply concerned with the welfare of his fellow humans, Moneim Fadali takes pains to show how the eating of animal flesh contributes mightily—not only to the colossal toll of animal suffering—but also leads to untold damage to the consumers of flesh themselves, resulting in preventable sickness and death on a grand scale. The depth of his sincerity and commitment in this regard is never more clear than in these passages, sprinkled through the book. He writes as a man of medicine, but also as a long-standing vegan, that is, one who neither eats nor wears nor consumes any animal products whatsoever.

On a personal note, I have known Moneim Fadali for many years. There are many words which come to mind when I think of him, but perhaps the most important is *wise*. By this I mean something much more than someone with the gift of intellect, the fruits of education or the mastery of knowledge. All of these attributes are present in him in generous measure, but wisdom in my sense of the word requires much more. Outstanding among these necessary requirements are moral character, enlightened compassion, and impressive courage. Moneim Fadali meets this test. His willingness, indeed compulsion, to stand up for what he believes in and to expose himself to attack from his peers and political adversaries are the marks of a true visionary. He is a teacher in the grandest meaning of the term. I commend him for writing this book, and I highly recommend it to all, but especially to those just becoming dimly aware that humanity's relationship with nonhumans betrays an ethical blind spot of monumental proportions. *Animal Experimentation: A Harvest of Shame* will open your eyes to vital information you may have missed, or perhaps have avoided for long enough. Even more importantly, this book will provide you with a healthy and inspiring alternative vision of what that relationship—and the planet we share with other animals— could be like in a truly humane and civilized world.

Foreword

by

Pietro Croce, M.D.
Professor Emeritus, Pathology, University of Milano, Italy
Member of the American College of Pathologists
Member of the American Society of Clinical Pathologists
Hon. President, Doctors in Britain Against Animal Experiments

"Love is ink for this book." In which page? you ask. I could easily answer you with cold, impersonal numbers. I prefer not to. This ink flows through the entire book; it meanders through every page, every single phrase, through even the most technical and scientific information. Love, passionate love for Nature, animals, mankind. So, don't please ask me on which page you will meet "love is ink. . . ."

And you—what solutions can you suggest? This question is prompted by a world which is living, surviving rather, in a jungle of uncertainties, of never answered or eluded questions. Fadali suggests not just one but two decisive answers. First, he tells us what we should not do; second, he suggests what, in order to be rational, we should do.

1. Not offend nor exploit Nature and the creatures nursed in her bosom.
2. Live in a way which "does good to the body, the mind and the whole lot"; refrain from eating animals and

their products (eggs, dairy produce) and follow Vegan principles. "Trust me," he says. "I am one—a Vegan."

One of the gravest offenses against Nature is vivisection, which is worse than death because to the destruction of the individual (animal or man), it adds mistreatment, anguish and wanton cruelty.

Vivisection is tackled from the side most congenial to a surgeon, and the most efficacious, since it encompasses all people who are capable of thinking and of possessing a sound sense of responsibility. Vivisection condemns animals and humans to the same hell. The reality of damage to humans is stressed and documented in the first four chapters, but it pervades the whole book. Even the most cynical, the most indifferent, egocentric, anthropocentric must ponder the assertion: "Vivisection is a state of mind, violent, egocentric, evasive." The adjectives "violent, egocentric, evasive" compare viviseciton to war. Isn't that the truth?

Fadali has an amazing talent for representing his thoughts cinematically. Here is a touching, delicate picture of a vivisectionist at home: "An 8×10 glossy photograph of a researcher petting a pretty dog with one hand and affectionately holding a child with the other." But then the tender picture is complemented (please, turn over!) by a biting, unexpected, bitter irony: "Soon the dog will be snuffed out, and that won't help the child." Again, animal and human are associated in the same anguish. Reader, don't bother to leave your easy-chair; your cinema is here!

A widely-spread commonplace asserts that a sense of humor is a hallmark of the British. But you, Dr. Fadali, as far as I know are not British, so where does your pungent sense of humor spring from?

Here is your description of how vivisectors put their self-protection into practice: "Vivisectionists, with no leg to stand on, duck down or fly all over you; and when the facts throw them flat on their backs, they roll over and play dead, waiting for the rising tide of murky waters to lift them up.'' Don't tell me that this is not ''British'' humor!

It is certainly also wrong to do as the vivisectors do and treat euphemistically—wrapping them up in velvet and painting them in happy colors—alarming and scientifically proved realities such as ionizing radiation and toxic chemicals which are known carcinogens.

''I don't eat anything with a face'' denotes the inability to endure the piercing gaze of a living victim. Mark Twain said: ''Man is the only animal capable of blushing. . . . but he is the only one who has plenty of reason to do so'' and implicitly introduces a most embarrassing question: why should we drop our eyes before the accusing gaze of a chimpanzee or a dog but not in front of a frog, for instance—a less expressive creature but not, for that, less capable of suffering and worthy of compassion?

Animal experimentation leads inevitably to human experimentation. This further and unequivocal pillar of our struggle against vivisection is repeatedly stressed, starting from Chapter One, which states that, ''Animal experimentation is harmful to human beings.'' This means also that *Animal Experimentation: A Harvest of Shame* was not conceived solely or even mainly to protect animals. On the contrary, the author is fully aware that it would be pointless to convince those who already have proper feelings towards animals or who least respect them; but all the efforts of the antivivisection movement should be focused on those who are not blessed with such noble sentiment, and on the followers of Darwinian and Cartesian philosophy who need a timely jolt to awake them from their centuries-long sleep.

Fadali builds his antivivisectionist pyramid on a base which rests on this statement: vivisection has never nor in any way played a part in the technological progress of medicine, which owes its most impressive developments to other methods:

1. In diagnosis, to the discovery of X-rays, computerized axial tomography, magnetic resonance, the discovery of radium, the invention of the optic and electronic-microscope, cardiac catheterization, artificial kidney and pacemakers. (Incidentally, not all the above medical breakthroughs are of a strictly medical nature, a proportion being due to engineering and physics).

2. More pertinent to medical activity are many breakthroughs in therapeutics: for tuberculosis, the discovery of streptomycin and for heart diseases, the discovery and utilization of digitalis, nitrates—and plenty of others that you will meet in the course of reading this book. For all these technical breakthroughs, Fadali gives an appropriate and technically qualified description, synthesized and within everyone's grasp.

But what about the positive contribution of animal experimentation? Not only is it nothing at all—no benefit whatsoever for mankind—but even less than negative, having led researchers astray from their proper scientific path and, moreover, very close to losing forever boons such as penicillin. And who knows how many other conquests, beneficial to man and animal we have lost? We don't know, we shall never know. What doesn't exist, or has gone, lost forever doesn't make history.

Fadali is a man of an immense culture, and that not only medical. However, don't be put off! He also has an immense capacity to make himself understood, to adapt himself to the knowledge level of the average reader. This is the endowment of a true and mature culture, and a further act and proof of love. Fadali ends with an exortation: "Stop Vivisection. NOW. Persevere upright!"—and with an assertion which resonates with promise: "The task is not impossible."

"I abhor vivisection. It should at least be curbed. Better it should be abolished. I know of no achievement through vivisection, no scientific discovery that could not have been obtained without such barbarism and cruelty. The whole thing is evil."

—Dr. Charles Mayo, one of the founders of the world renowned Mayo Clinic, one of America's most skilled and highly respected surgeons. A surgeon's surgeon.

Preface

Here's how it all began. One day, my eyes met Carmen's eyes. Looking into Lisa's eyes, I instantly read what she had just read in Carmen's eyes. There and then I knew I was destined to write this book. You speak of choice! Ha! On this one I had no conscious choice. Within the vast realm of one's subconscious, I believe choices, inklings, preferences and dispositions do exist, sooner or later to surface at the conscious level. The stimulus frequently is a conscious perception such as the one I have just mentioned. Nothing is totally spontaneous. When the conscious and subconscious are in harmony, freely communicating, spontaneity comes on uninvited, as it were. Matter of fact, the division between conscious and subconscious (unconscious) is artificial. In essence, in reality, the two are one; our analytical methods and fragmentary thought processes slice and partition. An immense data base lies beneath the surface, its circuits and interconnections are active, very active, quietly, or so it seems. Actually, when one sees things as they really are, there is no choice then. Pen in hand I began with, "To Carmen and to Lisa" and ended with, "Persevere upright. The task is not impossible."

Let the chips fall where they may. Let the pundits, scientists and pseudo-scientists condemn or commend, refute or salute, approve or disapprove, ignore or regard. Truth cannot be hidden any longer. For this would be a betrayal of my friends, human and fellow non-humans. Truth is never in hiding; it is right here, it is there, everywhere, amidst us. Truth is within, without, and beyond, all the time, every moment, but often we decide to look the other way, or in our habitual apathy or blind conformity, we fail to see and recognize its manifestations. Truth cannot be pursued. In pursuing truth, we alter it, denature it and fit it to our mental schemes, preconceived notions and built-in biases. On its own truth comes to the free, and by truth the mind is freed. Mutually interdependent, inseparable, truth and freedom are one, but we are shackled by our own prejudice, pride, fear, ambition, greed and, most importantly, brain conditioning. Our brain conditioning is the primary culprit, a deeply implanted mechanism that instantly molds and distorts what our unbiased senses receive—most notoriously, what we see or hear—falsifying reality. Yet we go on our ways believing it's all real. It isn't. The conditioned mind is a cage; its bars are unseen by most, thus incarcerated they remain. The skyline of the open mind stretches to infinity, but by matter of habit we accept what is handed to us as factual, correct, unquestionable, unchallengeable. Gullible, aren't we? Psychologically lazy, yet restless, silly at times, dazed most of the time; naive in one way, devious in many other ways. Excuse me! What is it then? Where is our sobriety? And, along rough roads and circuitous paths we continue to travel, embracing violence, war, cruelty and injustice not only to our fellow humans but also to animals, plants, earth and environment. Justifying and rationalizing as we go along, and one can only justify what is unjust and rationalize the irrational. Humans' long, bloody path is paved with justification and rationalization. And there isn't a crime or atrocity the human mind cannot justify or rationalize. And all will smell like roses. Luster and veneer. Innocence lost, all goes awry. And unless we see this clearly, very clearly, sorrow—personal and universal—will not end.

Vivisection* is one of those evils grafted on the human mind by the false prophets of science and reason. While some agile minds have rejected the ominous graft, others have accepted it as an article of faith, not to be questioned, let alone carefully looked at or seriously examined. And the verdict had been, is, and always will be: in harming others —human and non-human, sentient and nonsentient, knowingly and unknowingly—we harm ourselves. All while being misled, all while longing for peace, harmony, longevity, security and bounty. Longing won't do it for us. Hope procrastinates, cowardice defeats, blind obedience corrupts; figures of authority must be questioned and held accountable; and, the burden of responsibility is individual, nontransferable. Payday isn't light years away. It is here, today. Payday is now! Just look, even a cursory glance will do; see our unexplained boredom, chronic fatigue, recurring anxiety, self-imposed loneliness, debilitating stress, continuing conflict, easily-provoked anger, bloody violence, unending wars and perpetual fears. Penalties. All penalties. Look, just look. Count, account. You are always paying for what you do and for what you don't do, for what you commit and for what you omit. Omission is commission.

Fully aware of the cruelty and evil of vivisection, witnessing the calamities it has inflicted on humans and animals alike, I vowed to do my share in cleaning up the mess and washing the slate. A journey I must take. And I am not asking you to believe or disbelieve; all I am saying is see for yourself and consider. Find out. But to find out, one must harness and muster the energy needed. The awesome energy spent on diversions, wasted on trivia and drained by

---

*Practically speaking, "vivisection" and "animal experimentation" are synonymous. Claude Bernard, the prince of vivisectors, founder of experimental physiology, coined this term which implies all sorts of animal experiments, whether they involve cutting or not.

conflict—inner and outer—must be saved and put to better use. It is precious, very precious, available if not squandered. Don't let it drain. Don't let it drain.

Here is the book's agenda broken into ten chapters to be brought in as we meet on its pages.

Chapter One: Animal experimentation is harmful to human beings. Let me repeat this one: Animal experimentation is harmful to human beings.

Chapter Two: Animal models differ from their human counterparts. Conclusions drawn from animal research when applied to human disease delay progress, mislead and do harm to the patient.

Chapter Three: Animal experimentation inevitably leads to human experimentation. This one too I must repeat: Animal experimentation inevitably leads to human experimentation.

Chapter Four: The argument that clinical research involving human subjects is unethical and inaccurate is misleading. On the surface it has the cloak of morality and concern, at its depth, ignorance and naivety. Animal experimentation is a cover-up hiding and legitimatizing human experimentation. Animal experimentation does not prevent human experimentation. A de facto license to kill and bruise humans without being accused, questioned, arrested or punished, merely serving as a precursor, a prelude to the human misadventure. Vivisectors may try it on animals a thousand and one times, but the moment they move on to the human condition they will be experimenting on humans. See Chapter 3.

Chapter Five: The claim that we owe most of our advances and breakthroughs in medicine to vivisection is false. Even whatever little, minuscule benefit came out of the infamous chamber of horrors (the animal laboratory) it could have been obtained by other means, better means. I wholeheartedly concur with Dr. Charles Mayo's statement, ''I know of no achievement through vivisection, no scientific discovery, that could not have been obtained without such barbarism and cruelty.''

Chapter Six: Alternatives to animal experimentation are many, versatile, available, better, more reliable, and scientific, not pseudoscientific like vivisection is. Animal experimentation is not only wasteful and unnecessary but also unjust to humans and animals alike.

Chapter Seven: Learning surgical technique by practicing on live animals is a sham, unnecessary, imprudent and cruel. It has never produced a great surgeon.

Chapter Eight: Animal experimentaiton is inherently cruel and unscientific, useless and harmful to us as well; therefore, continuing it is senseless, heartless, mindless. Unforgivable. It must be outlawed. Banned. The infamous chamber of horrors (the animal laboratory) must be vacated, dismantled, never to be rebuilt or ever permitted to reopen and reoperate again. What the vivisectionists call "necessary evil" is evil, period. Unnecessary. Evil is not necessary— evil leads to evil. The notion that some good may come out of evil is immoral, shallow and cruel; justifiable to some, but not just. And ends cannot—should not—justify the means. Means must justify themselves, otherwise the rising tide in humanity's vast lake of sorrow will never ebb.

Chapter Nine: Animals have rights, the most basic being their right to life. They all long to live, and all, including the lemmings, are incapable of suicide. In the land of compassion there is no superior, there is no inferior and, unless we respect and sanctify life in its TOTALITY, we are doomed. Homo sapiens, live up to your name; sapiens means wise, and tell me please, where and when did you lose your sapiency? Was it on the way to the forum where your innocence was deflowered? Homo sapiens, wouldn't you rather be a shepherd than the executioner you are? You have killed your brothers and sisters. You have organized and perfected mass slaughters and rationalized single, multiple and mass murders. Recover your original face, opt for life and rise. All we are saying: Give compassion a chance.

Chapter Ten: Survival of the fittest not the strongest. Let's take charge of ourselves, stay healthy, live better and longer. Fitness is survival's magic tool. Mere strength frequently dooms.

My motion is to adopt the above 10 chapters. Let us now open the discussion, sift fact from fable, weigh the evidence. I'll present my case to you, basically, an eyewitness account of a cardiovascular and thoracic surgeon who has been practicing for over 20 years, still in active practice and has journeyed through the infamous chamber of horror experiencing its hell and enduring its profanity. I hope you will second my motion, for in adopting the above resolutions we shall redress grievances, make amends, heal and reconcile.

"Hell begins," said Gian-Carlo Menotti, "on the day when God grants us a clear vision of all that we might have achieved, of all the gifts which we have wasted, of all that we might have done which we did not do . . ." For me, the concept of hell lies in two words: "Too late!"

ALL WE ARE SAYING:
GIVE COMPASSION A CHANCE.

CHAPTER ONE

Animal Experimentation Is Harmful to Human Beings

Animal experimentation is harmful to human beings. Its toll on human life and well being is awesome, yet rarely mentioned or denied and ridiculed.

Our first article is not a theory or a point of view. It is a fact. A fact so startling, so vivid, so ominous that it has to be continually denied, maliciously ridiculed, deliberately distorted and willfully hushed by animal researchers. The awesome toll vivisection exacts on human life and well being is rarely mentioned, hardly ever seriously discussed, thus barely receiving the attention it deserves. The colossal damage, the incriminating evidence is inhumed in a vast necropolis. Removed from the blessedness of the sun and the balm of the air, the felonious seeds develop into a tree. Partaking of the fruits it bears corrupts and precipitates the Fall, individual and collective. The tree is the proverbial tree of Knowledge; Knowledge that is conceived in cruelty and false premise, hence its fruits are forbidden. Among its depraved fruits are: vivisection-generated papers, books, tapes, videos, articles, products and institutions. Thorns and thistles, not remedies, not restoratives. The vivisectionists are not lonely rangers;

1

their strange bedfellows are a well-armed squad of health organizations, federal agencies, pharmaceuticals, universities, medical schools, misinformed well-meaning philanthropists and a knot of good-hearted, misguided charitable groups. In order to continue their fictitious, harmful trade, they fully realize that two fallacies must be implanted in the public mind. The intent is to transform the public from inquiring witnesses to a cheering crowd.

Fallacy Number One: Vivisection is essential to our own survival and well-being. Stopping it will bring the splendid wheel of medical progress to a grinding halt. Who dares challenge such a benevolent, noble-sounding proposition and the deadly warning that goes with it? Who has the nerve to stand in the way of progress? Only the crank, the imprudent, the suicidal, the mischievous and the moronic. Duck out, folk. See!

Fallacy Number Two: Essential and useful, how can vivisection be harmful? Sounds Aristotelian, Platonic even. The two assertions cannot serve as the basis for a good argument. A logical conclusion cannot be drawn. The crafty bunch knows full well that their protocols and rituals must not offend the sensibility or sensitivity of pet owners, and the millions who fancy themselves as animal lovers. So they recite a ceremony of platitudes, polemics and deceptions while courting the credulous to the path of the believers, trusting that the doomed, abused animals have the best of all worlds, martyrs, not victims; hence, no sense of guilt, and no feeling of shame. Here goes one of their familiar refrains: The animals in our facility are not in harm's way, they do not suffer, they do not protest or complain, they are well-treated, like one's own pets, pampered and cuddled. Housed in expensive cages. Well! Well! Hold it right there; since when has the four-letter word ''cage'' become a metaphor for house or home? And what qualifies vivisectors to speak of animal suffering? Did they ever feel it? Did they ever contemplate, reflect or seriously look at animal misery? Bet you not, for if they did, they would have forsaken the bad habit. They claim the animals in their custody are well-fed, yet the menu is often an experimental diet carefully sorted out of a so-called scientific manual. Animals are anesthetized if the experimental protocol permits. What if it doesn't? Let me tell you: that won't stop a painful experiment. And why anesthetize in the first place? The experiment is wasteful and reprehensible. But, those fellows are pretty determined. Their head is set, "torture nature's secrets from her," executing the will of Francis Bacon, the willful, hallowed father of the empirical method of science. Make no mistake: in animal laboratories worldwide, animals are handed diseases they never had before, designated surgical operations and given medications they never cared for, never needed, bled some, transfused a bit and infused at will, cut, bruised, scratched, starved, and you know what? They are put to death when the executioner deems it is high time to harvest what he or she has been seeking to fetch the prize. Death and mutilation proffers the dowry and the requital. Animal sacrifices at the capricious notion of wrathful gods of opportunity. It is said that every man or woman has his or her whims; theirs are pretty bad though.

Enough of this. I don't want to turn you off, but, come to think of it, unless we keep our eyes, ears and all senses open we won't learn or change. Every serious scientist and philosopher has found out that our intellect is the one more likely to make errors than our senses do. Manipulators and opportunists have taken stock of this fact. By eliminating visual and auditory accounts of violence—military, civil, animal, environmental, etc., etc.—the public will accept violence, won't even fully recognize its disguised countenance and eventually will grow accustomed to it. The sanitized, varnished account is taken rather than witnessing the event itself. It's easier, the gruesome won't be seen. And if it doesn't offend or hurt, it won't evoke reaction, passion or sense of guilt, and the burden of responsibility, the obligation to act is done with, and life will roll by bedecked or blemished with its routine pleasures, mundane diversions, and annoying boredom; treadmill's endless belt pointing the way, getting us nowhere. Here is an example: Many meat-eaters will relish their steak or prime rib, enjoy it as long as the steer or cow—what used to be a steer or cow—was not slaughtered, butchery being murderous, inhumane and savage. Gassing or stunning is for the cultured and civilized. The former cow or steer was gently put to sleep, humanely, just went to an everlasting slumber, dazed, not killed! Just don't mention the pernicious word: Killing. Words matter the most; they stand by themselves, on their own, doesn't matter that much what they symbolize, mean and imply. And, may be used as a cover. The veil of words. Language for a guise. And on their dinner plates, in good appetite, with joyous complacency they are served a choice portion of the sleeping beauty, manicured with butter, zesty sauce and other ingredients of the garnish. I know of many who have turned vegetarian when the real hideous scene played back in their minds, in their conscience. I am one. And the beautiful, sad eyes of farm animals haunt me no more; and no fish, bird or four-legged animal shall perish to satiate my lust for the consummate and exquisite. Affectionately they all range the latitudes of my consoled mind. "I don't eat anything with a face."*

Retracing lineage and ancestry, humans have diverged from the chimpanzee nearly seven million years ago. For most of those seven thousand millenniums we were vegetarians subsisting on gathering native and wild nuts, fruits and

---

*A quote attributed to former Beatle, Paul McCartney.

vegetables. Our teeth are perfectly shaped to grind, cut some, rip a little. We lack claws or teeth sharp enough to tear open animal skins, bite off and chew their tough raw meat. And, animals in the wild run much more switfly than we can. To catch them we had to resort to hunting or trapping. Hunting and trapping had to await the development of certain tools and devices. Homo erectus evolved 1.6 million years ago, invented an assortment of stone implements, and wandered further than the end of Africa to China, Indonesia and Southern Europe. Homo sapiens succeeded erectus; in possession of a larger brain and better tools, he kept on walking, making his way to Northern Europe and chilly Siberia, later crossing the Bering Strait to North America 30,000 to 50,000 years ago. Only recently in Syria and Egypt did man domesticate animals (8000 B.C.) and invent the wheel (3500 B.C.).

Hunting tools probably were first used 350,000 years ago by the Peking man or earlier by the Java man about 500,000 years ago. Apparently at about the same time Prometheus stole fire from the gods* and Homo erectus began using fire domestically to light the hearth, to cook, heat and burn. And, humans' sumptuous banqueting on other animals began. Jollified, the feasted senses started to numb.

Surprisingly, despite seven million years of estrangement, the genes of humans and chimpanzee differ by a mere 1.5 percent. Humans' gastrointestinal tract and metabolic pathways have not yet learned how to cope with much of the stuff we eat and drink: the beef, the pork, lamb, calf, fowl, fish and their products. Their failure is manifested as ''diseases of civilization'' such as heart attacks, strokes, cancer, diabetes, arthritis and obesity. All are substantially preventable by abstaining from eating meat, eggs and dairy products.

---

*Myth had it.

Technology and biology immensely differ. Our brain, musculoskeletal system and senses can quickly learn and master new technology, be it the chariot, a car, aeroplane, telegraph, photography, telephone, computers, and the many, many weapons of limited and mass destruction. When it comes to biology, the wheel of biologic adaptation turns slowly, very slowly. We are running ahead of the wheel, way ahead. Beyond doubt, we are not ready for our contemporary culinary feast. It is absurd! Our organs and metabolic pathways have not made the necessary adjustment. And, the wages of our blundering are hefty.

Clearly, the right diet for humans is vegetarian. Dairy products, eggs and meat-centered menus do not make any sense. Our bill of fare is hurtful and mischievous.

Recently, war has been transformed into a video game and the pilots who push the buttons don't get to see the myriads of people they blow away. Imagine if they did! And the couch-bound public watches edited, embellished versions rhapsodized with music, sanctified by flags, graced with ocean waves, trees, prayers, church bells and . . . oops! Here comes a harmless, cute looking, target-seeking missile hitting an inhabited made-empty-looking building or softly, humanely, piercing through a demonized version of a humanoid; the truth-seeking, peace-loving missile must surgically excise, eliminate. And excise, it does; you may multiply this by many thousands if you are, wish or dare to be realistic, but you only get to see one, a neat, nifty one. No sweat, no angst, no offense to millions of viewers watching the evening news or the after dinner Pentagon specials. No wonder, in a recent survey, most children questioned did not associate the 1991 Gulf War with death, contrary to their perception of others wars.* Closing our eyes, turning a deaf ear, disconnecting our senses threatens our human-

---

*A Purdue University study quoted in *Newsweek*, December 9, 1991, p. 6.

ity. And they know it. So the vivisection establishment shows us its own version, cleansed, softened to mellow, brushed and polished to ornate. An 8×10 glossy photograph of a researcher petting a pretty dog with one hand and affectionately holding a child with the other. Soon the dog will be snuffed out and this won't help the child. I say, if we love our children—I mean really love them—end vivisection and never send them to wars to kill and be killed. And remember, wars do not spare animals, they can't hide; in thousands, in millions they perish, starve, unattended, their injured agonize till the last breath, till the last beat of their innocent, gentle hearts.

To end violence to humans and animals alike—vivisection being a form of bona fide violence—we must look violence in the eye. In looking at violence with full attention, with complete awareness, we will not be desensitized or grow numb to the bloody, the grievous and the tragic, but we will bring it to an end for it is absolutely horrible, intolerable, utterly insane. Looking at violence apathetically, lightly, in cold emperial detachment, without thoroughly understanding it or fully grasping the horror and experiencing the pain of what we are looking at or wandering away behind the blinding veil of the mundane, we are likely to get seduced, drawn in, and desensitized. By running away from violence, it won't go away. Not seeing it, not hearing it, not feeling it will not end it. It'll continue, it'll come back, sooner or later to engulf the attached and the detached. Looking with complete attention and full awareness, with one's whole lot is the key to ending violence.

Good intentions, peace conferences, listening to speeches, fabrications and lies will not bring peace or harmony. Never did. And, humans and animals alike will continue to suffer and lose. To end sorrow we must understand sorrow. Hiding from it, explaining it away, or rationalizing and justifying it will only perpetuate it. The crucial step is not to remain on the receiving end, half asleep, half awake while watching one tragedy after another unfold and explode. See, hear, touch, smell, taste, think for yourself. Don't let them feed your senses their own sweetened blend, garnished recipes, fragrant soaps, patriotic slogans, evil thoughts and cruel gimmicks. Friends, we didn't stray. It's all part of the tragic, the subject matter; and unless we talk about it and communicate it to one another, vivisection will continue to thrive. Vivisection is a state of mind: violent, egocentric, evasive. We must get to its roots, a twig here or there won't do it. Those abhoring violence, really abhoring it and are truly serious about it, cannot, will not vivisect, cannot, will not support wars, will not fight wars. Humans, animals, plants, and environment are war's cannon fodder. The stains of Adam's sins are not the faint smudges on the moon visible to the naked eye as had been thought in the middle ages. They are here on earth, right here, in, on and around. A vivisector's rite of passage is to kill animals. Our rite of passage is to stop it. Here are some facts to affirm and confirm the above:

While three animals die every single second in animal laboratories across the United States (the annual toll being approximately 60 million animals), it is estimated that one in every three Americans can expect to contract cancer in their lifetimes. Cancer, a disease which—according to our National Cancer Institute—is 80% preventable. Death from breast cancer in American women is steadily rising and the death rate from all cancers per 100,000 has climbed from 163 in 1970 to 206 in the 1990s; birth defects have quadrupled over the last four decades and the Grim Reaper still claims 800,000 American lives every year from heart disease and stroke. Vivisection, what did it do? Why didn't it help? Why isn't it helping? I am afraid it hindered. The toll has been rising. Focusing on the wrong thing, paying little attention and allocating minimal resources to prevention, designing invalid experimental models, wrong conclusions are drawn. The caravan has strayed and

*everyone pays the awfully dreadful price, and I am not even talk-
ing billions of wasted dollars, I am mourning the dead, recalling
wasted lives, advocating for the bruised, pleading for sanity.
Celebrating life.*

HOW DID VIVISECTION HARM OUR HEARTS AND BLOOD VESSELS AND WHY ISN'T IT HELPING TO STEM THE MENACING KILLER TIDE OF HEART AND BLOOD VESSEL DISEASE?

First and foremost, never lose sight of the grim fact that
heart attacks kill approximately 600,000 Americans every
year; yet, in individuals with a blood cholesterol of less than
150 milligrams, heart attacks are extremely rare. This has
been confirmed time and again, especially by the Framingham study, which encompassed thousands of individuals
followed for many years. This meaningful U.S. study is still
active, reaffirming the significant role of high blood cholesterol in causing heart attacks. None of the human participants were lanced, cut open, kicked, injected, bruised,
starved, incarcerated, sacrificed or even slapped on the
wrist. A serious study, ethical and not unkind. Low fat diet,
moderate exercise, nonsmoking, stress reduction, detecting
and lowering high blood pressure are key preventive measures. And let me pass on to you a formidable fact: meat-
eaters have ten times the incidence of heart attacks when
compared to vegetarians. Amazing, yet rarely acknowledged, quickly forgotten. Please don't let go of it, take it to
heart, to mind, for if you do, your heart will last longer and
your mind will have less to worry about. The enterprise is
open to everyone, make your own steps; this stretch must
be walked by you. One more thing: clinical observations
have conclusively shown that meat-eaters and sweets- and
fat-addicts are not happier, are not more energetic or more

successful than vegetarians and discrete eaters. Matter of fact, the latter—vegetarians in particular—have fewer burdens to bear, ache less, nurture fewer cancers, live longer and are less frequently hospitalized. And let me state here that those who do not eat beef, pork, veal or lamb, but eat chicken and or fish are not vegetarians. Talking to people, I am amazed how many with a straight face and resolute frame tell me: "Oh, fish is not meat, chicken is not either!" and the majority of them are well educated! To this heresy I promptly retort in an equally straight countenance and equally resolute manner that fish and fowl are not plants, and, of the known living creatures, what is not plant is animal. It is worth plugging here that the best way for vegetarianism is the Vegan, that is, not consuming animals or animal products such as eggs and dairy products. The healthiest of all, the most compassionate way for sustenance, it does good to the body, the mind and the whole lot. Trust me, I know it; I am one.

In clear conscience and scientific truth, I hereby unequivocably state that heart and blood vessel diseases—essentially arteriosclerosis or atherosclerosis commonly known as hardening or blockage of the arteries supplying blood to the heart and other organs of the body—are largely preventable and to some measure reversible by relatively simple measures totally within our reach and under our control. Animal research won't prevent the largely preventable, partially reversible, widely prevalent, wildly lethal malady. And, for its unfortunate victims the medical and surgical treatment available is not the product of animal research, be it bypass surgery, angioplasty (dilation of narrowed blood vessels), thrombolytic therapy (dissolving blood clots) and transplantation among other modalities as we will find out in another chapter. The real challenge is one of Right Seeing: In our modern times, more than ever, image has replaced the real thing, incomplete information is taken as complete, information is confused with knowledge and half truth (half lies) well-stated sound true, look genuine. Unfortunately, we generally believe the message if the messenger is believable, and it has never been hard for most to look believable. And many believable ones—vivisectionists, politicians, leaders to mention a few—are not telling it like it is, knowingly and unknowingly. In a certain sense, some of them are victims, misled, brainwashed. Brainwashed means blindfolded.

Let us move on to Galen, considered the founder of experimental physiology; with him I have a gripe. Time to air it. This Galen had a bad, repugnant hobby, a nasty obsession, that of dissecting live animals, especially pigs and monkeys, occasionally goats and other innocent, harmless beings. I don't know what grudge he had against these beautiful creatures that never claimed to tell about man. Was it all misunderstanding on his part? It all happened way back during the second century A.C. Long gone, I have no way to interrogate the man. Death being a mandatory statute of limitation, but unanswered, weighty questions never die. In this case let his own actions and their results testify on his behalf. Unfortunately, several centuries elapsed before many of Galen's conclusions were proven wrong. Dead wrong.

Galen extrapolated his vivisection findings—from monkey, pig and goat—to humans and concluded that blood flows from the right side of our heart to the left side through an opening in the wall that separates them. False. Normally, there is no such hole; the septum (intervening wall) in the human heart is intact. Blood must journey to our lungs to be aerated (oxygenated) first before returning to the left side of the heart which then pumps it to every station: brain, liver, limb, bowels, everywhere, not missing tongue or heart. And thank God for that. Blood's pilgrimage to our lungs ensured our survival. His erroneous conclusions misled the Western world for 11 centuries. Imagine that: 11

centuries wandering on the wrong road, a gift of animal research. Thanks! And for this and some other notorious animal exploitations, Galen was proclaimed founder of ex- perimental physiology—physiology being the science of finding out how our organs, tissues and vital processes work. What a way to find out! The highly-decorated phy- sician is still revered in the open forums and off limits con- claves of the scientific establishment. Incredible, isn't it? How long can disciples and successors remain genuflected, hypnotized by the master? It happens all the time. Inciden- tally, that icon, Galen, was also chief physician for the glad- iators of Pergamum (modern Bergama, Turkey). An apt part-time position for a renowed vivisector. Imagine the mil- lions who must have suffered or died as a result of treatment programs based on Galen's false assertions. From icon-level to eye-level comes down the champion. Record seriously ex- amined, many heroes fall. Galen's forays were grim, to be remembered for what they are; to be retold. And in the vast ambience of your compassionate, open mind, let enter the many animals that died for the vainglory and spiritual and mental ignorance of man.

Interestingly and amazingly, the ancient Egyptian Ebers Papyrus (1550 B.C.) included a surprisingly accurate descrip- tion of the human circulatory system, depicting the existence of blood vessels throughout the entire body and the heart functioning as the center of the blood supply. Fascinating! Look back, read the scroll, now unfolded, telling. But, will the seeker seek? And, is the seeker free or bound? The famed German Egyptologist, George Ebers discovered the document in 1872.

While on the subject of our ancestors, Imhotep of the 27th Century B.C. in Memphis, Egypt, the first physician in the history of humankind, builder of the Sakkara or step pyr- amid, the oldest monument of hewn stone known to the world, realized the significance of the human pulse, and cautioned that wounds of the heart are not necessarily fatal for they can be mended using a muscle graft, a surgical technique the West came to employ only as late as the latter part of the 19th century. Physicians of ancient Egypt recommended treatment of arterial aneurysms (ballooning of the arteries), a serious condition causing rupture of blood vessels, leading to death. Quoting the Ebers Papyrus (1550 B.C.), ''Then thou shalt say: This is a vessel swelling; a disorder I will treat.'' Those physicians of ancient Egypt were not vivisectionists, yet they made great contributions and medical and surgical breakthroughs. In the Odyssey, Homer said, ''In Egypt the men are more skilled in medicine than any of humankind.'' Imhotep, the mortal, was elevated to a full deity and was regarded as the god of medicine in Egypt and in Greece. While Imhotep was a mortal human like you and me, Asclepius, the ancient Greek god of medicine and healing, son of Apollo, had no terrestrial existence.

The celebrated Muslim scholar ar-Razi wrote in the 10th century an in-depth treatise on the venous system, accurately describing the function of the veins and their valves. In 1240 A.C., Ibn Al Nafis discovered the vital human pulmonary circulation. He was director of the Nasiri Hospital in Cairo, Egypt and his dissections were performed on cadavers obtained from the cemeteries of Cairo and Damascus, Syria. He found that blood circulates from the right side of the heart to the lungs, where it is aerated (oxygenated) before returning to the left side of the heart. Andrew Cournand gave Ibn Al Nafis credit in the book ''Circulation of Blood—Man and Ideas,'' published in 1964. Cournand shared the Nobel Prize in Physiology–Medicine with Richards and Forssmann for their work on heart diseases in 1956.

Without violating or harming a live animal or human, Ibn Al Nafis discovered a fundamental anatomical and physiological fact about the workings of our heart and blood circulation, while Galen brought falsehood. The difference being: Galen was a vivisectionist, Ibn Al Nafis was not. Galen is still remembered, Ibn Al Nafis largely forgotten. How about a Nobel for Ibn Al Nafis? Too late I'm afraid. Galen, step down from your pedestal? Roll over, will you? Under your spell we have been mesmerized for too long.

William Harvey (1578–1657) completed Ibn Al Nafis' work on the heart and circulation of blood. His findings stemmed from his observations of live human beings including himself, and on cadaver dissections. But true to the tradition of their master, the sons and grandsons of Galen credited Harvey's work to animal experimentation. Typical behavior, misbehavior. Harvey himself was slack on the matter. He was too famous, too comfortably seated, too busy to correct the score. And the mantra for many continued to be, "Why think when you can experiment?" attributed to John Hunter, an 18th century celebrity, a part-time vivisectionist as well. Hunter's licentious admonition spills the beans, exposing what vivisectionists do best: experimenting and experimenting with little provident thinking in between loathsome, detestable experiments. And, rather than repent and amend, they thumb their noses at us. Is it arrogance? Is it self-preservation? Ignorance?

In search of a surgical solution to arteriosclerotic heart disease, Beck of Ohio, U.S., and Vineberg of Quebec, Canada, took their ideas to the animal laboratory, a convenience facility annexed to almost every university. Each devised more than one procedure, envisioning success based on their animal data. Not long after, their recommended operations were performed on many thousands of patients worldwide. What were the results? To say the least, unworthy. To put it bluntly, a fiasco, a total failure. And many patients were harmed, yet neither Beck nor Vineberg were vilified by the medical hierarchy, and helpful surgical procedures and breakthrough medications did not originate in the animal laboratory. I am a witness to many of these events and the least I can do is speak out. And here I am reiterating in capital letters: ANIMAL EXPERIMENTATION INEVITABLY LEADS TO HUMAN EXPERIMENTATION. This is the verdict, yet despite the harsh sentence, the grim toll continues to mount on both sides; humans hurt and die, animals tormented and sacrificed; killed is the right word though. Can't we see? We will elaborate more on this shocking, utterly dismaying observation in other parts of the book, and will discuss how heart valve surgery and organ transplantation were hindered, and unscientifically pursued in the animal laboratory, inevitably inflicting human harm that could have been largely avoided.

Atromid (clofibrate): a medication that was widely used to lower blood cholesterol, caused deaths from cancer, pancreatitis and gall bladder disease in humans. The so-called "wonder drug" was tested and retested on animals, and based on that it was released by the Food and Drug Administration (F.D.A.) for human prescription. Ironically, to my knowledge, no study to date has conclusively shown reductions in fatal heart attacks among Atromid users.

Eraldin (practolol): a heart medicine; patients who received it suffered diarrhea, eye problems, including blindness, and there were many deaths.* Ultimately the manufacturer withdrew it from the market and compensated more than 1,000 victims. Again, it is animal experiments which permitted passing a highly noxious drug on to patients.

Quoting from Newsweek: August 7, 1989, "Last week a University of Pennsylvania researcher reported chilling

---

*Venning, G.R., *British Medical Journal*, January 15, 1983, pp. 199–202; January 22, 1983, pp. 289–292.

results: two prescription drugs for heart arhythmias, approved in 1987 after regular trials, may have killed as many as 2,000 people."

The spectrum of vivisection is bleak. The above is merely a sample of loss and damage that have been extensive. Rich possibilities for more tragedy unless we correct the incorrect and right the wrong. Our habitual euphoria with vivisection must end; our complacency and dupery must stop. We are harming ourselves, others as well.

VIVISECTION:
WHY DIDN'T IT HELP TO PREVENT CANCER?
WHY DID IT FAIL TO FIND A CURE FOR CANCER?
AND WHY IS IT DOING HARM?

Cancer is dreaded by all. It runs a close second to heart attacks as a cause of death in the U.S. When it comes to the role of animal experimentation in cancer, vivisectionists present a creative blend of the spurious, the fantastic and the ludicrous. A frenzied litany, monotonous, ambiguous, deceitful. Despite all the vivisectionists' hullabaloo, the fact of the matter is: vivisection is cancer's Bermuda Triangle in which our realistic hopes, faithful expectations and confidence in our research institutions have mysteriously disappeared.

Here are the three sides of the treacherous triangle:

THE FIRST HARM

Focusing on the trivial, the substantial automatically goes out of focus; dangling rosy expectations, the public overlooks the handy and the usable. Freakish promises of miraculous cures and phenomenal early detection devices waiting at the end of a short tunnel. Thus, available, effective preventive measures shy away, shifting to the backseat, though according to our National Cancer Institute, approximately 80 percent of all cancers are preventable. Wow! Music to my ears. And, I am going to tell the good news to everyone I know or meet. You too should. Smoking, excess dietary fat, environmental pollutants, low fiber in the diet predispose our bodies to cancer. Fortunately, all of them are avoidable. A little bit of effort, not a little bit of luck is needed except for environmental pollutants where several mega- and global corporations have acted irresponsibly and continue to contaminate our air, water and soil. In dealing with omnipotent entities, Congress and government have been timorous and accommodating. This is unfortunate.

Smoking alone accounts for approximately 30 percent of all cancer cases. Tobacco's favorite cancer is reserved for the lungs. The unholy smoke causes the majority of lung cancers, and the more and the longer you smoke, the higher is your chance of contracting the deadly disease. And, it doesn't make a bit of difference whether you are a male or female. Nicotine is not sexist. Our tax dollars subsidize tobacco growers so they can profitably grow more cancerous lungs and harvest many more destroyed lungs. A harvest of shame. Tobacco kills more than 300,000 Americans annually from cancer and emphysema. And if you add its grim contribution to heart and blood vessel problems, the appalling body count could exceed 500,000. Undoubtedly, tobacco is the number one single cause of preventable death in the country. On the tobacco victims' disability and medical care billions of dollars are spent.

Recently, lawsuits have been filed against tobacco companies by several states seeking to recover health care costs related to smoking and a giant class-action suit was brought by about 60 law firms on behalf of all American smokers who said they were addicted. There are charges of fraud alleging that the tobacco industry has manipulated and concealed scientific data on the addictive nature of nicotine. Five grand juries are looking into possible perjury and malfeasance by industry executives. Make no mistake, a cigarette is nothing but a drug-delivery device hooking and consuming the ones who light and inhale. Thanks to the hardihood and mettle of whistle-blowers such as Victor DeNoble, former researcher for Phillip Morris, the largest tobacco company; and Jeffrey Wignad, a former Vice-President of Brown & Williamson, the highest-ranking tobacco executive ever to blow the whistle. And, an antitrust investigation is being conducted by the Justice Department into an alleged conspiracy to stifle development of a fire-safe cigarette. It is estimated that the tobacco industry sells $250 billion worth of its product worldwide every year. A formidable business with dreadful global reach. (Much of the information in this paragraph has been drawn from newsmedia during the month of March, 1996, in particular, the *Los Angeles Times*, the *Daily News*, *Time* Magazine, and *The Nation*.

In Jacksonville, Florida, Friday, August 9, 1996 rolled in, hot, slow and humid; then came a throb and a rapid beat. A jury of five men and one woman spoke: Brown & Williamson, the country's third largest tobacco company was found liable for negligence and for making an unreasonably dangerous product. The magnificent six awarded a lung cancer victim $750,000 in damages ($500,000 for plaintiff, Grady Carter, and $250,000 for his wife). Truth or dare, truth and dare; a verdict of great consequence dealt the powerful maker of a cancer-producing, heart-attack-inviting, stroke-promoting gadget its first real loss in more than four decades of cigarette litigation, if the verdict stands on appeal. A long delayed punitive strike for the manufacturer of Lucky Strike.

With the well-documented fact that nicotine is addictive, any competent attorney can bring similar cases and prevail. The sizzling disclosures in industry documents suggesting that top executives had concluded by the early 1960s, that nicotine was addictive, which they publicly deny to this day, added insult to injury and brought dishonor and disrepute. ''We are then in the business of selling nicotine, an addictive drug,'' stated former Brown & Williamson general counsel Addison Yeaman in a 1963 memo.

Following the verdict, Wall Street had the jitters. Phillip Morris, the world's largest tobacco company called the outcome, ''certainly disappointing,'' while its stock plunged, knocking a hefty $11.25 billion off the value of its shares. RJR Nabisco Holdings Corp. plummeted, and shares of other tobacco companies dipped or nose-dived. On August 23, 1996, our faint-hearted government approved some timid regulations to curb tobacco advertising and limit teen-agers access to cigarette purchasing.

The tobacco-induced catastrophe isn't a natural one. It isn't hurricane Andrew or a Loma Prieta earthquake or an overwhelming Mississippi River flood. It isn't God sent. It is artificial, iatrogenic, human-made, home-grown. Avoidable. Still we are unable to get our government or elected officials to end tobacco subsidy and put our dollars to better use. They have grown accustomed to bad spending; this one is pretty awful. Unforgivable. Their personal perks, favorite toys and dough-givers receive first attention. Their set of priorities differs from ours, yet we have elected them; on thee we have bequeathed the power to effect, sway and control. I feel betrayed, a predicament many experience and endure. We couldn't even get R.J. Reynolds, the mega-tobacco company, to retire their knotty, witty camel, Uncle Joe. For many years the talking camel did ambush the minds of many young ones. Uncle Joe didn't cause cancer though. It is innocent, it doesn't smoke, it doesn't lie, and its diabolical call to death is the sound of man.

Our newsmedia, ever pretending to hold public interest at heart, avidly and shamelessly advertise the lethal stuff.

Co-conspirators, sports promoters and tycoons have joined the bad company. Major sports events are held under the flirtatious, approving gaze of sexy, magnetic role models with bombastic themes like "We'd rather light than fight," and "You've come a long way, baby" polluting the air and seducing many longing for self-esteem, personal growth, empowerment or glamor. Our "bottom line" has been going up and up. I see it has risen to a plane higher than our moral plane shading the eye of the mind.

Incidentally, the cause and effect relationship between smoking and cancer was not discovered in the animal laboratory. Readers, beware, whenever vivisectionists claim credit for something good, doubt it, research it; you may call the Physicians Committee for Responsible Medicine (tel: 800-US LIVES or 202-686-2210, P.O. Box 6322, Washington, D.C. 20015).

Fat and other dietary factors: are estimated to account for from 35 to 50 percent of all cancers, fat being the principal culprit. Meat and dairy products consumers have 10 times the risk of contracting cancer of the colon when compared to pure vegetarians. For men who eat meat and dairy products, prostate cancer is 3.6 times higher than in pure vegetarian men. The same goes for breast cancer in women—only the figure is higher, 5 times.

The American diet typically draws 40 percent of its calories from fat, while in Japan and China only about 15 percent of their diet's calories come from fat. Japanese and Chinese women suffer substantially less breast cancer than American women. The natural hormone estrogen fuels many different cancers. Here is the reason: a rich fat diet increases estrogen production, a fertilizer of sorts, stimulating cancer cells to grow, multiply and flourish. According to the World Health Organization, the average age of puberty in Western countries in 1840 averaged 17 years. Today girls reach puberty at 11, 12 or 13. Early puberty appears to result from increased estrogen secretion caused by high fat diets. Estrogen increases the risk of breast cancer. Way back only the rich could afford fat, rich meals, but nowadays the entire population is getting high on fat, growing fat, getting heavy, slower as well.

Another danger of high fat diets: they facilitate absorption of carcinogens into the body. Carcinogens cause cancer. They also weaken our immune system. German researchers found that vegetarians have more than twice the natural killer cell activity of nonvegetarians. Natural killer cells are specialized white blood cells that survey, intercept and destroy cancer cells.

A word about a new fad: non-fat dairy products such as milk, yogurt, cottage cheese and ice cream aren't all that benign. Caution! Lactose is milk sugar; our body breaks it down to galactose, another sugar, and galactose is broken down further by specific enzymes. When dairy products intake exceeds the enzymes' capacity to process galactose, it builds up in the bloodstream with a noted increase in the risk of ovarian cancer in women. This is what Dr. D.W. Cramer found through studying hundreds of women with ovarian cancer, comparing their diets in detail with a group of women who were similar in age and demographic variables. The women with cancer had eaten dairy products—especially yogurt—much more frequently than women without cancer. *This and other helpful information included in this chapter aren't outcomes of animal research.* Human studies, solid, clean, ethical, do not harm anyone. The information they generate is credible and promotes the human condition. What more can I say? I guess truth must dazzle those unaccustomed to its perpetual, natural light; they can't look straight anymore, so they shift and the eye of the mind goes blank.

Mammography: plays a role in the early detection of breast cancer in older women, but it does not prevent a single cancer. It does not reduce the incidence of breast cancer. True, self-examination and a mammography do pick up smaller cancers. Smart, but much smarter is to avoid the cancer altogether in a large number of those who would get it otherwise. And it isn't all that hard to do.

In addition to a low fat diet, high fiber diets (whole grains, legumes, brown rice, vegetables and bran) and avoiding alcohol, lower the chances of developing breast cancer.

You see the vivisectionists, their cronies, mentors, benefactors and beneficiaries, link cancer diagnosis and treatment to mammography, chemotherapy, surgery, radiotherapy and research on animals; and this is what the people hear and perceive when the alarm bell rings. If their trickery works, our mind will keep lumping them together. Prevention, which is highly effective, is conveniently dropped out in favor of medical or surgical handouts. Prevention requires some effort and a measure of discipline, but you know how most of us go about it, procrastination and inertia winning. A conscious, conscientious discipline once understood for what it is and established goes on smoothly and efficiently, "just like that." Effortlessly flows the river and on a butterfly's wings the disciplined dancer soars. The disciplined!

"We'll lose the fight if those cranks, the anti-vivisectionist zealots get their way" goes their familiar battle cry. Hysterical. Deceitful! Can't they see? Their declared war on cancer has already been lost, their soldiers of fortune have been mistaken, fighting the wrong battles, their weapons misfire, the innocent get hurt. Dear reader, whoever you are, wherever you happen to be at this very moment, contemplate, seriously reflect in the quiet solitude of your own mind. War on cancer, war on heart disease, war on birth defects, war on drugs, war on crime, war on poverty, war on violence, war on war, and, they haven't won any. Always war declarations by vivisectionists and by others, every one of their pet projects is wrapped in a flag and sanctified by the flammable unruly passion of combat. A standard rap. By invoking war scenarios, they charge our adrenalin pump and trigger the primitive parts of our brain to spew and fire, but, in the tempest's rising dust, our vision dims. Hammered and overwhelmed, our individual perception, inquiring mind and free spirit grow numb and rusty from disuse. And the herd does what it is supposed to do: follow. Trapped. Is there an exit?

Revive the withering parts lest they atrophy and die. The tombstones of the young are filling the land, many could have lived better and longer. Premature death has never been a good proposition, and, the purpose of life is to live it, not to strangle it. The quirkiness and distortion of the vivisectors and their allies we must dispel.

Not all foods are steak, hamburger, fish and chicken: whole grain, legumes, beans, lentils and tofu (soybean) are pretty good stuff. Pastry, ice cream and pies, sweet as they may be, are harmful. Fruits, sweet and juicy, are not forbidden and generally good for you. And remember, all the drinks on your table are not martinis, wine and sodas; still, there is something wholesome about water. And next time you invite a friend or a business associate for a drink, forget not that alcohol is not a drink, it is a drug, powerful, toxic. And smoking must be banned in public places. Passive smokers (those in the vicinity of smokers but who are not smoking) inhale one-third or so of the stink. Smokers have no right to light, exhale and harm nonsmokers. Their death wish is not ours. We want to live. And there are better things to inhale than tar fumes; fragrance of flowers for one, the aroma of freshly baked bread for another. And for the young ladies ''who came a long way,'' I'll tell a secret: several physicians —myself included—have noted that smoking, besides causing cancer and heart attacks, leads to early wrinkling of the skin and incontinence of urine in a high number of women who smoke. Who needs these? Both are nemesis to beauty, and Nemesis (Adrastea) is the goddess of divine retribution! You may pass on this secret if you like, but please don't forget it. Cheers! Buddy, will you please extinguish your cigarette, pass the jug of water. Thirsty, I can use a drink!

On to something else. I am beginning to enjoy this book. I started with commitment; with joy added, my right hand will not tremble and I'll have no difficulty summoning the words, the thoughts.

THE SECOND HARM

Shamelessly, the vivisectionists state and restate: without animal experimentation we won't discover new drugs to kill cancer; give us more money, more time, more attention; silence the opposition and we will ''deliver the goodies on a silver plate.'' Untrue. Utterly False. Well, generation after generation, they have been blurting the same monologue. After all, they have no goodies to deliver, their silver plate remains empty and we'd rather go for the gold. Unfortunately, their worn-out record still plays, and their old graffiti keeps on blemishing unwashed walls, and many of us got habituated to their fictitious refrains. So what shall we do? And, where shall we go from here?

Here are some observations splendidly defying the rule: the bat is a mammal, but it flies; the ostrich is a bird, yet unable to ride the wind; the dolphin is aquatic, but it breathes air; and in Australia they have egg-laying mammals; and, we are creatures of habit, still we are capable of observing directly, thinking clearly and reasoning soundly.

On anti-cancer drugs, here is the dismal record of vivisection: Despite screening over half a million compounds as anti-cancer agents on laboratory animals between 1970–1985, only 80 compounds moved into clinical trials on humans. Of these, a mere 24 had any anti-cancer activity and only 12 appeared to have a "substantial clinical role." Actually these so-called "new" active agents were not so new: they are analogs of chemotherapeutic agents already known to work in humans.* Failure by any standard. Mediocrity to say the least. It lends credence to a saying frequently echoed in research circles, "A drug is a substance when injected in a rat will produce a scientific paper." In other words, "A scientific paper—I should say most—is produced by injecting a substance in a rat." Or, "Rats are used to produce scientific papers by injecting them with substances." Syllogisms, deductive logic of sorts. They may substitute the rat with the monkey, the dog, the guinea pig, the cat, whatever! You see, anywhere near a vivisectionist, no animal is safe. And human safety is endangered as well.

When you inquire, truly inquire and seriously talk to those engaged in real scientific research on cancer, many will admit that not a single effective anti-cancer drug has come solely as a result of animal research. The reasons are: **Animal models differ from their human counterparts. Conclusions drawn from animal research when applied to human disease are likely to delay progress, mislead and do harm to the patient**. See Chapter Two in the Introduction and detailed discussion in subsequent chapters. Thus, Chapter Three emerged; it states, **"Animal experimentation inevitably leads to human experimentation."** And bear with me, I'll quote from Chapter Four, **"The argument that clinical research involving human subjects is unethical and inac-**

---

*Ronald Allison, M.D., quoted in *Physicians Committee for Responsible Medicine*, No. 1, Vol, 8, 1992, p. 6.

curate is misleading. On the surface it has the cloak of morality and concern, at its depth, ignorance and naivety." Clinical studies are the legitimate cornerstone for understanding and treating human illness. FDA regulations mandate that a new compound must be tested on animals first before it is tried on healthy human volunteers and patients. Sounds good, but animal testing never ensured safety or effectiveness in humans, a step that is misleading and harmful. All it does is import a false sense of security, the "we care" placebo ethics. The "Preclinical" testing phase on animals is but a cover up, disguising and legitimizing human experimentation. A protective shield absolving researchers from responsibility whenever humans are harmed. You can try it on animals a thousand and one times, but the moment you move on to the human condition—a new environment—you will be still experimenting on humans. See Chapter Four in the Introduction. And Chapter Five turns out to be valid, **"The claim that we owe most of our advances and breakthroughs in medicine to vivisection is untrue."**

We have already mentioned the role of tobacco, diet, environmental pollution and alcohol in preventing cancer; furthermore, hormonal treatment for breast and prostatic cancer, some chemotherapeutic agents being used, even radiation and surgery; all are not the result of vivisection.

Even if we concede some achievement came out of animal experiments, I should add that it certainly could have been accomplished by other means without resorting to cruelty and wretched savagery. It's like calling your boss at 8 A.M., with the bad news that you cannot get to work because your cantankerous car refused to start. Well that ought not to be the end of it. There are several alternatives. Here are some: take public transportation, bus, train, or street car, call a taxi cab, ask a neighbor, a friend or a co-worker to give you a lift, rent a car or walk if feasible. More than one way. If you sincerely try, you will get to work one way or another regardless of whether your car drives or not. And if you miss that day, you better remedy the situation soon, or you will be canned. Glued to a path, we grow blinders on the right and on the left; other paths are not seen.

In another chapter, we will talk about the ethical and more credible alternatives to vivisection that have been available all the time and discuss some newer ones such as cell line cultures, clonogenicity and some responsible applications of genetic engineering.

Vivisectionists, with no leg to stand on, duck down or fly all over you, and when the facts throw them flat on their backs, they roll over and play dead, waiting for the rising tide of murky waters to lift them up. Still, I remain optimistic; good reason, good science and compassion for all will one day dawn.

THE THIRD HARM

This one is a direct one. While the first and second harms incurred by vivisection on cancer prevention and possible cure are for the most part indirect, are no less harmful, more so, perhaps. Indirect harm, many a time, injures its victims without being recognized. Years, even decades or centuries may elapse before an indirect harm is identified. Whether it will be corrected or not, it all depends! Not knowing the source, we search many places, look different directions and consider a multitude of possible causes. Not infrequently, we end up pointing an accusing finger at others, other places, other causes. Consult the archives!

Here are but some examples of the direct harm caused by vivisection in relation to cancer:

Diethylstilbestrol (DES), a synthetic estrogen to prevent abortion in humans was first tested in animals, then given the stamp of approval. What did it do thereafter? It caused vaginal cancer in daughters of mothers who received the drug; even their grandchildren were not spared, they developed genital defects.* Despite the tragic outcome, DES failed to prevent abortions; even some statistics showed that it did increase abortions, premature births and neonatal deaths.** Always ending in the same place; no happy endings there. Stripping off of the mask: a pailful of deception, cruelty and utter contempt for life and the living.

Atromid (clofibrate), a medication to lower blood cholesterol, as we mentioned earlier, caused deaths from cancer and other serious maladies.

Ionizing radiation and toxic chemicals are bona fide carcinogens, meaning cancer producing. Thanks to animal research, we have been betrayed, victims of humbug and scientific chicanery. Imagine two of the most nocuous and lethal agents life has ever encountered, wrapped in velvet and painted happy colors. Trivialized or given official approval, they may kill or harm you, your family and friends, but you won't be eligible for compensation. Tolerable, endurable, livable, so said row after row of test tubes with faces and whiskers: the animals. Rats, guinea pigs and other experimental animals don't lie, and courts and compensation boards did not hear them testify. They didn't do it to us. They themselves were done in. All while studies of human

---

*Herbst, A.L., et al, *New England Journal of Medicine*, April 22, 1971, pp. 878–881. Vanchieri, C, *Journal of the National Cancer Institute*, vol. 84, 1992, pp. 565–566.
**Dieckmann, W.J., et al, *American Journal of Obstetrics and Gynecology*, vol. 66, 1953, pp. 1061–1081. Brackbill, Y. & Berendes, H.W., *Lancet*, September 2, 1978, p. 520.

populations actually exposed to hazardous ionizing radiation and toxic chemicals in the work place or in their living environment are largely ignored. Case in point: ''at Hyde Park and many other dumpsites, including Love Canal and the West Valley nuclear dumpsite, the residents and workers have been repeatedly assured by state and federal agencies that their low-level exposures were harmless,'' wrote Dr. Irwin D. Bross, the President of Biomedical Metatechnology, Inc., in the November 1988 issue of the *Anti-Vivisection* magazine. For 20 years Dr. Bross had been Director of Biostatistics at the Roswell Park Memorial Institute for Cancer Research in New York, for 7 years acting head of Epidemiology at RPMI, and for more than a decade he had been studying ''technogenic cancer''—that is, cancer caused by the misuse or abuse of radiological or chemical technologies. Harm and kill us they do, and millions of Americans have been unnecessarily exposed to these hazards. While animal testing may occasionally shed dim light on acute toxicity of chemicals and radiation, when it comes to ''mutagenecity,'' the remote danger, animal testing is meaningless and utterly useless. Misleading. All it does is import a false sense of security. Mutagenecity means genetic damage. Genes carry genetic information and they are found in every cell nucleus; 50,000 to 100,000 of them determine a person's make-up, what have you, what not. Mutagenecity causes cancer years, many years, after repeated exposure (chronic exposure) even to minimal doses, the minuscule quanta deemed safe by government agencies and regulators.

The false sense of security is supported by the lame animal experiments (vivisection). A dreadful example of a direct harm incurred by vivisection. If this isn't, what is it then?

Even though governmental and congressional agencies might once in a blue moon get caught in truth's vast ambience, the clever, slick bunch manage to sneak out where the air is not clear. To some, truth liberates, to others, truth incarcerates. Here is an example: the Congressional Office of Technology Assessment (OTA) recently did a critique on the Environmental Protection Agency's report on "Habituality of the Love Canal Area" and the Centers for Disease Control. It found serious scientific errors in collecting, analyzing, reporting and evaluating information. In a rare instance of candor, OTA was unusually blunt in criticizing governmental procedures at dumpsites, and failure to protect public health. OTA stated, quoting from Dr. Bross' report, "Technical standards to determine unacceptable levels of contamination are, on the whole, lacking." Further, the agency added, "Epidemiology is the only method that establishes association between a substance and human toxicity." Hurray! Finally it came out of the horse's mouth, an affirmation of a time-honored scientific standard. A little bit later though, OTA reneged, regrettably stipulating, "(the testing in laboratory animals) is the backbone of current toxic substance identification." Itself lacking of backbone, the congressional agency did not dare condemn animal studies, despite their manifest utter failure. In focusing on acute toxicity rather than mutagenecity, the latter being more of a serious health hazard, animal experimentation was used to cover the more hazardous, the most lethal, the one that strikes at and plunders the building blocks of life. In the hallowed congressional chambers there appears to be a frequently used dumpsite, ocean-deep, where public interest is dumped, buried in favor of organized and well-heeled lobbies of polluting technologies. With such a "backbone" (animal testing or vivisection) highly publicized, acknowledged and sanctioned by the government and legislature, their efforts to protect our health from technogenic hazards are but a sham and a shameful deception. All while paying homage to the indispensable bond of empathy!

The horror story, the sinister plot isn't over yet. Here is

some more: When a court order mandates clean-up of a dumpsite, it considers two options, "capping" or "excavating." Excavation involves digging out the toxic chemicals and shipping them out, a pretty expensive proposition. Capping is much less costly to the polluting entity. Capping would diminish acute toxicity, but not mutagenecity. So, they hurry to animal researchers in order to do their mischievous bidding. The polluters are not scientists, are not physicians; some of their cronies are. So, to talk health and human safety, they run to the keepers of the nation's health. On to rodents to find out, and a whole array of animal models; many, very many, are assembled, and each model system brings out a different result. In practical terms, whatever you have in mind, animal research can do it for you. The medium is complacent, compliant, and under control. After all, the researcher is the one setting the agenda, designing the experiment, choosing and choreographing the model, observing, recording and interpreting the results. They have it all, go for it. A rubberband, not a wand. Scientifically proven, the model itself profoundly modifies the result of any experiment. In the book of good science, modifying and altering are one and the same. Models model our thinking, and actualize our intent. And, under the coaching of the charitable sponsor, the data are released. And, the band "plays misty for me," for all of us. Stripped of romantic connotation, misty means blurry, dim.

In obedience to authority, the laboratory mouse loses weight when exposed to those chemicals at low levels; mind you, these low levels are not lethal for the period of the experiment. They measure acute toxicity not mutagenecity. Deception, isn't it? The mouse has spoken. So, mice and men: What to do next? Hurry up, cap it, bury it, out of sight, out of mind. A dumpsite is but an enormous sponge that takes on human-made lethal substances and deadly filth, nurturing them, an offering to the seed, the harvest, the worm, the livestock and the underground water that flows about in a fascinating network man has yet to fathom. And it stays, and stays on, willed to our loved children and their loved ones after them, a bequest, a legacy by last will.

Here is something that'll make you laugh; it will hurt though. For their calculations—I should say, miscalculations—researchers have coined a mind-catching phrase, "quantitative risk assessment." Sounds terrific, but those who are in the business have a more apt phraseology, "Mickey Mouse arithmetic." Sounds like "voodoo economics" and "collateral damage"; the first is a myth, the second is real: war's massive casualties; the injured and the dead, humans and others, and others. After punching their numbers and equations—arithmetic of sorts—that bears no relation to the real endangerment of the Hyde Park residents, the Love Canal and West Valley nuclear dumpsite communities, and many other unsuspecting, unnamed communities nationwide, worldwide, what comes out of it? All are caught in the same predicament. Cheated, bruised, diminished. Killed. The infamous Love Canal in Niagara Falls isn't very far from Hyde Park (or Bloody Run) dumpsite. There is no Love there, there is no Park either, and, New York State has the dubious distinction of hosting both. No wonder the "Big Apple" is rotting. At this time a number of other states have similar problems. These dangers are real; we must never ignore or underestimate their peril. They used to be hidden, now uncovered, bare, staring us in the face. Alas! for long legitimized and domesticated through vivisection, still are. Don't you think the whole damned thing is evil? Don't you think that all reasonable men and women should condemn vivisection? Now.

EXAMPLES OF OTHER DRUGS THAT PASSED ANIMAL TESTING BUT FAILED THE HUMAN TEST

Thalidomide: a tranquilizer that was granted the safety emblem based mainly on animal experimentation; yet among pregnant women who took it in their first trimester, the drug led to the unfortunate birth of at least 10,000 babies with missing or stunted limbs, mere feet where legs should have been and flippers replaced arms.* Alternative testing available at the time in the late 1950s and early 1960s—such as human cell culture—could have averted the colossal calamity. Some pain cannot be overcome!

Oraflex (Opren): an antiarthritic drug meant to alleviate the pain and frequently crippling limitations of arthritis; was found safe in nonhuman primates, at 7 times the maximum tolerated human dose for a year. It caused death in a number fo elderly patients, mainly from liver damage,** subsequently it was withdrawn from the market in 1982. you see, even testing on nonhuman primates won't ensure the safety of human primates.

Butazolidine: a pain killer; caused kidney and red blood cell damage.

Chloramphenicol: caused bone marrow destruction and fatal aplastic anemia which is not reversible,*** though human cell culture could have found what animal testing has failed to show.

---

*Keller, S.K. & Smith, M.K., *Teratogenesis, Carcinogenesis & Mutagenesis.* Vol. 2, 1982, pp. 361–374.
**Eason, C.T., et al, *Regulatory Toxicology and Pharmacology*, Vol. 11, 1990, pp. 288–307.
***Spriet-Pourra, C. & Auriche, M., *Drug Withdrawal from Sale*, PJB Publications, 1988.

Isoprenaline aerosol: during the 1960s, thousands of young asthmatics died following the use of isoprenaline aerosol inhalers.* Animal tests did not show nor predict the dangers; matter of fact, cats could tolerate 175 times the dose found dangerous to asthmatics and the adverse complications could not be reproduced in guinea pigs, dogs and monkeys at doses much higher than the recommended dosage.**

Eraldin: a heart medication; some patients who received it suffered intestinal and eye problems; blindness and many deaths resulted (see page 15).

Clioquinol: a primary ingredient of Enterovioform and Mexaform used to treat diarrhea; caused a major epidemic in Japan where no fewer than 10,000 people contracted a new disease entity, SMON (subacute myelo-optic neuropathy). The nerve damage caused weakness in the legs, paralysis and eye problems, including blindness among other horrible things.*** The drug was tested on rats, cats, beagles and rabbits with no evidence of neurotoxicity. Japan banned the drug in 1970 and several years later it was withdrawn from the world market.

Phenformin: to treat diabetes; caused 1,000 deaths annually until withdrawn from the market.****

Amydopyrine: a pain killer; caused a nasty blood disease.****

---

*Inman, W.H. In *Monitoring for Drug Safety,* Ed. W.H. Inman, MTP Press, 1980.
**Carson, S., et al, *Pharmacologist,* vol. 18, 1971, p. 272.
****Lancet,* March 5, 1977, p. 534.
****Kupsinel, R., *Vivisection: Science or Sham,* p. 8, Publication of PRISM.

Reserpine: to treat hypertension; may cause restlessness, nightmares and depression, pancreatitis, severe anemias and kidney failure. A number of epidemiologic studies pointed to an increased risk of breast cancer in women.* It may cause fetal harm when given to pregnant women.*

Methotrexate: to treat leukemia and psoriasis; caused intestinal hemorrhage, anemia and tumors.*

Mitotane: for leukemia; caused kidney damage.*

Cyclophosphamide: used for cancer and transplants, but it led to liver and lung damage.*

Urethane: for leukemia; caused cancer of the liver, lungs and bone marrow.**

Kanamycin: an antibiotic; caused deafness and kidney damage.**

Methaqualon: a tranquilizer; caused severe mental disturbances. An exorbitant price just to stay cool.**

Maxiton: diet pills; caused damage to the heart and nervous system.**

Valium: a popular tranquilizer; can be addictive in moderate doses.*** Already we have a sackful of those. Do we still need more?

---

*Physicians' Desk Reference, 1995, published annually by Medical Economics Data, a division of Medical Economics Company Inc. Montvale, N.Y. 07645.
**Kupsinel, R., Vivisection: Science or Sham, p. 8, Publication of PRISM.
***Petursson, H & Lader, Dependence on Tranquilizers, Oxford University Press, 1984.

Accutane: for acne; in pregnant women taking the drug, even in small amounts for short periods, there is a very high risk of birth defects.* Hepatitis, inflammatory bowel disease and increased levels of blood lipids were reported with Accutane administration.*

Halcion: a hypnotic; reports of severe psychic problems with its use are surfacing which prompted Britain to ban its use. I think France followed suit; U.S. still asleep!

Tegretol: for epilepsy. Two potentially fatal blood diseases: aplastic anemia and agranulocytosis are 5–8 times more likely to occur in patients on Tegretol than in the general population. Epidemiologic findings suggest an increased incidence of birth defects when pregnant women used Tegretol.*

This isn't a complete list by any means but it serves to focus our attention on some of the very serious health problems vivisection has been inflicting on us. A shabby record, to say the least.

Quoting Dr. Robert Sharpe, "An analysis by scientists at the pharmaceutical companies Pfizer and Rhone-Poulenc revealed that at least 80 products had been withdrawn on safety grounds from one or more of three European countries (France, West Germany and United Kingdom) and the U.S. between 1961 and July, 1987. The most common adverse reactions which led to withdrawal were liver damage, blood disorders and neurological problems.** Pretty serious

---

*Physicians' Desk Reference, 1995, published annually by Medical Economics Data, a division of Medical Economics Company Inc. Montvale, N.Y. 07645.
**From Dr. Robert Sharpe Address at the General Assembly of the International Association Against Painful Experiments on Animals, Philadelphia, June 24, 1989.

stuff emanating from two pharmaceuticals highly regarded by most.

The Food and Drug Administration (FDA) still requires drug testing on live animals. In God's name why? Can any sane individual tell me? And, who is benefiting? Us? Well! You must be kidding, or your mind must have been made up and unwilling to be confused or persuaded by facts. And the poor animals did not volunteer for the ghastly enterprise. Animals are incapable of suicide. Lemmings are thought by many to plunge into the sea in a deliberate death march. The lurid tale is fiction; their migration to the sea isn't a rite of passage through the straits of martyrdom, nor a grim sacramental ritual of mass suicide. Seasonal habitat changes calling the shots.

The amazing fact remains, Homo sapiens is the only animal capable of suicide. Of course, our gruesome ability for homicide is mind boggling and frightening. Dishonoring. Many shame it out; yet, many others are proud of it; for a medal they wear it with no guilt or shame.

On Silicone Implants, a Tale of Tragedy, Arrogance and Greed: September 1, 1994, a judge in Birmingham, Alabama, granted final approval to a $4.25 billion pact between women and manufacturers of silicone breast-implants. The largest product-liability settlement in U.S. history. Some analysts claim that as much as $200 billion is required to satisfactorily compensate implant recipients. The pact involves nearly 60 companies, none of whom admitted any wrongdoing; self-conceit or legal maneuvering or both, I presume. More than 90,500 women have made claims. They reported notoriously serious damage to their breasts, other body organs and health in general. Silicone and its polymer have been animal tested in many labs, innumerable times. It's a hoax my friends; mock science. The offering: a pailful of ruin. Are we still asking for more?

For an epilogue: Gail Armstrong, a spokeswoman for the National Breast Implant Plaintiffs' Coalition, said members are watching to see if the judge follows through on promises to keep lawyers' fees and administrative costs at $1 billion. Good luck, Gail!

CHAPTER TWO

Animal Models Differ from Humans

Animal models differ from their human counterparts. Conclusions drawn from animal research when applied to human disease delay progress, mislead and do harm to the patient.

What are those differences? I am going to begin with a statement of a generic nature: For most human diseases we do not know what produces the disease process itself, the majority of cancers being a glaring example. Yet we dare inflict those diseases on live animals, diseases they didn't have before, and boldy venture opinions and proclaim conclusions, all along confusing information with knowledge. Doesn't make an iota of good sense.

Another relevant consideration is: Spontaneous diseases—naturally evolving rather than artificially induced or iatrogenic—progress, linger, halt or regress differently and the host reacts to them in diverse ways. A whole distinct ball game, dissimilar, thus not permitting valid conclusions to be drawn.

The animal model is not a natural one. It is designed for the experiment to be executed. Conditioned at conception, biased from its inception, contorted in its development, therefore, invalid.

Because the experimental and spontaneous processes and the animal and human conditions are at variance, extrapolation has become a necessary component of animal experimentation. Extrapolation means, estimating or inferring value or a quantity or an outcome, beyond the known range on the basis of certain variables within the known range, from which the estimate value is assumed to follow. In other words, when we extrapolate, we are not inferring or drawing conclusions from direct observations—what we see—but from the unseen, the unobserved. Predictions of sorts. Like seeing behind the bend of a road. Even though the road might be familiar, yet many a surprise may be hidden beyond the swerve ready to spring out or furtively keeping out of sight. Even economic, seismologic and weather forecasts based on extrapolation, frequently prove faulty. The extrapolation gap between the actual (the real) and the inferred (the assumed) is a trap in which we fall, knowingly and unknowingly. There, researchers attempt to adjust for species differences. It proved misleading and harmful not only in medicine, but also in politics, sociology, economics and other disciplines.

One more basic, inherent defect in animal experimentation methodology is the "rare event." An animal-model (excuse me for using the term animal-model, a misleading metaphor; in reality, it is a live animal being experimented upon, confined and given all sorts of nasty, nocuous penalties while alive) many a time may have, say, a low cancer-producing potential. Extremely high doses of the test chemical are used by researchers to compensate for this in order to bring forth a "rare event." Clearly, a "rare event" is not a common event, besides being manipulated and contrived. How can any sane person take such pretzel logic seriously, let alone use it in monitoring, judging or mending human affairs, failings and infirmity.

SOME IMPORTANT DIFFERENCES IN ANATOMY AND PHYSIOLOGY BETWEEN ANIMALS AND HUMANS

1. Comparatively speaking, dogs' coronary arteries (the blood vessels supplying the heart with blood) have smaller connections with one another and the left coronary artery dominates, while in humans the right is dominant.
2. The heart conduction system along which the impulses that synchronize and regulate the heartbeat travel is different. Having another pattern of blood supply, researchers encounter great difficulty in experimentally producing heart block in dogs. Heart block occurs frequently in humans and is much easier to induce.
3. Dogs' blood coagulation mechanism is unlike ours; therefore, testing prosthetic devices and valves in dogs is unrealiable. Human diasters followed when the lessons learned from canines were used to design and provide heart valves for humans. Oral contraceptives increase the risk of blood clots in humans; not so in dogs; the opposite happens.
4. After massive blood loss, a dog's intestine is congested with stagnant blood, while in humans the reverse occurs, pallor and ischemia (lack of blood supply) are observed.
5. Human heart tissue accumulates less calcium than rabbits and dogs.
6. Acetylcholine—a substance normally secreted by the body—dilates dogs' coronary arteries while constricting those of humans.
7. Human blood groups are not encountered in animals.

Despite those important differences, dogs are still being extensively used in heart and blood circulation research.

8. In many animals—for example, the mouse, a frequent captive and prey of cancer and immunology research—the crucial locus is the H-2 system which is red blood cell-based, while in humans it is the HL-A system which is white blood cell-based.

9. Certain cancers and sarcomas develop spontaneously in some animals and may spontaneously regress. Those happenings do not duplicate the human experience; for example most spontaneous mice malignancies are sarcomas arising in bones, muscles or connective tissue, while in humans, they are carcinomas originating in lining membranes.

10. The rabbit is an ineffective animal in atherosclerosis research; it rarely develops spontaneous atherosclerosis.

11. The rat is totally an unsuitable model for studying essential hypertension. They use it!

12. There is no valid animal model whatsoever for cystic fibrosis.

13. AIDS is uniquely a human malady for which there are no animal models. Even chimpanzees do not develop the disease when injected with the human virus. The Simian AIDS virus (S.I.V.) is not H.I.V.

14. Alzheimer's disease is also uniquely human; it is shared by no other species. Forgetting this fact—I guess—several researchers in renowned universities use rats in Alzheimer's research. Never learning from the past, ever reliving history, human sorrow knows no end. I wonder if Alzheimer's disease is an obligatory human trait?

15. Many animals—particularly the popular, yet loathed rat—tolerate intraabdominal sepsis (pus producing infections) much more than humans do.

16. Addiction to drugs, for example, cocaine, PCP, alcohol, tobacco, etc., is not an animal disorder, yet the loathsome, odious experimenters contrive and conduct all

sorts of oddly odd experiments with drugs on animals. Finding a cure to human addictions is their morbid excuse for so doing. Are we reluctant or afraid to look at parks and street corners in our big and small towns? Affluent and poor communities in the U.S. suffer the pangs and spasms of drug addiction. Income, race, rank, sex or age does not seem to matter.

17. The rabbit's eye commonly used in the Draize Test to test cosmetic and household items has many differences compared to the human eye. The pH (a measure of acidity or alkalinity) of human tears (7.1 to 7.3) is much lower than that of rabbits (8.2). A 1-point difference on the pH scale means a 10-fold difference in the acidity or alkalinity of tears. The rabbit's cornea is about 30 percent thinner than the human cornea. The "third eyelid" (nictitating membrane) rabbits have, humans do not. They blink and tear at rates very different from humans and while the cornea represents 25 percent of a rabbit's eye surface area, it is only 7 percent in the human eye.

18. There are important differences in kidney structure and ability to dilute, concentrate and eliminate.

19. Their endocrine system isn't exactly ours; all shades of difference exist.

20. Our gastrointestinal system reacts, digests and absorbs in ways that are not truly similar.

21. Lemon juice is harmful to cats.

22. Prussic acid fumes which kill human beings are an appetizer for sheep and toads.

23. Parrots and parsley don't get along. The latter kills the former, yet innocuous to humans.

24. Of mice and men, botulin poison kills both, yet cats seem to love it.

25. Unscrupulous producers of alcoholic drinks blinded many by adding methyl alcohol to their products,

yet the chemical spares the eyes of most laboratory animals.

26. For many years coal dust was not linked to pneumo-coniosis (a serious form of lung fibrosis whereby scar tissue forms) in coal miners. Thanks to animal experiments that misled and victimized thousands of workers.

27. Asbestosis, a lung disease caused by inhaling asbestos may cause lung cancer in humans. Animal studies failed to establish the link between lung asbestosis and cancer.

28. The link between smoking and lung cancer in humans was denied for many years based on vivisection data. Health warnings were delayed for all those years.

No wonder, drugs activity in humans and animals vastly differ. The following table illustrates this; relatively long, yet not complete, the actual list is much taller, and broader. A jamboree where the joker is the highest of all.

Drug	Activity in Animals	Activity and Possible Complications in Humans
1. Accutane (for acne)	Safe	Birth defects
2. Acetycholine (a natural body chemical)	Dilates coronary arteries of dogs	Constricts the coronary arteries
3. Aminoglutethimide (Elipten)	Anticonvulsant	Cortisol inhibitor
4. Amydopyrine (pain killer)	No important side effects	Blood disease
5. Amyl Nitrate	Glaucoma (high internal eye pressure)	Reduces internal eye pressure
6. Antimony	Fattens swines	Fatal

Drug	Activity in Animals	Activity and Possible Complications in Humans
7. Arsenic	Safe in large quantities in sheep	Kills
8. Aspirin	Kills cats. Causes birth defects in dogs, monkeys, rats and cats.	Analgesic and retards blood coagulation
9. Atromid (to reduce blood cholesterol)	Different	Caused deaths from cancer, gallbladder disease and inflammation of the pancreas
10. Bradykinin (a body chemical)	Contracts brain blood vessels in dogs	Relaxes brain blood vessels
11. Butazolidine (for arthritis)	Does not harm the bone marrow	Aplastic anemia due to bone marrow damage, frequently fatal
12. Chloramphenicol (an antibiotic)	Safe	Irreversible damage to the bone marrow
13. Chloroform (was used in general anesthesia until the 1950s)	Danger is one of asphyxia	Commonest cause of death is heart failure
14. Chlorpromazine (Thorazine)	Antimotion sickness	Tranquilizing and may cause liver damage
15. Chymotrypsin (for cataract)	Corneal perforation and severe damage to rabbit's eye	No serious complications
16. Clindamycin (an antibiotic)	Safe when tested in rats and dogs	Diarrhea, sometimes fatal
17. Clioquinol (antidiarrhea)	Not reported	Blindness, paralysis and death
18. Clonidine (Catapres)	Nasal decongestant	Anti-hypertensive also prevents or limits narcotics withdrawal symptoms

Drug	Activity in Animals	Activity and Possible Complications in Humans
19. Cortisone (antiarthritis and antiallergy)	Birth defects in pregnant mice and rabbits	Endocrine problems, high blood pressure, psychosis and other major complications. No birth defects.
20. Cyanide	Safe for owls	Kills
21. Depo-Provera (an injectable long-acting contraceptive)	Cancer; breast and uterine infections in dogs	Considered safe
22. DES (to prevent miscarriage)	Safe	Cancer in daughters of mothers who received DES and birth defects in their grandchildren
23. Digitalis (for heart failure and abnormal heart rhythm)	Causes high blood pressure in dogs	Not so
24. Dinitrophenol (for obesity)	No cataracts	Causes cataracts
25. Diptrex (an organophosphate pesticide)	No nerve damage	Nerve damage
26. Disulfiram (Antabuse)	Antihelminthic (against some parasites)	Creates toxic reaction after drinking alcohol
27. Domperidone (to treat nausea and vomiting induced by anticancer drugs)	No changes in heart rhythm	Serious heart irregularities (arrhythmias)
28. Encainide (for irregular heart)	Safe	Heart attacks and deaths. Together with flecainide 3,000 individuals may have died after taking these drugs. Withdrawn in 1989

Drug	Activity in Animals	Activity and Possible Complications in Humans
29. Eraldin (practolol) (a heart drug)	Fairly safe	Corneal damage including blindness, also digestive tract damage and death. Withdrawn in 1976
30. Fenclozic acid (Antiarthritis)	Safe in rats, mice, dogs and monkeys	Liver toxicity. Withdrawn from humans
31. Flecainide	Safe	Heart attacks and death. Up to 3,000 people could have died after taking Encainide and Flecainide. No more used since April 1989
32. Fluoride	None	Inhibits dental caries
33. Furmethide (eye drops to treat glaucoma)	Safe, even when instilled in rabbit's eyes for months	Permanent obstruction of the tear passages in the majority of patients where the drug was used for periods exceeding 3 months
34. Furosemide (Lasix, a diuretic)	Liver damage in mice and others	Not so
35. Glutethimide (Doriden)	Anticonvulsant	Sedative and hypnotic
36. Halothane (a general anesthetic)	No liver damage	Liver damage and death of many
37. Holofenate	Hypolipemic	Hypouricemic
38. Ibufenac (anti-inflammatory)	No liver damage, only in rats a minor effect when exposed to lethal doses	Liver damage and death. Withdrawn
39. Imipramine (Tofranil)	Depressant	Antidepressant

Drug	Activity in Animals	Activity and Possible Complications in Humans
40. Iron sorbitol (injectable iron to treat anemia)	Cancer at injection site	No cancers developed
41. Isoniazide (for treatment of tuberculosis)	No liver damage	Can cause liver damage
42. Isopreterenol (as a spray inhaled for relief of asthma)	No important side effects	Thousands of deaths were caused
43. Ketoconazole (antifungal)	Safe	Liver damage, some died
44. Kanamycin (for some infections)	No great side effects	Deafness and kidney damage
45. Maxiton (diet pills)	Different	Damage to the heart and nervous system
46. Methyldopa	Does not lower blood pressure	Very effective in lowering high blood pressure
47. Methylsergide (for migraine)	No serious side effects	Retroperitoneal fibrosis which can be life-threatening by obstructing blood vessels and ureters. Damage to heart valves is reported
48. Mianserin (antidepressant)	No blood disorders	May cause fatal blood disorders
50. Morphine	Renders cats manic (morphine mania)	Analgesic and respiratory depressant
51. Opren (Oraflex) (for arthritis)	Safe in large doses in non-human primates	Liver damage and death, withdrawn from the market in 1982
52. Oral Contraceptives	Bleeding in dogs	Thrombosis, heart attacks, strokes and liver tumors

Drug	Activity in Animals	Activity and Possible Complications in Humans
53. Penicillin	Kills guinea pigs	Very useful antibiotic
54. Pentazocine (Talwin)	Narcotic antagonist	Analgesic
55. Perhexiline (for angina)	No liver damage	Liver damage and deaths occured. Withdrawn
56. Phenacetin (pain killer)	No important side effects	Kidney and red blood cell damage
57. Phenformin (for diabetes)	Different	Many deaths
58. Plaxin and Pronap (tranquilizer)	Different	Killed many babies
59. Prenylamine (used for angina)	Reduces heart rate in many	Ventricular tachycardia, a very serious type of fast heart rate. Withdrawn
60. Prostaglandins (a group of natural body substances)	Different effect on the force and rate of heart contraction	Different
61. Strychnine	Does not kill guinea pigs or monkeys	Kills humans
62. Psicofuranine (anti-cancer)	No heart damage in mice, rats, dogs and monkeys	Heart toxicity. Trials discontinued
63. Selacryn (diuretic)	Safe	Liver damage and fatalities. Withdrawn
64. Suprofen (for arthritis)	Safe	Major kidney problems. Withdrawn
65. Tegretol (for epilepsy)	Safe	Potentially fatal blood diseases and epidemiologic findings suggest an increased incidence of birth defects
66. Thalidomide (a safe tranquilizer)	Safe	Birth defects and fetal death

Drug	Activity in Animals	Activity and Possible Complications in Humans
67. Trilergen (antiallergic)	Different	Hepatitis
68. Zimelidine (antidepressant)	Safe	Fever, liver problems, joint aches, nerve damage and paralysis. Withdrawn in 1983
69. Zipeprol (Cough depressant)	Deemed safe for humans	Severe neurologic symptoms at high doses—seizures and coma

Sources:

1. *Physicians' Desk Reference*, published annually by Medical Economics Data, a division of Medical Economics Company Inc., Montvale, N.Y. 07645, 1995, 1994, 1993 and other editions.
2. *Vivisection or Science: A Choice to Make*, by P. Croce, M.D., Buchverlag CIVIS Publications, 1991.
3. Dr. Robert Sharpe Address at the General Assembly of the International Association Against Painful Experiments on Animals. Philadelphia, June 24, 1989.
4. Sharpe, R. *Science on Trial: The Human Cost of Animal Experiments*, Awareness Publishing Ltd., London, 1994.
5. *Bulletin of the International Associations Against Painful Experiments on Animals*. Autumn/Winter Edition, 1987.
6. *Vivisection: Science or Sham*, by Roy Kupsinel, M.D. Published by PRISM (People For Reason In Science And Medicine) Woodland Hills, California.

CHAPTER THREE

Animal Experimentation Leads to Human Experimentation

Animal experimentation inevitably leads to human experimentation. Animal experimentation is human experimentation because the first leads to the second; therefore, the first and second are one and the same.

Animal experimentation inevitably leads to human experimentation. True. Absolutely True. Animal experimentation is human experimentation because the first inevitably leads to the second; therefore, the first and the second are one and the same: The law of inevitability.

One can design any kind of model, experiment on all sorts of animals, repeat the experiment 1,001 times, more or less, but as one moves to the human condition, still, it is all experimental, plain and simple for the following reasons:

First reason: Animals are different, in many ways: their anatomy differs, their physiology is not similar to ours, their behavior is not the same. And as you go down to the nitty gritty, to the cellular and the sub-cellular levels and down, down, down—I should say up, up, up—to the genes, to the RNA and DNA structure, there are manifest variations.

51

Therefore, applying what you find or learn from animal experiments to humans is incorrect.

A well-known fact is: Any slight alteration in an experimental model, subject or methodology alters the result significantly.

Second reason: The diseases we give or induce in animals are not natural ones. They are generally illnesses that do not affect them, artificially created. Even if we give animals a disease that is known to afflict them, the natural evolution of a disease is unlike its experimental induction. It is all dissimilar and diverse.

Given the above two facts, how can anyone in the right frame of mind expect vivisection to tender information that is applicable to human beings? It is an impossibility. No wonder this faulty approach proved harmful. The scroll of hurt and loss engendered by vivisection is lengthy and protracted, shocking and unprecedented, not only in its cruelty, but also in its absurdity and lack of visibility. Chapter One unrolls the infamous parchment displaying the shameful record.

As a physician, I have taken the position that continuing vivisection by the medical community violates the basic tenets of the Hippocratic oath, a solemn affirmation taken by students about to receive the M.D. degree. A promissory oath not to knowingly or willfully harm patients, to seek knowledge and use one's proper faculties and moral values in attempting to heal and alleviate the suffering of those who seek his or her knowledge and skills. Predating and transcending the Hippocratic oath is the "Do No Harm" principle. Timeless, immemorial, universal. Ego checked at the door, blinders cast away, I have ceased participation in any vivisection, given up eating or consuming animals and animal products. And, in atonement, I speak, write and divulge what I have known. Reconciliation at last. Enmity to other fellow creatures has long gone, clearing my being. In their company, I am joyous and guiltless. And, they are safe. Music swells, book of songs opens, energy doubles.

Bow to the province of Bolzano, Italy. On July 21, 1986 Bolzano adopted the provincial law of July 8, 1986, No. 16, entitled: Regulations for the Protection of Animals.

Article One decrees: The autonomous province of Bolzano has decreed that within its own sphere of competence, animals of all kinds should be protected. Article Seven Section B of the same law states: The same penalty applies to anyone who carries out experiments on living animals even just for scientific or teaching purposes.

Bolzano is way ahead of the U.S. Congress, the World Court, the World Health Organization and legislative and religious counsels worldwide. I am not giving in, for my cause is right and I am not giving up on them either. And, I am not about to quit or cede the rights of animals or the rights of humans; the two are inseparable, in reality, the two are one.

''Those who experiment on animals should never be able to quiet their own conscience by telling themselves that these cruelties have a worthy aim.'' So said Albert Schweitzer. True: no worthy aim. For more than 51 years, Schweitzer continued to work in Lambarene, western Gabon, until his death in 1965 at age 90. Natives of Lambarene were utterly helpless and desperately ill; he founded his hospital there and made Lambarene his home. The Nobel Prize came in 1953, money from which went to buy more supplies for the hospital. His compassion embraced all, ''The human spirit is not dead. It lives on in secret. It has come to believe that compassion in which all ethics take root, can only attain breadth and depth if it embraces all living creatures and does not limit itself to mankind.'' That is Albert Schweitzer's credo. Compassion does not sort out, does not discriminate, does not exclude; there are no "others," there are no aliens, all belonging to one planet: Gaia (Earth).

Claude Bernard (1813–1878) the "Prince of Vivisectors" was awarded the dubious distinction as father of experimental physiology, had a defection from his close ranks: his own wife. She couldn't take it anymore—Marie Francoise Martin was an animal rights advocate. In 1883 she founded the first French league to combat vivisection. Victor Hugo became the first president of the French anti-vivisection society. Predating the French society, an anti-vivisection society was founded in Britain thanks to George Hoggan, a young physiologist who attended the institute chaired by Claude Bernard. After spending four months with the wicked elf, he returned to England, condemned the obscene cruelty of the father of experimental physiology stating that ". . . of the experiments, which I had witnessed, not one was justified or necessary . . ." On the evils of vivisection Victor Hugo stated, "Vivisection is a crime." And I second the motion, "Vivisection is a crime." The story of George Hoggan is quoted by Hans Ruesch in his book "Slaughter of the Innocent."* The patriarch was seriously challenged by spouse and disciple.

Given all the above and the obvious harm inflicted: Why is vivisection still practiced in medical schools, colleges, high schools, hospitals, pharmaceutical companies, institutes of health and the proving grounds of the military? And don't forget the Food and Drug Administration, which mandates live animal experimentation before proceeding with experiments on human beings, including healthy volunteers—a shady practice with which I disagree. The answer is: Brain conditioning has created a blind spot in the mind's eye.

---

*Ruesch H., *Slaughter of the Innocent*. New York: Bantam Books, 1976.

Within the sightless speck, real ignorance breeds species arrogance, cruelty, inertia and unawareness. Add to this, ambition and greed. Dr. J.D. Gallagher, Director of Medical Research for Lederly Laboratories offers an explanation, "Animal studies are done for legal reasons and not for scientific reasons. The predictive value of such studies is meaningless—which means our research may be meaningless."* Taking on some risk, I dare substitute "is" with "may be," candidly stating our research (vivisection) is meaningless.

So, for those of us who still believe that animal experimentation protects humans, time to see things as they are; this belief has no foundation, a misleading fabrication. Vivisection doesn't protect human health and well being. It endangers. It is merely a license to harm and diminish us, all while its icons and perpetrators are reaping a constellation of benefits including the luxury and comfort of escaping punishment and confinement.

Chapter five will show and prove that the breakthroughs which brought forth, nurtured and shaped modern medicine and surgery did not result form vivisection. Chapter six will discuss at some length a multitude of available, viable, reliable alternatives to vivisection that are cruelty-free as well. Please refer to them, then make up your own mind. And, when you do, reach out, let your new state of mind, state of heart touch members of your own family and embrace your friends, acquaintances, the human consortium as well. Along the journey there is joy, beneficence and light. Our first step will switch on energy, fortitude and sustenance. The rekindled inner flame will endure and keep the dynamo running.

---

*Journal of the American Medical Association, March 14, 1964.

CHAPTER FOUR

Clinical Research Can Be Ethical and Precise

The argument that clinical research involving humans is unethical and inaccurate is misleading. It has the veneer of morality, yet, ignorant and naive. Animal experimentation is merely a prelude covering up and legitimizing human experimentation.

The argument that clinical research involving human subjects is unethical and inaccurate is misleading. On the surface, it has the cloak of morality and concern; at its depth, ignorance and naivety. After all, animal experimentation is but a cover-up hiding and legitimizing human experimentation. Matter of fact, animal experimentation does not prevent nor preclude human experimentation; on the contrary it perpetuates it, boosting momentum and conferring spurious legitimacy. Armed with misleading data and bogus conclusions drawn from their animal experiments, researchers and disciples are permitted to sow the mendacious seeds into the keenly longing firmament of human anguish and infirmity. What about harm that wreaks, the ache, the bruise, the wound, parts depraved, lives nullified? Whom to blame? And, where is the culprit? In this case, animal experimentation is a prelude and a waiver. Accountability expires along with the die hard laboratory animals. No one is indicted, nobody is accused and no experimenter or sponsor will be questioned, arrested, demoted, fired, incarcerated, or penalized. Vivisectionists may try their notions, procedures and gadgets on animals as many times as they deem necessary, but the moment they penetrate the perimeter of the human condition, still, they will be experimenting.

I am not here advocating shameful, contemptible undertakings such as the Tuskegee syphilis study. All its subjects were black Americans. It took place in the United States, begun in 1932 and continued for forty years thereafter, ending only when an Associated Press reporter broke the demeaning, brutal tale. U.S. Public Health Service, Alabama's Department of Health, Tuskegee Institute, the Tuskegee Veterans Administration Hospital, and Alabama Macon County Health Department all participated in the clandestine scandal. The 400 black men were poor, mostly cottonfield sharecroppers. The stages of the disease were observed by the so-called scientists and physicians from the initial chancre, to the rash, to the arthritis, to the destruction of the nervous system, heart valves and major blood vessels; all despite the well-known fact that if not treated, syphilis is fatal; all regardless of the discovery of penicillin and its proven efficacy in the treatment of syphilis.*

For years a number of physicians in the U.S. injected large doses of plutonium into the veins of individuals without their prior consent or knowledge of the sinister experimental protocol.** And, are you ready for this? "A report released by the U.S. Department of Energy disclosed that human radiation experiments conducted from the end of World War II into the 1970's were far more extensive than was previously known. About 16,000 people participated—often unwittingly—in the tests; many were from 'vulnerable pop-

---

*Newsmedia including *Newsweek*, April 6, 1992, p. 23.
**Time Magazine, August 28, 1995, p. 21.

ulations' that included prisoners, pregnant women, children, mentally retarded people and comatose patients."* Alas! On its vulnerable populations our government wreaks its malignity and wrath. Desire to harm is overwhelming; malice aforethought; â priori. Not to be surpassed, the U.S. Central Intelligence Agency slipped LSD into bodies of unsuspecting subjects and years ago bacterial cultures were released in the New York subway, all while more than 200 nuclear tests were secretly carried on in the U.S. by our own government.* This is but a short version of a high-rise order of heinous crimes committed behind the wall of secrecy by lofty institutions under the approving gaze of authority.

According to the FDA protocols, experimenting on volunteers is a stage to follow animal experiments. Why harm the healthy? I question the validity and morality of experiments the subjects of which happen to be in good health. The claim that participants tender their informed consent after receiving full explanation of the procedure or test to be performed with its possible risks, alternatives and objectives is a sham. Goal-oriented, win, win-obsessed staff of pharmaceutical companies and medical schools are adept at persuasion and dangling rewards to entice would-be candidates to sign on. The art and craft of manufacturing consent is rampant, practiced ad libitum by governments, mass media and institutions that reign. Throughout history, stirring up fear, ambition and greed, leaders readily herd their clan, tribe or nation to war, destroying their lives and lives of others. How much does a clerk, a technician, a law student, art or engineering apprentice know about creatinine phosophokinase, alpha feto-proteins, immunology, splenic functions, cancer, the liver, kidney or hemopoietic system? The machinery that manufactures consent is serviced regularly, always ready to weave, spin and make believe. Beware!

---

*Newsmedia including *Newsweek*, December 27, 1993, pp. 14–20.

HOMOLOGOUS EXPERIMENTATION

Homologous experimentation signifies trying new diagnostic or surgical procedures or medicines on patients. A very delicate area indeed, widely open to abuse. Strict guidelines can help eliminate blunder and mischief:

1. The experiment subject must be suffering the specific disease entity for which the tested procedure is intended. Tryng methods or medications on patients with different diseases on the assumption that they, too, might benefit without strong evidence to back such a claim is unethical.
2. The diagnostic procedure or drug must have certain qualities that render benefit to the ailing subject likely. Of course, vivisection is out. It is a fraud, a poor predictor heralding false prophecies. There are other ways and means: Please refer to chapter six on alternatives. Keen, multiple observations—not experiments—on human beings can contribute valuable information. On this, I will elaborate later on in this chapter.
3. The patient must give an informed consent. If the patient is incapable of providing such a consent for one reason or another, the legal guardian or the courts should undertake this responsibility.
4. The new therapy or diagnostic technique should be tried only if other alternatives do not exist.

Under no condition should such a trial be carried out on a given patient in order to help others, the community or humanity at large. We cannot allow nor condone sacrificing one individual so that another or many may benefit—a slipshod immoral philosophy that has imported danger and brought disgrace to humankind.

Choices, are they narrowing? Roads are they dead-ending

or leading to nowhere? Where shall we go from here? We have been satiated by the "Experimental Method" despite its numerous shortcomings and serious pitfalls. In every scientific discipline—physics, chemistry and others included —observation of natural phenomena goes hand in hand with experimentation. More so in medicine where the questions raised pertain to life, dynamic as it is, replete with mysteries hard to fathom and comprehend. Keen observation is the key. And, right here, epidemiological methods play a crucial role.

Matter of fact, great advances in medicine took place through direct observations by astute observers. A few examples should bring this important point home. The following extraordinary feats were the product of remarkable observations: the discovery of digitalis (a breakthrough heart medicine), penicillin (the keynoter for all antibiotics), cephalosporin (the forerunner of most newer antibiotics), aspirin, quinine, X-rays, antisepsis, tobacco (causing cancer), ultraviolet predisposing to skin cancers, occupational cancer such as the landmark discovery of scrotum cancer in chimney sweepers by Percival Potts, anticoagulants, ether (the harbinger of all anesthetics), several newer anti-hypertensive drugs, coronary arteriography and many, many others. Please consult chapter five; it lists more, telling how each was discovered.

Naturally, an observation has to be substantiated and confirmed by other observations, then comes the role of investigation, collection of data, thinking, all in accordance with the discplines of the science of epidemiology.

At this juncture, I'd like to quote from professor Pietro Croce's book, *Vivisection or Science, A Choice to Make*,* "Medical science was born at the same time as philosophy; in the

---

*Croce, P.: *Vivisection or Science: A Choice to Make*. Buchverlag CIVIS Publications, 1991, p. 137.

Western world, at the time of Thales, in Greece. However, it has run two irreconcilable courses; observation on man and the attempt to use the animal as a model for man. The second method has overwhelmed the first and led it astray. Its influence has been powerful because it gave the illusion of being a short cut to clinical and anatomical/pathological observation. It is an illusion welcomed in these hectic days of the idolatry of Formula One and of travel by Concorde. It is like someone who, seeking a shortcut through an unknown forest, cannot even find his way back home.''

Dr. Croce is a respected pathologist from Italy; his field is cancer. ''Torture is useless because it makes people confess to crimes they never committed. Vivisection is equally useless because animals have nothing to confess. However, it does serve to confess human stupidity.'' Dr. Croce, I wholeheartedly concur.

While pathology is the science of studying diseases of the individual, epidemiology is concerned with the study of diseases of world population. Epidemiology is derived from the Greek, *epi*, meaning upon or among; *demos*, meaning people; and *logia* means study or to speak. It is not a mere collection of data and compilation of observations. Done properly, it stands to decipher the causes of disease and methods of control. Unfortunately, we got hooked on the experimental method despite its inherent limitations and deficiencies. Even in physics, chemistry and biology, the experimental method has shortcomings, more so in biology, the science of life, where rigidity and a mechanistic approach can twist and deceive.

To elaborate on the indispensable role of epidemiology I will resort to a question/answer format.

Question: How can we study human beings?
Answer: By observing human beings.
Q: What do you mean by observation? Just observation?

A: Observing what occurs spontaneously in a large number of individuals.

Q: What about experimenting on human beings?

A: We are not talking about experimenting. Forget about the experimental method now; we have dealt with it earlier in this chapter.

Q: Is there a human experimental model?

A: Scattered all over the globe, the human model walks, talks, and stalks; consumes, pillages, atones and does it again; subject to transiency and a number of existential decrees, options and opportunities. The core of epidemiology is to observe spontaneously occurring phenomena in those live models, right there, in their natural habitat. The number of observations must be large enough to arrive at credible conclusions analogous to the laws of physics and mechanics.

Q: Can you give us some examples?

A: I am going to mention a few, though risking repeating what I have said earlier:

1. Semmelweis observed in the wards of Vienna that childbed fever is spread from one patient to another when the physicians and attendants did not wash their hands between patients. This laid the foundation of the science of antisepsis.
2. The much higher incidence of skin cancer in Europeans living in the tropics. Dark-skinned people have much lower rates because the pigment melanin protects them from the harmful effects of ultraviolet light.
3. Cancer of the scrotum in chimney sweepers.
4. Tobacco causing cancer. As a matter of fact, it causes at least one third of all cancers.
5. Dr. John Snow (1813–1858), an English anesthesiologist

who with the help of a map of the city of London pin-pointed the areas of cholera infection, found an infected aqueduct as the source.

6. The Framingham study was conducted in Massachusetts in the 1960s, lasted for many years and involved thousands of individuals. It proved that those most susceptible to heart attacks are smokers, consumers of relatively large sums of animal fat, sedentary persons who scarcely engage in physical exercise, obese and hypertensive ones.

7. Seventh-Day Adventists who abstain from tobacco and alcohol have low-incidence of cancer of the lung, larynx, esophagus, mouth, bladder and cervix compared to the rest of the population.

8. Cancer of cervix is frequent in prostitutes, rare in nuns, while cancer of the uterus is encountered more commonly in countries with a higher standard of living.

So don't let them fool you. The primary source of knowledge about ourselves is ourselves. Advances in medicine and surgery emanate from us. It is us. Homo sapiens, within your very ambience, your frame, core and entrails the whole truth regarding your very being hybernates.

Q: Why is epidemiology not used more often?
A: Epidemiology does not give instant, extravagent returns. It takes time. The endeavor is serious, demanding sincere participation and cooperation on the local, national and, on occasion, the international level. Its scientific papers lack the pomp, the high-flown soundbites, elaborate models and the fanciful stipulations displayed in vivisectionist publications. But fortunately, in these days of computers, microchips and intrepid global communication epidemiology's job can be facilitated by gathering data readily available in health institutions worldwide.

Vivisectionists and their influential allies and collaborators credit animal research with lengthening life expectancy by 20.8 years. Utterly ridiculous. Incorrect. Credit duly goes to public health measures, particularly sanitation and improved food distribution. In his book *Man Against Disease*,* Dr. Muir Gray states, ''The decline in mortality can be attributed more to the prevention of disease than to the development of specific therapies. . . . In the 20th century, many effective cures have been developed, but most of this advance has taken place in the years following the second world war during which no great improvement in the rate of increase in the expectation of life can be detected.''

In this regard, the renowned Dr. Dennis Burkett's comment begs to be restated, ''We got rid of infectious diseases, by increasing resistance and by getting rid of the causes . . . clean water, clean milk, adequate sewage disposal, and so on. Doctors and drugs had nothing whatever to do with the conquest of infectious diseases.''

Live animal experimenters' erroneous claims remind me of the fiction of the golden apples kept by a dragon taken from the serpent which tempted Eve. The golden apples allegory proffers rich possibilities for insight, great works of art, poetics, sumptuous debates, magnificent temptations or even a third rendition of the *Divine Comedy*.** Not so with the vivisectionists' pretention; it ends in itself, by itself.

---

*Gray, M., *Man Against Disease*, Oxford University Press, 1979.
**Al-Maarri, the eleventh century Syrian poet and seer, composed the first *Divine Comedy*, known in the West as *Risalat al Ghufran*, translated into English by G. Brockenburg in 1943. Three centuries later Alighieri Dante wrote the second *Divine Comedy*.

CHAPTER FIVE

Vivisection Did Not Advance Medicine

The claim that we owe most of our advances and break-throughs in medicine to vivisection is false. Held sacrosanct by many, the fictitious notion should be laid to rest. Discarded.

The claim that we owe most if not all of our advances in medicine to animal research is not only untrue, but also preposterous and absurd—an outright lie. It's like giving credit to Masters and Johnson for discovering the joy of sex, or reprehending flambeau, lascivious Madonna for inventing lewdness and burlesque, or such and such saint or guru for finding God, or claiming that Freud was the first to study the basic instincts of man and unravel mysterious disorders of the mind. What shall I say? Here is generally how the malarkey goes: they, the vivisectionists, figure out some experimental condition or a test of sorts, design an experimental model (the model is nothing other than a live, healthy animal sentenced to contract disease, injury and, in most instances, death). They experiment, re-experiment, model, remodel, alter, re-alter, then let fly data, graphs, posters and publications. Now, all they need to do is speak loudly enough, frequently enough and lay claim to credit and breakthroughs. And, as Darwin's maxim goes, credit goes to the man who convinces the world. Convincing they certainly do, lots of it. Clad in starched white coats with degrees and professional rank pinned onto their eager breasts, cast in a halo of light with the right sonic settings, whining intonations and well-composed pronouncements are uttered. Add to the impressive facade the awesome clout of the high institutes that nurture, cover and sponsor. Exhortations and whispers by high walls, and automatically, they become believable. Veneer shines and hides; artificial flowers lure anxious lovers. News media join the circus providing time, air waves, pages and color. And lo and behold, Cretins grow in stature and acquire authority and the high ground, the false priesthood of science in the making. And the show goes on, icing more cakes, but they haven't baked any.

One of their powerful allies is the pharmaceutical industry with its access, outlets and corporate schemes. Slick, market-oriented, profit motivated, they dress up the bride, make-up, perfume, vows and a heavenly walk down the aisle. The soft ditties, the band and the rest of the saga, you know it! This reminds me of the standard good news/bad news joke—the good news is, we have a miracle drug tested on animals and proven safe. We'll take care of you. The bad news is, it has side effects, oops! A few accidental deaths, "collateral damage," the mandated cost of progress, you know, nothing for nothing. But, for the safety of our dear customers we are going to withdraw the miracle charm from the market. We care!

Need I apologize for my sarcasm? Its grain is truth, its essence is fact. I am told, in the right measure, sarcasm is good medicine. So, I hope the right dose has been delivered. Will leave it at that.

Let us recall events largely forgotten, facts conveniently ignored, mischievously altered, adroitly covered. Spread the word for we shall reap what we sow: End of Vivisection.

LET'S GO FOR THE FACTS:
THE DISCOVERY OF HEART FUNCTION,
BLOOD VESSELS AND CIRCULATION OF BLOOD

We did not discover through vivisection the inner chambers of our heart, and the life-giving flow of warm blood in our veins and arteries. As we mentioned in Chapter One, the Ebers Papyrus (1550 B.C.) includes a surprisingly accurate description of the circulatory system, depicting the existence of blood vessels through the entire body and the heart functioning as the center of the blood supply. In 1240 A.C., Ibn Al Nafis discovered the pulmonary circulation. His dissections were performed on cadavers obtained from cemeteries in Cairo, Egypt and Damascus, Syria. He proved that blood circulates from the right side of the heart to the lungs, where it is aerated before reaching the left side of the heart. Thus, Galen's theory that blood flows from the right side of the heart through an opening in the intervening septum was finally laid to rest. Galen, the 2nd century A.C. physician, is considered the founder of experimental physiology. His erroneous conclusions, which misled the Western world for 11 centuries, were based on animal research. Imagine the millions who suffered or died as a result of treatment based on false premises, as well as the animals that perished in vain. Too late to counsel him. But, in making amends, I hope his 20th century disciples and future ones as well will awaken and change their path, a path without heart, without mind. That Galen, in ravaging the warm, vibrant interiors of live animals, strayed. The fallen ones, our own dead, had the true information, the map of our heart, the trails of our blood vessels beneath their cold skin, within their stilled interiors, yet he didn't visit with them. You see, not all makers of history are legend-worthy. Big names, don't let 'em fool you. Like us, heroes are made of clay; they err, their slate is not immaculate, their scroll is not infallible.

William Harvey (1578–1657) studied medicine in the University of Padua, Italy. At that time, the majority of its curriculum was based on Ibn Sina's and ar Razi's textbooks. Ibn Sina's* *Canon of Medicine* and many other books of his as well as ar Razi's texts were regarded as the only authentic references in much of Europe up until the 18th century. Earlier we mentioned that in the 10th century, ar Razi accurately described the venous system and the function of its valves. Harvey returned to England and completed Ibn Al Nafis' work on the heart and circulation of blood. His findings stemmed from his observations of live human beings, himself included, cadaver dissections as well.

Harvey's discovery was a momentous breakthrough. A graduate of Padua University, he must have been instructed in the landmark, colossal works of his predecessors who had already discovered the circulation of blood and the layout of our heart and blood vessels, but he got all or most of the credit. Not the first, won't be the last, where a bronze medalist gets the gold! Makes me wonder: to whom do the laurel and wreath belong? Hung on a door, the garland is questioning; around a forehead the chaplet is quibbling. Vivisectionists, true to their bad habits and faulty agenda, claim that Harvey achieved the breakthrough through animal experimentation. Wrong. Wrong. Dead wrong. Vivisectionists, take a walk. You can use some fresh air. Some insight.

CARDIAC CATHETERIZATION:
A CORNERSTONE OF MODERN CARDIOLOGY

This breathtaking development is not the result of animal experimentation. It gives us a fascinating still and dynamic display of the heart chambers and the great blood vessels

---

*Ibn Sina (980–1037) is known in the West as Avicenna.

enabling us to discern their topography, contour and anatomical relationships and to observe and follow the impact of changes caused by different disease conditions and diagnose disorders previously undiagnosed. Surely this radically changed our approach to maladies of the heart and blood vessels and gave birth to many surgical advances. Werner Forssmann (1904–1979), the German surgeon, was the first to insert a catheter (a tiny wire-like long tube) into a vein of his own forearm; he advanced the tip of the catheter under fluoroscopy into the right atrium, one of the heart's four chambers. Fluoroscopy enables one to see on a screen radio-opaque objects such as the catheter Forssmann used. Noteworthy, fluoroscopy itself is not a product of animal research, even by the stretch or overstretch of the tempestuous imagination of some. Our bag of tools is not equipped in animals labs.

Coronary arteriography made coronary bypass surgery possible. Thousands, many thousands with blocked arteries, heart attacks and disabling chest pain reaped benefit from this surgical procedure. Same goes for angioplasty where a narrowed blood vessel is dilated by a special catheter carrying a balloon at its tip, thus minimizing the risk for those with tightly narrowed blood vessels who failed to respond to medical treatment alone. Arteriography provides portraits and motion pictures of the blood vessels supplying the heart. This pearl was discovered in the Cleveland Clinic by Mason L. Sones in 1961, while catheterizing patients for valvular heart disease. Sones' discovery was a happenstance, timely and far reaching. No animal sacrifices. The sacrament was unction; blood of the innocent was not spattered. Not even one! Not even one! Again, vivisectionists grabbed this jewel, recycled it, still recycling into thousands of animal lab-made publications adding very little if any information and sacrificing (killing) as many animals as they can afford to. In the rowdy arena of animal research, the number of publications more or less is directly proportional to the number of animals put to death. And, the appearance of scientific authenticity of a vivisectionist's publication is generally strengthened by executing more animals. You see, there is an incentive to kill! And, on the rungs of the bewitching academic ladder they ascend propelled by the minuscules and minuets of information; hot air balloons and flying kites. On the "win, win" trail, means are meaningful, but this is not where it all finally rests. Means Must Ultimately Justify Themselves.

To experimenting on the dog, the ape, and many others in between and around, we do not owe such a fascinating breakthrough. We owe nothing. We beget nothing but grief, angst and ache. Again, vivisectionists are wrong. Do you think they'll ever listen?

THE DISCOVERY OF X-RAYS

On November 8, 1895, a little after 5:00 P.M. in a basement laboratory in Wurzburg, Germany, something happened. Earth shaking! And it wasn't a tremor or volcano eruption. Well! More formidable. A star was born. And, at the risk of overstating a wee bit, I'll say: A whole galaxy came to be; modern physics. And medicine has never been the same since. It took a giant leap.

Wilhelm Conrad Roentgen (1845–1923) discovered the energy which, in view of its uncertain nature then, he named X-radiation. Later, in his honor it became known as Roentgen radiation. It all happened while he was experimenting with electric current flowing in a partially evacuated glass tube (cathode-ray tube). When the tube was in operation, a nearby piece of barium platinocyanide emitted a spark of light. Wow! A spark of light! What a spark that was! Many materials became transparent to this new form of radiation which also affected photographic plates. For his discovery, Roentgen received the *first* Nobel Prize for Physics in 1901. Among the very first X-ray plates were his own hand and his wife's hand. Roentgen, I want to shake your hand.

COMPUTERIZED AXIAL TOMOGRAPHY (CAT OR CT SCAN)

This is Body Section Roentgenography, an X-ray technique by which details of body organs appear in one plane after another, thus showing details and particulars previously unseen by conventional X-ray techniques. While the X-rays are directed through the patient, the machine rotates about an axis, the patient remaining stationary. Thanks to EMI (Electronic Musical Instruments) the British recording company that sponsored the Beatles, it took on this challenge as well and in the early 1970s it offered the world the first CT scan. On this one, Allan Cormack of the U.S. and Godfrey Hounsfield of the U.K. were awarded the 1979 Nobel Prize for Physiology or Medicine. And animals in the forest, in cages, in alleys, pet and the wild cheered. Celebrated. None was murdered, hit, crushed, maimed or exanguinated to summon the breakthrough. Vivisectionists, stay out of this one; Beatles, don't stop the music. Sing. Sing. Extol. Thanks, EMI.

MAGNETIC RESONANCE

A magnificent tool, no relation to animal research. Atoms possess a unique quality. Placed in a magnetic field they absorb special frequencies of radio and microwaves, hence came a miracle machine: Magnetic Resonance. Truly it revolutionized the investigative work and therapy for many conditions in different organs and parts of the body. Reliably and noninvasively, that splendid gadget dips into the enchanting world of the minute, down to the cellular level; further, it enabled us to visualize blood vessels, small and large, without resorting to arteriography. Unlike magnetic resonance, arteriography is invasive, involving sharp instruments, requiring professional dexterity and dye injections and is fraught with a number of complications. Magnetic resonance's impact on the practice of medicine is now unfolding, far and wide, breathtaking. Its horizons are rapidly expanding.

Not outgrowing the party line, vivisectionists will claim and mud wrestle. They won't distract or waste our time, we have to move on, a lot remains to be said, to be done.

THE DISCOVERY OF RADIUM:
THE MAGNIFICENT FOUR

Radium, a radioactive chemical element that was discovered in 1898 by Pierre Curie, Marie Curie and an assistant, G. Bemont, occurs naturally as a disintegration product in the radioactive decay of thorium, uranium and actinium. It is used in luminescent paint, for meter dials, clocks and signs that must be read in the dark, but the most important application of radium is in medicine, mainly for the treatment of certain cancers, by harnessing the gamma radiation. Less costly and more efficient radioisotopes such as cobalt-60 and cesium-137 are now available, but the discovery of radium was a landmark. Vivisection did not do it.

Two generations of the Curies of France influenced the development of modern physics: Pierre and Marie Curie, their daughter, Irene, and son-in-law Jean Frederic Joliot. All awarded the Nobel Prize. Wow! What a clan! To those decrying their own station in life, yearning to be someone else, don't rush; reconsider, reflect. It isn't all laurel and smiles. Marie Curie died of leukemia caused by radiation on July 4, 1934; Irene died of the same disease in 1956; Pierre, was killed much earlier; in 1906 he was run over by a dray in Paris and died isntantly. Grim Reaper, be not proud. Pierre's death, a tragic blow to Marie, became a decisive point in her career. She doubled her energy to fulfill the scientific projects they both embarked on. At this somber moment, I won't allow vivisectionists to desecrate my temple of solitude. Silence is due.

THE MICROSCOPE AND THE MICROSCOPIST

Playfully yours, exhulted a libidinous, brawny sperm as it pierced through an ovum's defense. Dividing and multiplying, spreading their subculture to the suspecting and unsuspecting, importing doom or bloom; not all bacteria are bad, you know. And, protozoa, always agile, some mischievous, some beneficent. Mighty is the minute! All seen through Antonie van Leeuwenhoek's lens, lives within lives, energy, the vital force, the gentle, the sacred, the tempestuous and profane. Notoriously splendid, all and a zillion others, previously unseen by the unassisted human eye.

In the latter part of the seventeenth century, Antonie van Leeuwenhoek, an outstanding Dutch microscopist, took microscopy for a full-time work, an engaging hobby. The busy bee ground no less than 400 lenses during his lifetime. A secretive hermit though, he never revealed his microscopy techniques. They remain something of a mystery. I presume he knew for a secret to remain secret, don't entrust it to someone else; take it with you. But, the Dutchman permitted us to see what he saw; scenery never sighted before.

Vivisectionists, what are you going to say to this one? Your tales, your fables make politicians look good.

THE ELECTRON MICROSCOPE

More to fathom, wonder on and behold. Hopelessly invisible behind noncandid, opaque walls, intracellular mitochondria, nucleoli and many other cellular structures go about their vital tasks, their whereabouts, details and entrails shielded from an inquisitive Homo sapiens' eye. Not for long. Rending the veil happened in 1937, when physicist Erwin Wilhelm Muller brought the Electron Microscope into being. The great image magnifier enlarges by as much as one million times. Think of the multitudes added to our visual sphere since! Imagine the scientific and medical advances that were made as a result! Muller wasn't a vivisectionist. Thank God! And, later, in 1951, the same Muller offered the world one more fabulous invention, the intriguing field-ion microscope used to study crystals and gas absorption. Luminous, open and diaphanous, our cells have now become. Revealing what goes on at the basic primordial level has greatly enhanced our ability to examine ourselves, witness our minute anatomy and comprehend our physiology as well as the behavior, metamorphosis and characteristics of viruses that cause disease and epidemics.

Punching a hole in a pussycat's skull, or tying it by the tail, smashing a dog's torso, opening an obscene window to an ape's bowels or brain, wholesale burning of guinea pigs or wreaking ghastly spasms on some other animals (all and many more atrocious experiments in a vivisectionist's manual of arms) didn't invent an electron microscope or create a CT scan, didn't discover the X-ray or decipher the circulation of blood through our bellows and the chambers of our heart, nor teach us how to cook, communicate or contemplate. Yet, animal researchers keep on blowing their own trumpet—tunes to which we will not dance. Only the uninformed and misinformed will pay attention, wiggle and concede.

ANTICOAGULANTS

The advent of anticoagulants made complex vascular surgery, cardiac surgery and organ transplantation possible. None could have happened without them. Blood banks rely on anticoagulants to keep their blood inventory in a fluid state till the time of transfusion. The lives of thousands of patients with kidney failure depend on regular (usually three times a week) hemodialysis. The dialysis machine does for them what their kidneys have failed to do, filtering and purifying blood. Without anticoagulants, blood in the machine will clot, cease to flow, filtration becomes impossible, and harmful byproducts will accumulate, devastate and eventually kill their subject. Obstruction of blood vessels can be devastating or even fatal. If coagulation of blood is the cause, such obstruction—in a large number of cases—can be cleared by the administration of anticoagulants, saving life and restoring function.

Anticoagulants came primarily through keen observations, serendipitous knowledge, collective experience and in-vitro (test tube) testing. Animal experimentation has nothing to do with the discovery of any of them. But, even on this one, obvious as it is, vivisectionists came with a tooth fairy, but they have no right to treat us with contempt. When it comes to testing these compounds, there are several alternatives without having to harm animal or human—without distortion and scientific mediocrity. Didn't know, but I am finding out that animal experimentation is a habit, a form of addiction. And, some got hooked. Cure it we shall, for we can't run away or hide to escape responsibility. Within a clear conscience, there is no place to hide and responsibility cannot be ignored or delegated. Animal rights have been entrusted to a shepherd, Homo sapiens. Where is he? Where is she?

At this juncture, some basic information on the four principal anticoagulants is due.

Back in the 19th century, it was common practice to use leeches to suck blood out of an animal or human in order to cure or ameliorate certain conditions for which there was no definitive treatment then. Hirudin is secreted from glands situated near the leech's suckers; its anticoagulant property prevents blood from clotting, thus allowing the unweaned suckler to draw blood, and bleeding from the subject's skin continues for some time even after the glutted leech is removed from the skin. Man and the leech. Interesting! No harm was done. Why can't we all live together, give and take, take and give, akcnowledge, all in mutual interdependence and compassion (compassion means equal energy for all). Planet earth is but a Noah's Ark created to provide refuge for all the species. The Ark has been punished and reviled by the ill will of man. What shall we do if it slips anchor or runs adrift? The tidal waves of our ignorance and cruelty can do just that.

Another anticoagulant, citrates, was discovered in the 18th century. Sailors were plagued by scurvy due to vitamin C deficiency. Lemon and lime juices were used to treat scurvy. Something happened though; spontaneous hemorrhages were noted among sailors who consumed large amounts of lemon and lime. At that time, it was also known that these fruits contained high concentrations of citrates. Besides this clear evidence, test tube reconfirmation would have been sufficient and absolute. Yet, blindly, as though in a reflex response, vivisectors took their case to the animal laboratory and falsely claimed that we owe discovery of the anticoagulant propety of citrates in 1890 to their deeds, oblivious to the existence of test tubes and other ways and means. Sure-handed, not even-handed.

Coumadin, a very important anticoagulant, is frequently used worldwide. Veterinarians have noted, for some time, that cattle that ate "sweet clover" suffered spontaneous hemorrhages similar to those in sailors who freely consumed lemon and lime juice. Sweet clover was found to contain dicumarol, the parent substance from which coumadin is derived. On this, human and cattle have agreed; still on many others, they go their separate ways. To affirm and confirm, animal sacrifices aren't necessary, never were. But, strange how fads make it to our brain cells, displacing common sense, eclipsing good judgment.

Heparin, a monarch among anticoagulants, is a native substance naturally secreted by the mast cells of the reticuloendothelial system of humans and other animals. Jay McLean discovered Heparin in vitro, without animal experimentation. Heparin is indispensable to performing major vascular and cardiac surgery, and the drug of choice in treating acute thrombotic conditions.

Newer agents keep coming adding more therapeutic tools, such as thrombolytic therapy using streptokinase, urokinase and other agents. Trying to credit animal research for this modality discredits those who so argue and assert.

BLOOD TRANSFUSION AND THE BLOOD GROUPS

Severe hemorrhage may be caused by many diseases including stomach or intestinal ulcers, blood disorders such as hemophilia, accidental injury or in the course of some major, complicated surgical procedures. An otherwise healthy individual can cope with and compensate for small or moderate blood loss, but a previously unhealthy individual may succumb. A massive blood loss can be rapidly fatal for anyone. Blood transfusion came to the rescue whereby the ruddy warm water of life can be directly infused into the veins of bleeders saving their lives and restoring their stamina and vigor. For blood transfusion to be reasonably safe, donor's blood must be screened for certain diseases; besides, donor and recipient must belong to the same species (homologous) and should have the same blood group. If a blood group A patient receives blood drawn from a group B or AB individual, severe reactions are bound to happen; even death may follow. Blood transfusion between different species was practiced in earlier times and was fatal in the majority of instances. In elective situations such as a future major surgery, a portion of a patient's own blood (autologous) may be withdrawn ahead of time, and stored in the blood bank up until the time of surgery when it can be returned to the patient as needed. If not promptly used, blood can be frozen and maintained viable for years.

Before the discovery of blood groups, blood transfusion was fraught with serious immediate and remote complications. Karl Landsteiner, while working as a research assistant at the Vienna Pathology Institute, noted the severe reactions and fatalities resulting from transfusion of whole blood from one human to another. In 1901, he discovered the three major types of human blood; the following year, he discovered the fourth. 1901 and 1902 were very good years. Here we are: blood incompatibility, matching, blood banking, grouping, administration, the whole works, all materialized without committing animal experimentation. This extraordinary discovery was a milestone that reshaped and upgraded the art and science of medicine and surgery. Blood groups are also utilized in legal medicine as an admissible evidence in paternity cases and murder trials. Blood types were found to be inherited by way of specific genes; this fact gave the study of human genetics a substantial boost.

The quartet includes the drummer; theirs ravishly beats the drum and tampers with the beat. Informed, we won't march, enlighted we won't swallow vivisectionists' hogwash.

ANTISEPTICS, ANTIBIOTICS AND
BACTERIOSTATIC AGENTS

Antisepsis means preventing infection by inhibiting the growth of microorganisms which cause infection. It goes without saying that prevention of infection is one of the main pillars of any good health care system. Antibiotics and bacteriostatic agents have become an integral part in the treatment of many infections that would otherwise cause serious harm or even death. In the United States, as recently as the 1940s, bacterial infections alone caused 25 percent of all deaths. Today they are responsible for less than 3 percent. Unfortunately, we are now besieged by a new epidemic, AIDS (acquired autoimmunodeficiency syndrome). We don't know for sure how the menace broke out, let alone how and when it will end or be brought under control. Despair, apathy and hostility will not cure AIDS. With no remedy on hand, preventive measures are now the only shield we have for combat. This includes: sex educaton before adolescence; avoiding anal intercourse and multiple sex partners; the use of condoms; total abstinence from intravenous drugs; screening blood donors for the virus; and transfusing blood and blood products only when absolutely necessary. Whenever possible, if major surgery is anticipated, timely provision should be made for one's own blood to be drawn, safely stored and transfused as needed during and after surgery. This process, called autotransfusion should be talked over with your physician. A cure, a solution will one day come, but it won't be through animal research. Matter of fact, animal research will mislead, delay and hinder as it has done time and again. Yet the licentious devil has seduced many. And, to the misbegotten altar of sorrow they gravitate, blinded by fabrications, energized by false hopes. Human-made is the devil; anthropomorphic, the tempter moves about, surreptitiously stalking ambient and abode.

When it comes to antisepsis, credit duly belongs to Dr. Ignaz Semmelweis. In the 1840s, he established the aseptic technique. His keen observations of childbed fever in women (puerperal fever) were crucial. At the Vienna General Hospital he noted that a large number of women developed chills and fever, and often died within a few days after delivery in the hospital, while those women who delivered on their way to the hospital were the fortunate ones; they rarely contracted the fever and survived. You see, a hospital isn't always a safe place for you. In the same infirmary, one ward had several deaths from childbed fever, while the second ward had only a few. Semmelweis became convinced that obstetricians and nurses were the vehicle through which puerperal fever was transmitted from an infected woman to a noninfected woman. He recommended that all obstetricians and nurses must wash their hands with a watery solution of chlorinated lime after examining women who had been infected with puerperal fever. To everyone's surprise, the ritual of washing-of-hands did the trick. It dramatically lowered the death rate in the unsafe ward to that of the relatively safe ward. Despite the obvious, the senior obstetricians rejected the principle of hand washing. Their arrogance and stubbornness inflicted death on untold numbers of women. Shameful how the lives of others grow irrelevant the moment someone's ego comes in between. Amazing how serial large scale killings committed by rulers, leaders, kings, queens and scientists are overlooked, accepted, even hailed, while petty or single offenses perpetrated by John or Jane Doe are condemned and passionately avenged. I guess it all depends on who did what, not on what was done. The scales of justice suffered a permanent tilt. Scoliotic they remain. Oliver Wendell Holmes, Justice of the U.S. Supreme Court, once remarked to his clerk, "I don't do justice, I merely apply the law." It says it all; the whole thing is a sham.

To prove what had already been proved, Semmelweis was pressured by some of his supporters to experiment on rabbits. Poor rabbits! Even this unnecessary, gruesome cue failed to convince the bone-headed, insolent professors. Finally, Semmelweis was dismissed from the Vienna Hospital, only to return later, as a patient, in the psychiatric ward (where else?), with the diagnosis of insanity. They broke his heart and let me tell you: when hearts break, everything else follows; the whole lot. Irascible heart, exultantly pounding in my bosom, do you realize how vincible you are?

It took 20 years to get the point across. Imagine that! In the 1860s, Pasteur isolated the specific bacteria that caused puerperal fever and innoculated them into laboratory animals. Louis Pasteur merely followed the usual writ: menacing live animals to prove what had already been proven. In the interim—a 20-year time span—thousands, possibly millions of women worldwide continued to succumb to the frequently fatal infection. Their lives were wasted and could have been saved. A classic example of wholesale malpractice gone for 20 years. Pasteur could have used other means to reaffirm and pontificate. What shall I say? Even individuals of high mettle and intellectual fortitude cannot escape the straitjacket of mind conditioning. It takes more than mere intellectual skill—much more than vast oceans of conventional knowledge.

Doctor Sigismund Peller, medical statistician and historian, stated in an article quoted by Brandon Reines in his book *Heart Research on Animals* published by the American Anti-Vivisection Society, in 1985, pp. 48–49, "In a world that had not been stultified by the idea that only animal experimentation and only the laboratory can provide proof in matters of human pathology, the battle against puerperal fever would not have needed to wait for the discovery of the cocci (bacteria). The experts who, during the 1840s, opposed and prevented the initiation of a rational program of combatting the disease should have been charged with negligence that resulted in mass killings. But they were not. They were not deprived of the position they had misused. Instead, they continued to enjoy the privileges and prestige previously accorded to them, while the benefactors suffered and paid dearly for their discoveries.''

This is not the only large scale disaster caused by blind obedience to authority. Authority itself is blind. And, the blind leads the blind. Mind's eye blinded, many habitually repeat the vivisectionist's mantra, ''Do not stop vivisection,'' while the tragic reality, ''Vivisection kills you'' is blotted out. Unseen.

And, it didn't all happen in the safe and unsafe wards of Vienna's infirmaries or the much hallowed scientific conclaves of Paris. Ancient Chinese, practical and adept, used iodine as an antiseptic. Of other people and cultures very little do we know. Once in a while it is good to cruise and travel beyond the perimeter, even through the silent, telling pages of a book or the faded leaflets of a distant scroll, or just by talking to others. There is more to our small world than just the U.S. and Western Europe. This may help dampen the blazing flames of bigotry and nationalism, a fatal disease in itself. Remember, we can't save animals if we can't save ourselves, others as well. As a direct result of our doings, the poor souls perish. Love, you can't fragment; fragmented, it ain't love. Bias would be more like it. Let us leave it at that!

THE DISCOVERY OF PENICILLIN

Penicillin, undisputed father of all antibiotics. For long the magic wand in the antibiotic arsenal. Penicillin still reigns, but due to predictable and unpredictable changes in the biology and virulence of microorganisms, his lineage—a long list—together with other new clans and subclans of antibiotics have come to the fore. And, it wasn't a chimney-mediated Christmas gift from Santa Claus. And, it wasn't through the dubious trails of the animal lab. Here is how the epoch discovery came to be.

In 1928, while working with staphylococcus bacteria, Alexander Fleming noted a bacteria-free zone around a mold growth, pencilium notatum, a fungus which contaminated the culture. The observation wasn't lost to the serious observer. Fleming isolated the ingredient in the mold that prevented bacterial growth even when it was diluted 800 times. He called it penicillin. In 1945, Fleming shared the Nobel Prize for Physiology or Medicine with Ernest Boris Chain and Howard Walter Florey. The Scotsman was also knighted in 1944.

Matter of good fortune that penicillin was not tested in guinea pigs, the all time popular experimental animal. The sweet, dainty creatures would have died and perhaps, penicillin would have been lost to humanity. God! Those guys must have deprived us of some other goodies.

STREPTOMYCIN
A GIFT OF THE SOIL

The second antibiotic to be developed after penicillin, and the first to be effective against a then prevalent and fatal infection: tuberculosis. Streptomycin works by interfering with the ability of the causative organism, the tubercle bacillus to synthesize some vital proteins. A gift of the soil where it is synthesized by one of its many benevolent organisms, streptomyces griseus. The discovery was made by Waxman and his colleagues in 1945. So, when we celebrate streptomycin's birthday, we won't let the vivisectionists dance around the birthday cake. Avid for merit and recognition, they experiment and experiment with the stuff, publish and publish, talk and talk, and when their noise level reaches a certain critical decibel, credit lands in their lap. A steal! So skilled at it, they are hardly apprehended. Stealthy! That is why this chapter became part of this book.

THE DISCOVERY OF CEPHALOSPORINS
A GIFT OF THE SEA

An extended family of antibiotics, prolific, now constituting the majority of antibiotics effective against many serious infections. A gift of the sea. They are semi-synthetic, primarily derived from a mold, cephalosporium acremonium. The auspicious mold was accidentally discovered in the stagnant marine waters off Sardinia, the Bay of Naples and Sicily. Thanks to Guisseppe Brotzu, an Italian physician. So when you sit on the dock by the bay, don't let the calm waters fool you. The first cephalosporin was isolated in 1961, sixteen years after Brotzu made his discovery. Vivisectionists, you have lost your fig leaf. Bare you stand, poised for the Fall.

THE SULFA DRUGS

Sulfanilamide was discovered in 1935; it inhibits or stops the growth of bacteria in cultures. More than 5,000 derivatives, known as sulfonamides or sulfa drugs were prepared and found to have antibacterial properties. Though superseded by antibiotics, sulfa drugs remain key to managing certain specific infections.

Again, members of the sulfa family were not born or reared in the animal research laboratory, yet someone from the ranks will surely be eager to adopt. Whose ranks? You know!

THE DISCOVERY OF ANESTHESIA

For centuries from the 1840s, relief from pain during surgical procedures was attempted through pressure on nerves, freezing of the part to be operated upon, acupuncture, inhalation of fumes from extracts of narcotic plants, alcohol stupefaction; even deliberate asphyxiation was practiced.

In 1842, Crawford W. Long of Georgia removed a small tumor from the neck of a youth who was under the influence of ether; reportedly, the surgery was painless, ushering in the successful use of anesthesia during surgery. From then on, anesthesia grew to be a science and an art, yet from its inception, its breakthroughs were not the brood of vivisection. Vivisectionists may claim otherwise, but facts refute their claims.

THE DISCOVERY OF ETHER: REMEMBERING GEORGIA'S FROLICS

From alcohol and sulfuric acid, Valerius Cordus synthesized ether in around the 1840s. "Sweet oil of vitroil," as he called it, turned out to be a hit and became known for its medicinal properties. Here's how it all began, a chance occurrence. Music, dance, food, balloons and the booze, wild parties, lots of fun, and let come what may. To exult and exhilarate, the medical students at Jefferson, Georgia used the stuff, the "sweet oil of vitroil." They inhaled, got high and leaped with joy. Poor things; they must have been utterly stressed. Those hellish fiestas became known as "ether frolics." Into one or some of them Crawford W. Long, a surgeon at Jefferson, wandered, stress-driven, perhaps. Good that he joined the boisterous crowd for he noticed that party villains who oozed and bruised were uncharacteristically oblivious to their pain. Sedate. Anesthetized. So, it dawned on him to try ether as an anesthetic for surgery. Try it he did; successful he was. Hooray, a milestone was laid, unblemished by vivisection, untarnished by cruelty to animals. Happenstance and clinical investigation put ether on the table. Thank God for "Georgia's Frolics" and Crawford Long.

THE DISCOVERY OF CHLOROFORM

It's liquid, it's heavy, odor pleasant, ether-like, it is chloroform. First prepared in 1831 and first used as an anesthetic in 1847 by Sir James Simpson of Edinburgh, chloroform proved to be a very useful agent. It has the advantage of being nonflammable, while ether is. But, because its margin of safety is narrower, its use greatly declined; still its discovery was a formidable step in the development of anesthesia. John Snow, the first physician to practice anesthesia full-time, administered it to Queen Victoria during the birth of Prince Leopold, her eighth child. The potent inhalation anesthetic can be prepared from various organic compounds, most often from alcohol or acetone.

DISCOVERY OF THE LAUGHING GAS AND SOME OTHER ANESTHETIC AGENTS

Whimsical and misty, in small doses nitrous oxide, when inhaled, relieves pain and frequently induces laughter. Hence, it's called the laughing gas. Around 1800, Sir Humphry Davy noted the anesthetic effects of nitrous oxide on himself.

Other anesthetics followed: Cyclopropane, Halothane (Fluothane), Methoxyflurane (Penthrane) and intravenous anesthetics. And, vivisection deserves no credit.

INHALATION ENDOTRACHEAL ANESTHESIA

It happened in Glasgow, Scotland in 1880. William MacEwan was called to remove a malignant tumor at the base of a patient's tongue. Using a mask for anesthesia, it would have blocked the surgeon's way into the patient's mouth, so MacEwan decided to insert a tube down the patient's windpipe to administer the inhalation anesthetic. For practice, MacEwan used a corpse, not laboratory animals. Common sense. He passed a tube into the patient's mouth, down through the larynx into the trachea.

A major hurdle remained: what can be done to prevent the lungs from collapsing when the chest is opened to perform surgery on the lungs, heart or esophagus? Dr. Ferdinand Sauerbruch, the well-known surgeon of Leipzig, Germany, thought of blowing air into the lungs to keep them inflated while the chest was open; in other words, insufflation or positive-pressure ventilation. Like his mentor, Paul Mikulicz, Sauerbruch had faith in animal experimentation, so he took his sound idea to an unsound place and tried positive-pressure anesthesia on animals. It was harmful to them, a mistrial that halted progress in this field for approximately four decades, from the early 1900s to the mid or late 40s. Sauerbruch was very influential, a superstar; obliged, many scientists and surgeons worldwide followed. Meanwhile George Fell of Buffalo, New York, as early as 1891, used forced respiration to resuscitate victims of drowning and morphine poisoning. In 1900, Matas, in the course of operations on the open chest, employed positive-pressure ventilation through a tube in the larynx. And it worked.

Sauerbruch's animal experiments were repeated by Samuel J. Meltzer in the early 1900s. The technique was found safe, and lungs could be inflated and deflated while the chest was open. Still, when Meltzer's work on animals was applied to humans, several problems arose. Gaining experience from extensive casualties in World War I, Ivan Magill and E.S. Rowbotham used bellows to blow air containing inhalation anesthetics into the patient's lungs through a tube lodged in the trachea (windpipe). This is essentially the technique of modern inhalation endotracheal anesthesia.

The road was long, developments were momentous. Animal experimentation did not bring them about; matter of fact, Sauerbruch's work on animals misled him and sound ideas were abandoned. Meltzer's animal experiments were of secondary value, their impact was even questionable. Pert and flippant, vivisectionists' folly won't change facts.

BLOCKERS, INHIBITORS, AGONISTS, ANTAGONISTS AND DIURETICS: THE DISCOVERY OF ANTIHYPERTENSIVE DRUGS

High blood pressure claims many lives, millions worldwide, due to accelerating arteriosclerosis (hardening of the arteries) contributing to narrowing and eventual blockage of blood vessels, kidney destruction and rupture of blood vessels in different parts of the body including the brain. A grim disease. A notorious, surreptitious killer. Some drugs have evolved and proven effective in treating hypertension in humans. They did not emerge from the chamber of horrors, the animal laboratory. The influential vivisectionist assembly will tell it differently, but their propaganda, snap shots, sound nips and endless literature should not persuade anyone. Facts disprove their claims. Those helpful medications are the product of keen observations made while thoughtfully monitoring the human condition in health and disease, subsequently supported by careful, ethical clinical investigation. When something shows promise, real or imagined, make-up artists hurry to the scene, choreography follows, sequence of events rearranged, a maze of statistics, tables, graphs and snatches of truth here and there to don legitimacy on the spurious and fictitious.

THE DISCOVERY OF ORAL DIURETICS IN THE TREATMENT OF HYPERTENSION

In 1937, Dr. Hamilton Southworth, while practicing at Johns Hopkins Hospital, noticed that patients began to breathe deeply after receiving the new miracle drug sulfanilamide to treat their bacterial infectoins. Later, he and Strauss confirmed the observation on a few normal human volunteers. Sulfanilamide led to diuresis and improved elimination of sodium and potassium by the kidneys. As a diuretic it offered relief to patients with heart failure. Soon a group of chemicals, namely chlorothiazides, evolved from the parent chemical. They proved effective and reasonably safe in treating hypertension in humans. Karl Beyer, a prominent researcher in this field wrote, ''We did not assess the activity of chlorothiazide in hypertensive animals prior to clinical trial.''* Matter of fact, diuretics do not lower the blood pressure in normotensive animals. Besides, it isn't easy to produce hypertension in rats or dogs. Interesting how breakthroughs come about. Amazing how facts remain beneath the surface, fabrications and misconceptions paving the way. All it needs is some digging and facts will readily emerge.

---

*Beyer, K.H., ''Discovering the Thiazides: Where Biology and Chemistry Meet,'' *Persp. in Biol. and Med.* Spring 1977, p. 417.

THE DISCOVERY OF BLOCKERS

Blockers play a substantial role in the treatment of high blood pressure in human subjects. Let us consult the archives where the true story hybernates. Dr. B. Pritchard was administering propranolol, a well-known "beta blocker," to patients suffering from angina pectoris (chest pain caused by narrowing of the blood vessels supplying blood to the heart). Pritchard noted that in addition to relieving the severe chest pain, the drug lowered the blood pressure of his patients. Quoting Dr. Desmond Fitzgerald, "Pritchard's tenacious studies on the hypertensive action of propranolol eventually paved the way for the extensive use of beta blockers in hypertension even though this therapeutic application was not predicted from animal studies."*

And it isn't just beta blockers; alpha blockers are also being used to treat hypertension. Beta and alpha blockers work in different ways on epinephine and norepinephine that are normally secreted into the blood stream. As in beta blockers, alpha blockers were used to treat hypertension based solely on clinical observations on human subjects.

CLONIDINE

A very effective agent, to treat hypertension. Its lowering of high blood pressure was accidentally discovered while being used to relieve nasal congestion in humans. Observation! Observation! An open eye (an open mind) deciphers, discovers, guides.

---

*Fitzgerald, D., "The Development of a New Cardiovascular Drug." In *Recent Developments in Cardiovascular Drugs*, Edinburgh, 1981, p. 13. Edited by J. Coltart and D.E. Jewitt Churchill Livingstone.

CALCIUM ANTAGONISTS

A very exciting recent addition to our armamentarium for controlling hypertension in humans. While this group of drugs was being administered to patients with angina pectoris, lowering of blood pressure was noted in addition to relieving chest pain. That is how their role in the treatment of hypertension evolved. And they proved effective.

Creatures of bad habit, animal researchers grab all the above, march to their altar, sacrifice animals, experiment and experiment, grind out myriads of so-called scientific papers; many get published. And, credit goes to those whose names perch on the page. All in the name of humanity. Ends justifying means: the ignoble cycle that has tarnished and bruised humanity. Drawn into its powerful magnetic field, humankind's wrath, illogic and lack of prudence have grown mighty, endangering itself, others as well. Is this a book of lament or amends? Well! of both; let it be, for I hope the latter will heal the former.

THE DISCOVERY OF DIGITALIS FOR THE
TREATMENT OF HEART FAILURE

Heart failure means that one's heart has failed to pump blood to the lungs, brain, liver, kidneys, extremities and other tissues and body organs. Untreated, heart failure ends fatally, always. When his majesty, the heart, declines, every other organ follows: kidneys, lungs, liver, intestines, muscles, brain, what have you. Fatigue, difficulty in breathing, nausea, indigestion, poor appetite, lethargy are some of the symptoms. One of the obvious signs is dropsy, meaning accumulation of fluids in the body. Literally and figuratively, one swells up, particularly noted in the legs.

For millennia plants have remedied the ills of man. There

the herbaceous figwort stands tall; a grand family of plants, one of its beneficent members is the foxglove. Native to Europe, the Mediterranean region and the Canary Islands, its drooping bell-shaped flowers bloom in white, purple, or yellow, but the offering is in the leaf. For centuries folklore tales made mention of miraculous cures of dropsy after consuming foxglove leaves. On William Withering, the anecdote and observation were not wasted. In the 1700s the good doctor extracted digitalis from the figwort and used it to treat dropsy in a number of his patients. Here is what Dr. Thomas Lewis wrote in *Clinical Science*: "To show by further example the completeness with which observations on man himself must govern the establishment of medical remedies, digitalis is named, than which there is no more valuable remedy in the pharmacopoea today."* Late on, it was found that the most potent action of digitalis is exercised through lowering the ventricular heart rates in cases where the auricles are fast as in auricular fibrillation. The ventricles are the two principal pumping chambers of our heart; the auricles are the other two chambers, basically receiving blood from different parts of the body and passing it on to the ventricles. The four chambers of our sacred heart act interdependently, harmoniously waiting for one another, dancing, synchronizing the indispensable cycle: circulation of blood. Back to Sir Lewis Thomas, "in this is an instructive example of how unwisely theory may be allowed precedence over immediately relevant experience. The most essential information, the profound effect which digitalis is capable of exerting in auricular fibrillation could not have been one through observation on the frog or normal mammal, but only, as it was won, by observation on patients."** It says it all. Are they listening though?! Are they?

---

*Lewis, T. *Clinical Science, University College Hospital, London*, Shaw & Sons, Ltd., 1934, p. 188.
**Ibid.

THE DISCOVERY OF DRUGS FOR
THE RELIEF OF ANGINA PECTORIS (CHEST
PAIN ORIGINATING FROM THE HEART)

With every heartbeat, the heart pumps blood to every organ and body part, near and afar, five quarts of blood every minute, 2,000 gallons a day. But, for the indomitable heart to keep pumping the water of life, itself must receive sufficient portion of the vital brew. The heart is supplied with blood by way of the coronary arteries, themselves are frequently ravaged by arteriosclerosis (atherosclerosis) which causes narrowing of those vital, dainty routes and diminution in the volume of blood delivered. With reduced blood supply, a heart may function perfectly well at rest, but during exercise things go different. More blood is needed to enable the heart to perform the extra work. If the coronary arteries are substantially narrowed, the laboring heart will not receive the blood quota it is asking for. Angina pectoris results, a severe chest pain red-signalling the underlying serious problem. A heart's anguished cry for help.

Nitrates represent a cornerstone in the treatment of angina pectoris. And, it wasn't animal research that gave us nitrates to relieve anginal pain in humans. Matter of fact, in 1867, Dr. T. Lauder Brunton tried amyl nitrate on himself when he was seized by an anginal attack. Amyl nitrate assuaged his ache; subsequently, he and Dr. William Murrel used the same drug to treat angina in patients. Sir Thomas Lewis, physician in charge of the Department of Clinical Research at the University College Hospital in London, wrote, ''The method of Clinical Science avoids all theoretical assumptions and the fallacies arising out of this, all errors originating out of complex technique and artificial circumstance; it brings us at once to the endpoint in a simple but crucial test in asking: Does this substance in fact relieve anginal pain? In its simple directness, and its capacity to produce the precisely relevant answers, lie the virtues of this eminently scientific inquiry (clinical science)."*

Dr. Maurice McGregor, a clinical pharmacologist, believes that animal research could have retarded rather than enhanced the development of effective medications for angina pectoris. Quoting Dr. McGregor, "Few would dispute that the most significant advance in the last hundred years in the treatment of angina pectoris was the introduction of the nitrate drugs by Lauder Brunton in 1867. This advance was the result of observing the anginal patient and did not depend on any experimental model at all. Departure from this approach may be largely to blame for much of the unprofitable effort expended in the search for better agents in the subsequent 99 years."**

Even this plain, direct one, they won't let it pass. The collective will of the vivisectionists has forged its signature on every page of the encyclopedia of medical advances and breakthroughs. We know it, we must let others know. Passing valid information on to others is a responsibility, a duty considered by the seers to be a most formidable consummation of charity. The enterprise is open to everyone. Begin now: The authentic data on this page and other pages are all yours to transmit, to dispatch.

THE DISCOVERY OF DRUGS FOR THE TREATMENT OF IRREGULAR HEARTBEAT (ARRHYTHMIAS)

That naughty heart; it keeps missing the beat. "He did not feel great discomfort during the attack, but, as he said, be-

---

*Ibid., p. 244.
**McGregor, "Drugs for the Treatment of Angina Pectoris." In *International Encyclopedia of Pharmacology and Therapeutics: Section 6: Clinical Pharmacology*. Edited by L. Lasagna. V. ii Oxford, Pergamon Press, 1980, p. 387.

ing a Dutch merchant used to good order in his affairs, he would like to have good order in his heart business also and asked why there were heart specialists if they could not abolish this very disagreeable phenomena. On my telling him that I could promise him nothing, he told me that he knew himself how to get rid of his attacks, and as I did not believe him, he promised to come back the next morning with a regular pulse and he did. It happened that quinine in many countries, especially in countries where there is a good deal of malaria, is a sort of drug for everything, just as one takes acetylsalicylic acid today if one does not feel well or is afraid of having taken cold." Wenckeback, the famed cardiologist wrote this in 1914.*

Cinchona bark, also called quinquina, most likely came from Peru in 1638 and has been successfully used for the treatment of malaria. Quinine and quinidine were extracted from the cinchona bark and were administered to malaria patients. Physicians noted that patients who received any of those drugs and happened to have irregular heartbeats were substantially improved. For the so-called rebellious palpitations, Jean-Batiste de Senec in 1749 used cinchona with satisfactory results.

From cinchona to cocaine: for a long, long time, physicians have acknowledged the local anesthetic effect of cocaine was brought by blocking the impulses traveling through nerves. This important discovery of the local anesthetic action of cocaine has nothing to do with animal experimentation, yet when it comes to its antiarrhythmic properties, it is being said that German investigators tried the local anesthetic effect of cocaine on the irregular heartbeat in dogs. Assuming this story is true, a drop in the bucket, which I am certain

---

*Cohen, S.I. "Current Concepts in Quinidine Therapy." In *Drugs in Cardiology*, V. I, part 1, p. 17. Edited by E. Donoso. New York: Stratton Intercontinental Medical Book Corp., 1975.

would have evolved as a natural outgrowth of its anesthetic action, an action that bears no relation to animal experimentation. From cocaine, procainamide came.

A potent widely used antiarrhythmic drug is lidocaine (Xylocaine). Dr. Louis Lasagna noted that lidocaine is among drugs whose effects "were not discovered except by serendipity after their clinical introduction for other purposes."* Here is a good example: During cardiac catheterization, Southworth noted in the 1950s that administration of lidocaine many times controlled ventricular fibrillation in patients, ventricular fibrillation being a rapidly fatal irregular heartbeat. On this Dr. Moss stated, "Subsequently many authors have confirmed the value of lidocaine in abolishing or preventing ventricular arrhythmias in animals and man under a variety of conditions."**

Dilantin has been used for the treatment of convulsive disorders such as epilepsy as early as 1938. Since then, its effect on irregular heartbeats in patients was duly noted and recorded on electrocardiograms. Later on, in 1950, Harris and Kokernot experimented with dilantin in the animal laboratory and claimed credit for the antiarrhythmic properties of dilantin. It has already been known, but that is the way some choose to confirm and affirm. A choice, the prudent declines to undertake. Vivisection is not a necessity. It is an easy pick by featherweights who shun accountability; for them alternate routes are harder to negotiate, though better, safer, kinder; hence their disdain.

---

*Lasagna, L. "Drug Discovery and Introduction: Regulation and Over-regulation," *Clin. Pharm. and Ther.* 1976, 20(5):507.
**Moss, A.J., *Antiarrhythmic Agent.* Springfield: Charles C. Thomas, Publisher, 1973, p. 47.

CORONARY BYPASS SURGERY AND
TRANSLUMINAL ANGIOPLASTY

Lonesome, solitary and pointing to the left, where the spleen is, the heart tends the well, life's reservoir where the water of life serenely flows in and tempestuously surges out. Behold the cosmic dance of your heart; with every beat, the divine dancer draws up warm blood, its offering to every viscus and body part. Still, even the gallant warrior is not exempt from the harsh articles of the divine constitution. With all others it is subject to infirmity, eclipse and retribution. When its lines of blood supply (the coronary arteries) are interfered with the well's steward thirsts, endures and suffers. Its proprietor experiences angina pectoris, a crushing and agonizing chest pain; the heart muscle itself may sustain severe damage. This is known as coronary artery disease or arteriosclerotic (atherosclerotic) heart disease which causes heart attacks and inflicts a grave toll, 600,000 deaths annually, in the United States alone. We have dwelt on the subject earlier, a revisit here is made to help connect the parts, the thoughts. To bring desperately needed blood supply to parched hearts, the bypass principle proved useful. A winner. Long in use for other parts of the body, it worked; basically going around (bypassing) obstructions, be they in the bowels, stomach, brain's aqueduct or other blood vessels.

In coronary bypass surgery, the patient's own veins—usually harvested from the thighs and legs—or a dispensable artery—commonly a mammary artery located behind the breast bone—are utilized to bridge the blockage in the coronary artery that impedes blood flow to the heart muscle downstream. Just like a river or a highway. For the most part, the operation relieves the symptoms of the disease, essentially the debilitating painful attacks of angina pectoris, patients can do more, and the quality of their lives is improved. As far as extending life, adding more days, more seasons, years, perhaps, this has materialized in those patients where the right coronary as well as the two branches of the left coronary artery are severely diseased, also in a critical group with tightly narrowed left main coronary artery, an ominous condition heralding impending sudden death. Animal research was not responsible for this development. Repeating: Animal research was not responsible for this development. It was a naturally grown fruit of Kunlin's work on peripheral vessels, principally in the lower extremities. In 1961, in France, Kunlin first used a portion of a patient's own vein to replace obstructed arterial segments. This gave birth to arterial bypass surgery for different parts of the body, including our indispensable heart. Mind you, earlier on we discussed what it takes to perform this operation: anesthesia, blood grouping and transfusion, anticoagulants, antibiotics, antiseptic/sterile technique, drugs to treat irregular heartbeats and many other disciplines including a big one: the heart-lung machine. In all of them, animal research either contributed nothing, misled or curtailed.

By contrast, the animal laboratory is credited—more appropriate to say discredited—with several surgical procedures to augment the blood supply to the heart; none of them worked out. All harmed. Briefly, I will tell of three. Beck's procedures included rubbing the surface of the heart with a sponge; crude, isn't it? Even sprinkling irritants and dubious chemicals on the poor thing with the mistaken notion that such a jumble will import blood from the heart's neighborhood. It failed. Another Beck's fiasco was constricting the principal vein draining the heart (coronary sinus): blood will thus back up and flood the barren heart muscle. Sorry, this one didn't work either; it added burden to a tired heart; the agile organ refused to go soggy. And it did harm. Another fancy of his didn't make it. Beck thought of supplying blood to the heart through the back door by forcing it under high pressure into its draining thoroughfare (the coronary sinus), in a retrograde manner. Like its predecessors retrograde perfusion backfired, went down to defeat. And the rendering was injury.

All Beck's procedures were born and nurtured within the shady oracles of the animal laboratory; dogs basically were the victims. Controlled clinical trials subsequently proved that none of Beck's forways was worthy. They imported iatrogenic damage, a vivisection-created disease. Malpractice.

Another baroque idea issued from Vineberg of Canada. A good salesman, his tortured design caught the imagination of cardiac surgeons in the 1960s and 1970s. Vineberg conceived of the heart muscle as a sponge, a porous mass capable of sucking or imbibing blood when served. It isn't. He theorized that by tunneling an artery—usually the mammary artery—into the heart muscle, the blood delivered by the implanted artery will nurse a heart in drought. Intoxicated with his idea, Vineberg went to the animal laboratory—where else!—a playground for those who could afford one. He knocked off many dogs, and came up exactly with the same conclusions he started with in the first place. A neat job! Self-fulfilling prophecies, tailored to a snug fit; no wonder those guys love the animal laboratory, it gives them what they want, when they want it, a shopping mall, just about. Ego realized; image aggrandized. Unfortunately, his experiments were copied in many other places with simlar erroneous conclusions. The dog ain't human. A chum and a perfect buddy, this for sure; still, it ain't human. Outcome: disastrous. Thousands upon thousands of patients had their hearts poked, damaged further, harmed more.

Being supercilious is not reserved for American and Canadian researchers; others share the untidy distinction. In the 30s and 40s, Italian researchers caught glimpse of a crazy cerebration: tying of the mammary artery. The mucky effluent was ferried to the animal laboratory and, naturally, the expected outcome came along: Hallelujah! An amazing feat with great promise; on to patients with initial wild claims—as always—shortly thereafter, inevitable impairment and other penalties of muckraking. No one knows as of this date how such a foolish idea could have worked out. Ill-advised from the outset, but this is exactly why we have vivisection, a proving ground for the ill-considered, the mistaken, the peevish and the chimerical. And don't forget, status-seekers, the infatuated and those with nothing better to spend their time, their life on.

MY NINE LIVES ON EARTH:
THE MIRACLE OF RESURRECTION
EXCUSE ME! RESUSCITATION
CARDIOPULMONARY RESUSCITATION (CPR)

"I advised him to take no more medicine, but to be electrified through the breast. He was so treated. The violent symptoms immediately ceased and he fell into a sweet sleep."* That was Reverend John Wesley, founding father of the Protestant Methodist Church in the 18th century. The Reverend was a proponent of "electrotherapy." "On the Recovery of the Apparently Dead," Charles Kite, a member of the English Royal Humane Society, wrote in 1774, "A Mr. Squires very humanely tried the effects of electricity on a child who had fallen from a window and being taken up for dead. Twenty minutes at least had elapsed before he could apply the shock, which he gave to various parts of the body without apparent success; but, at length, on transmitting a few shocks through the thorax, he perceived a small pulsation; soon after that the child began to breathe, though with

---

*Quoted by Wertenbacker, L. In *To Mend the Heart*. New York: The Viking Press, 1980, p. 178.

great difficulty. In about ten minutes she vomited. A kind of stupor remained for some days, but the child was restored to perfect health and spirits in about a week."*

If the heart stops contracting (cardiac arrest) or if it quivers (ventricular fibrillation), no blood could be pumped out. The heart must resume contraction within approximately five minutes, otherwise irreversible damage to the brain will result. A heart in fibrillation can many times recover its beat by applying an electric current as the Reverend and Mr. Squires have done more than 200 years ago, or by thumping the chest with a closed fist as many have done in earlier eras. An arrested heart needs an immediate massage. And the massage can be done with the chest open or closed. In most cases, electric shocks are needed in addition to cardiac massage.

More than a hundred years after its successful application in humans, Prevost and Battelli used electric current to reverse ventricular fibrillation in dogs. And, "open chest cardiac resuscitation" is not the result of animal experimentation.

In the early 1960s, Kouwenhoven, Jude and Knickerbocker experimented with cardiopulmonary resuscitation without opening the chest, known as "external cardiac massage." Their animal studies did not bring forth an effective method. They then began working on cadavers in the morgue. They compressed the chest of recently deceased humans and proved that blood could be made to circulate through external compression of the heart. Their technique was then tried on human beings, combined with mouth-to-mouth resuscitation; it has become a standard CPR technique.

---

*Kite, C., quoted in *To Mend the Heart* by Wertenbacker.

HOW CAN YOU MEND A BROKEN HEART?
THE HEART-LUNG MACHINE

How? And I am not talking sorrow, despair, the woes of falling out of love, the chill and bleakness of loneliness and other ill-fated liaisons of the meandering human heart. Those aches along with other burdens I have pondered and mused on in other books, *Coping and Beyond** and *Love, Passion & Solitude.*** In this book the subject is physical ailments that impound and impoverish the heart with outcomes, serious to fatal.

To fix an anatomically broken heart, such as leaky valves, abnormal openings in the intervening septum (wall) between the right and left chambers, or narrowings within the heart, the heart itself has to be opened, procedures collectively called: open heart surgery. Opening the heart is attended with two fatal risks: one, the patient will bleed to death unless blood is not only returned to the patient but also pumped to all body organs and tissues; two, blood has to be aerated (oxygenated), a vital function of the lungs. Therefore, for the surgeon to open a patient's heart, the work of the heart and the lungs must be carried out by an alternative heart and lung (a heart-lung machine); hence the procedure is called cardioplumonary bypass because the native heart and lungs are bypassed using a machine in most instances.

The idle, dronish mind would attribute the development of the heart-lung machine to vivisection. An inflated claim to say the least. Largely distorted. It is a twilight zone where

---

*Fadali, M., *Coping and Beyond: A Surgeon's Reflections on Medicine, Science, Art & A Life Worth Living*, Marina Del Rey, CA: DeVorss & Co., Publishers, 1990.
**Fadali, M., *Love, Passion & Solitude*, Los Angeles, CA: Hidden Springs Press, 1994.

fact and fiction swirl and merge to the degree that the up-right and incorrupt must exercise great caution and scientific veracity to decipher one from the other. Dear readers, to you, I vow to do just that.

For almost twenty years, Dr. John Gibbon experimented primarily on cats with his newly developed heart-lung machine. In the early 1950s his device was tried on human beings with a high mortality; two out of three died. Later on, several surgical teams, notably the one at the Mayo Clinic, tamed the fitful machine and rendered it serviceable for humans.

Advocates of animal research would buoyantly jump on their feet alleging that without animal experiments, there wouldn't be a heart-lung machine at all. Opponents of animal experimentation after rendering the whole saga full thought counterargue as follows: Programmed to view the animal laboratory as a testing field for new devices, newer drugs, and novel procedures, a vivisectionist or a misinformed physician or scientist will go ahead and test on live animals. The result as we have demonstrated in previous pages is a gadget, a substance or a procedure of sorts when put to human use, almost invariably ends in disastrous sequelae. Gibbon would have been better advised after assembling his machine to examine its mechanics: flow, resistance, energy, etc., then to move on to non-live models whereby blood and blood components could have been circulated to assess any damage the machine would incur on various blood elements, also to assay different membranes and other methods to bubble oxygen into the blood for oxygenation and to prevent foaming by adding anti-foaming agents. Anticoagulation levels, temperature requirements and a whole array of flow dynamics could be scrutinized. His next logical step would have been a trip to the morgue whereby corpses of the recently deceased could serve as facsimiles to perfect techniques and evaluate performance. I bet you, if this stepwise thoughtful methodology would have been followed, we would have had an efficient heart-lung machine within a shorter time span with lesser risk to the very first patients who were hooked to it. Their numbers ran in the thousands; many of them died or suffered strokes, multi-organ failures, devastating infections, anemias and a host of other dreadful complications. It wasn't all wholesome and invigorating. And many fatalities and serious handicaps could have been prevented. It takes rethinking, change of mind, real change, not modified versions of the status quo. To dare to differ demands immense moral courage; to observe freely without a preset or preconditioned brain takes magnificent fortitude. I have witnessed the tragedies that plagued the early phases of the heart-lung machine; I was there, a member of the crew. I am not relaying to you anecdotes, tales of the scholars, fast laboratory gossip or the ceremony of the ivory tower. I participated. This book is my way to make amends and to rend the veil. After twenty years or more sacrificing and wasting lives of cats and other animals, when humans were committed to the machine, the initial thousands were being experimented upon still. There were "experimental subjects" from the cat, dog or calf to the human; it is an experiment and you better know it. That is the way it is, but it is all camouflaged, thanks to vivisection, a most artful veneer, the perfect guise.

And please remember it isn't just having that splendid, complex device bypassing the human heart and lungs, it requires many other ingredients to perform open heart surgery. I'll mention a few: anesthesia, antibiotics, antisepsis, anticoagulants, X-rays, CAT scan, blood transfusion, etc., etc., etc. As stated earlier, they are not the harvest of the wicked, infamous seed: animal experimentation.

An important implement to open-heart surgery is the use of hypothermia, which means cooling the body temperature, thus less blood is needed to sustain organs and tissues and preserve their function while the operation is in progress. Vivisectionists would credit the animal laboratory for the introduction of hypothermia to the practice of open heart surgery. Truth is otherwise.

For thousands of years, scrolls, archives, folk tales and esteemed story tellers have recounted miraculous events of humans believed to be dead, and, lo and behold, days later they came back to life, joined the ranks, toiled, and leisured with the group. Their pilgrimage below the horizon, their excursion into the bewitched and the obscure and their final retreat where light prevails must have enchanted and entranced those who missed the adventure. A fascinating fairly recent example from McLeave's *The Risk Takers** begs to be told, ''The first authenticated record appears in the proceedings of the Swedish Academy of Sciences in 1757. This was the case of the Swede whose relatives nearly buried him alive. This peasant, who had drunk too much brandy, was bowled over by a strong wind on the 23rd of March 1756, collapsed in the snow and fell asleep. Uncovered the next morning, his relatives put him in a coffin and prepared to bury him. But before they could carry out the interment, their doctor Sven Naucler arrived unexpectedly and asked to examine the body.

The face, hands and feet were frozen, their joints locked with the cold, the eyes were fixed and staring, heart still and breathing no more. But Dr. Naucler thought he detected a small region of warmth at the pit of the stomach. He ordered the man's legs and arms to be rubbed while he placed hot towels on the stomach. To their general astonishment, the man gradually stirred, later sat up, and by the next day was recovering.''

---

*McLeave, H. *The Risk Takers*. New York: Holt Rinehart & Winston, 1962, p. 106.

Two more 18th century surgeons believed in the virtues of cold. Dr. James Currie, an imminent and observant Liverpool surgeon wondered what killed sailors who were shipwrecked in the Mersey. In 1798 he persuaded people to take prolonged baths in cold water and noted their temperature and pulse. As their bodies lost heat, Currie found the heart rate also flagged.

OF HEARTS: THE COMPETENT
AND THE INCOMPETENT
MENDING, REPLACING, FITTING
AND RETROFITTING THE VALVES

The four chambers of the heart: each is guarded by an exit valve which permits the forward flow of blood while preventing leakage or retrograde flow. Any appreciable backward flow will reduce the volume of blood to be pumped by the heart. Less blood will be delivered, as simple as that. For many reasons, valves may lose their competence and leak allowing blood to run back; orifices (openings) they guard may narrow, curtailing the egress of blood. Both conditions can stress and damage the heart, also, impair body functions such as breathing, staying alert, thinking, walking, digesting, what have you. In repairing or replacing damaged heart valves, progress has been made. Thanks to pioneers comprising several dedicated members of the medical profession. Vivisectionists, no thanks. Your best equation: an ounce of remedy for a pound of harm is untenable. A loser.

Between the left atrium and the left ventricle (the two left-sided heart chambers), there exists a valve called the mitral valve. Historically, this valve received most of the early attention by cardiac surgeons. Recapping the eventful story, Dr. Robert Platt wrote in ''Art and Science of Medicine,''

"Science is necessary for the advance of medicine. Some advances are still possible from the use of clinical methods alone, as the recent brilliant work on the surgery of mitral stenosis has shown."*

". . . despite all that had been learned through animal experimentation, only one of his four cases, the young girl on whom he had operated first, survived. . . ."** wrote Doctors Swazey and Fox in reference to Dr. Eliott C. Cutler of Boston's Peter Bent Brigham Hospital. He spent—wasted—years in the animal laboratory experimenting with mitral stenosis. The gratest challenge was to create mitral valve stenosis in healthy animals to no success; such a model could not be developed, yet Cutler maintained that he has learned plenty through animal tampering. Perhaps, but when he carried his newly-acquired knowledge to the human theater, results were disastrous. Obviously the animal laboratory didn't teach Cutler what he shouldn't do. That was 1923. Not a very good year, at least as far as animals and humans are concerned. Through the grace of intelligence Homo sapiens learn what to do, but in higher realms where prudence rears wisdom, we learn what not to do. Intelligence ripens into wisdom. Wisdom beholds the precept of Oneness of Seeing (perception)/Oneness of Being, Duality being an illusion. Thus, the wise do no harm. As for the intelligent, the skillful, the fool and the stupid, they share a malicious leer, spinning the wheel of misfortune every so often. And, no end to sorrow. I'm told wisdom's gate is always open; a gateless domain.

In 1925, Dr. Henry S. Souttar, then Director of Surgery at London Hospital, operated on a 19-year-old girl for mitral stenosis, successfully. He developed the surgical procedure

---

*Platt, R. "Art and Science of Medicine." *Lancet*, November 15, 1952, p. 978.
**Swazey, J.P. and Fox, R.C., "The Conical Moratorium: A Case Study of Mitral Valve Surgery." In *Experimentations with Human Subjects*, p. 317.

without resorting to any animal experiments. ''The patient made an uninterrupted recovery, and all present during surgery were 'struck by the facility and safety of the procedure.' To the best of his knowledge, Souttar wrote this was the first time a mitral valve had been reached by the auricular route, or that the interior of the heart had been subjected to digital examination.''* Only surgeons who examined the hearts of mitral stenosis patients at autopsy could gauge and fully comprehend the extent and details of the abnormality and could faithfully conceive what to do to correct or improve the anomalous situation. Their tenacity generates mending and rectifies techniques.

For leaky heart valves, various methods of repair to restore valvular competence have been devised. Some used the dog and pig for a test tube; not surprisingly their misadventures did not improve or boost the ongoing search for solution to a vexing problem.

When it comes to replacing irreparably damaged heart valves with artificial ones, the story is a blend of the comical, the bizarre and the tragic. None of those artificial valves worked in dogs, the blood clotted over them with calamitous results. Despite the dismal outcome in canines, some cardiac surgeons implanted them in human hearts with a fair degree of success. The procedure evolved to an art and has been helping an increasing number of patients worldwide. After valve replacement, many resumed work and leisurely activities. ''. . . concerning artificial heart valves, that probably man does not react as violently as the animal does in producing a clot at the interface between the myocardium and the artificial prosthesis. It may be that man is a better candidate for this type of thing than the animal.''** And,

*Ibid., p. 324.
**Comments made by George H. Clowes on a paper presented by Albert Starr, a cardiac surgeon. Starr, A., ''Mitral Replacement: Clinical Experience with a Ball-Valve Prosthesis.'' *Annals of Surgery*, 1961, 154 (4):740.

when they took occasional favorable outcomes seriously, and implanted their promising gadgets in human hearts, one disaster after another followed. Recently, a heart valve that was blamed for at least 360 deaths was subsequently taken off the market.* Would something of this scope inspire vivisectionists to reconsider and to focus on human well-being, even if they don't give a hoot to animal welfare or mere existence?

Xenografts (grafts, valves in this case, obtained from species other than human) proved helpful as a human valve substitute. One prerequisite, though, the valves must be harvested after the death of the donor animal and should be treated with chemical agents to kill their antigenicity. Antigenicity will lead to rejection of the implanted valve by its recipient. However, live animals should never be specifically sacrificed for this purpose. With homografts, both donor and recipient belong to the same species, for example, from human to human. Harvested from human cadavers, many long-term follow-up studies have shown that homograft valves functioned in a manner comparable to that of xenografts.

Dear reader, the audible tick of your artificial valve if you happen to have one, isn't broadcast out of the goodness of vivisection. The same holds true if your resolute heart tills with the help of xenografts or homografts. While artificial valves tick, others whisper, murmuring softly beneath your warm breath. You don't owe a thing to the vivisectionists. Demur!

---

*Los Angeles Times, Monday, January 2, 1995.

THE ARTIFICIAL HEART

Not in a poetic sense; lots of those are tempestuously grinding along, chaotic, venomous, remorseless. An actual artificial heart to replace an irreversibly damaged heart has been in the cards for some time; yet, despite more than forty years of relentless experimentation on animals from dogs to pigs to calves to monkeys, the artificial heart for all practical purposes remains a whimsy and a dream. From all that we know, continued work and grant allocation in this field are put to waste. Results won't be applicable to humans. Recent trials on humans all ended in spectacular failures. A grand circus with all the hoopla, masquerading and lewdness, no responsible soul can stomach. What do you expect?!

BORN TO LOSE
CORRECTION OF SOME INBORN
(CONGENITAL) HEART ABNORMALITIES

Made to order, yet some hearts are at fault, from the very beginning. A penalty, victim: innocent, not even one chance to err, loathe and stumble. Every conceivable and imaginable abnormality has been encountered when human hearts were thoroughly examined: being in the wrong place, beating at the wrong time, blocked outlets, double outlets, gigantic chambers, minuscule quarters, blood taking the wrong way home, blood delivered to the wrong address along salacious circuitous routes, walls too thick, walls diaphonous, mismatched rendezvous, arteries gone venous and veins that dared arterialize. Name it, misname it, it's all there in the tumultuous book of the congenitally abnormal hearts. For millennia, mutations threatened offsprings; at times though mutations have resulted in evolutionary enhancement. It all depends on the way ingredients of the dough get mixed and how it is baked. A roll of the dice, and, here you are: sink or float. But, with a little bit of help, many would-be sinkers will float. And, all waters have rafts.

On a glittering TV screen or the glossy fashionable pages of a glitzy magazine, you see a blooming, spritely child affectionately perched within the warm embrace of a loving mother with the caption underneath affectionately whispering: ''If it weren't for the animal research, my child would have been dead; he had an abnormal heart that the doctors fixed through knowledge and skills acquired in the animal laboratory.'' False. Surgical and pharmacologic advances made in the treatment of congenital heart disease are not the fruits of animal research; matter of fact, animal research by its very nature—faulty that is—can't help but retard, hinder, harm and derail. It's a gruesome game with many casualties; yet, the crowd stacked in the bleachers pay and cheer. Regrettably, for the past several decades, congenital abnormalities have been on the rise, be they defects of the heart, liver, lungs, limbs, blood, brain and other organs. A multitude of factors to blame: environmental, dietetic and a long list of toxic chemicals polluting the air, the water and the soil. All packaged as benevolent enhancers to sustain, heal and boost our lot along the eventful ride. Alas! Many believe the wicked anecdotes.

This monograph is not planned to be an exhaustive treatise on this subject, but some samples will help illustrate what we are talking about.

Out of a mother's womb, a neoborn might be blue rather than pink. In the dark-skinned, blue or pink can be noted on the nail beds, lips and other mucous membrances. One distinctive anomaly moving one's birth color to the bluish spectrum is Fallot's tetralogy, named after a French physician who described the dreary quartet—a combination of four inborn errors—that incapacitate and kill. Only a fraction of the circulating blood reaches the lungs for aeration (oxygenation). Dr. Helen B. Taussig of Johns Hopkins School of Medicine, a pediatrician, reasoned that delivering additional quota of blood to the lungs could correct the serious problem and allow blue babies to live. A surgically-created conduit should do the trick, Helen thought. Enthused, she took her idea with her to Boston for an audience with its famed surgeon Dr. Gross. But, little Caesar turned Helen of Baltimore down. Disappointed, not disheartened, Helen surveyed her own abode. And on to another date with another man: a surgical colleague on the premises right at Johns Hopkins, Dr. Alfred Blalock. Alfred had a knack for animal research. He took her gift of idea to his court, and on to full blast experiments with dogs. Matter of fact, the one who performed most of the experiments was Blalock's chief technician, Mr. Vivian Thomas, an interesting gentleman whom I have met while working at Johns Hopkins. More than once I revisited the saga of the blue babies with Dr. Taussig. More than once I recalled the eventful history with Mr. Thomas right in the very spot where he and Alfred did it to the dogs, on the twelfth floor of the Halstad Building. Detailed scrutiny of the canine experiments showed ambiguous results, discouraging rather than encouraging to the prospect of success for Dr. Taussig's concept. But, and here is the important thing with animal experiments, hundreds of them under his belt, Dr. Blalock and his platoon could march into the operating room and dare experiment with patients. With the ritual of animal sacrifices consummated, there is nothing to atone for. And, the operative procedure worked out. Sailed. Clearly stated: If Blalock and his entourage would have taken their dog experiments seriously, they wouldn't have come anywhere near the brittle, snappish blood vessels of blue babies. But they did. You see, time and again, animal experiments serve as a permit to execute the human experiment under the guise of ''it worked for animals,'' ''it was tested on animals.'' Well! Like artificial heart valves, it didn't work in animals, but it worked in humans. Yet in other experimental situations as we have seen earlier with drugs and other notions and devices, it works in animals but not in humans. A flip of a coin, zigzags and dancettes.

And herein as happens with many other ventures, they have ignored an unmistakable evidence staring them in the face, an already existing proof that Taussig's idea would certainly work for humans: Some babies with Fallot's tetralogy have survived without surgery. In a number of them the abnormality was not severe enough, while some others had another peculiarity in the form of a conduit (channel) to the lungs bringing additional blood for aeration. The abnormal conduit is called ductus arteriosus. Normally, right after birth, clamping the umbilical cord and the newborn's first few breaths trigger closure of the duct. Remaining open this channel (the duct) prevents Fallot's patients from becoming blue, saving their lvies. This is precisely what Dr. Helen Taussig had in mind when she took the trip to Boston for her rendezvous with Dr. Gross. She wanted him to mimic her majesty, Mother Nature. Dr. Taussig's only armor was her definitive clinical observations on patients correlated and confirmed by autopsy findings. The procedure she proposed to Dr. Gross was straightforward, sensible and feasible for any well-trained vascular or cardiovascular (cardio means heart) surgeon. Dr. Gross was a pioneer, but he backed down. He didn't buy into her concept nor critically examine the overwhleming evidence; besides he was too busy doing the exact opposite procedure, tying and intercepting the duct to correct another heart abnormality. And, here comes Helen with a plea to reclaim the duct. The haughty surgeon declined and turned down the lady's elegant proposition. As for Blalock, he seconded Taussig's motion, but following his brain conditioning, he had to reach the mortally-ill infants through the conditioned reflex of animal experimentation. Clearly, animal research is a paved road to justify and sanctify. A shield behind which they queue under the grand banner of ethics and protection of humans yet: Animal experimentation leads to human experimentation. To put it in another way: Animal experimentation legitimizes human experimentation. A third version would be: Animal experimentation allows human experimentation without tarnish, punishment or penance; it is human experimentation. Just like wars, to get rid of evil, to exterminate the bad, to cleanse mind, soul and land, yet thousands upon thousands of wars over the past thousands of years haven't eliminated evil or exorcised the bad; matter of fact, wars reared the first, nurtured the latter and disseminated both. Can't we see? And, the demon remains alive and well, surreptitiously moving about. Within. Is this the "Twilight of the Gods"?* The descent of man? And, woman? Hell, too harsh. Paradise, undeserved. Purgatory has two exits. Choose!

This book isn't a declaration of war on vivisection. No, it isn't, for this won't end the malady. Wars do not consummate virtue. Vivisection will end when we—collectively—realize it for what it is. As is, bare; tempera denuded, original unveiled, then and there, it can't be.

Another inborn abnormality is called coarctation of the aorta, whereby the aorta is the principal thoroughfare along which life-offering blood journeys to every parcel of the body through subsidiary branches (arteries). In some newcomers, life's central highway is throttled, ending up comletely shut off or severely narrowed to the sanguineous traffic. It was the early 1940s when Doctor Clarence Crafoord of Stockholm, Sweden, surgically removed the obstructing segment of the aorta, and connected the two ends back together restoring continuity to the vital stream. Obstruction

---

*In Norse mythology, the demise of gods and world destruction in a final battle with the forces of evil.

gone, baby's life spared, adolescent or early adulthood catastrophes blotted out. No grim epilogues. Animal experimentation wasn't in the ritual; common sense and reason prevailed. An accidental severe hemorrhage that happened in a previous patient of his forced Crafoord's hands to clamp the aorta in order to allow him to repair the tear. The emergency situation was well handled, the patient survived, and the operation to correct coarctation of the aorta was born. Learning of the idea and its spectacular success, animal researchers and their advocates followed their fictitious commandments designing experimental models. Wherefore? With no time to contemplate and receive reality, they experimented on animals, an unworthy tormenting expedition to prove what has been proven already. Mind boggling, disturbing as well that a critical analysis of their experiments could only invalidate what has been found valid, yet their tortured interpretations carry the day and their pretzel logic echoes. Alas! In dusty landscapes vision dims, and ghouls appear angelic.

Many other innovations such as balloon dilation of blood vessels and new medicines came along. Contribution of animal research to their development is on the order of a joke, in the same category with silly notions such as Mozart's contribution to Gypsy music or Rock 'n' Roll's bequest to the African beat. Come on! Wake up, fellows.

DOC! WHAT IS THIS SILLY WIRE
DOING IN MY HEART?
PACEMAKERS

Over the past forty years or so, pacemakers have undoubtedly extended life and promoted its quality for many individuals. Bearing witness and laboring without intermezzo or repose, human hearts may grow restless and weary, skip into erratic rhythms, their beat may quicken or go slow, they may play a King Lear on us, strike, quit beating for several seconds, then beat again; they better, or else. . . . The energy wave (an electric current) wayfaring the specialized heart pathways may face insurmountable resistance at one location or another imparting what's known as "heart block" bringing about grave consequences, such as dizzy spells, strokes, serious injuries or even death. A tiny electrode (a special wire made of specific alloys, coated with a particular coating) connected to an electric battery when applied to the heart can coerce it to contract more efficiently, redeeming rate, restoring rhythm and appropriate response to body needs. Pacemakers have grown sophisticated over the past decade; brainy, they can sense the heart's native impulse, adjust to it, let go or delete and pace the heart accordingly. Some can modify their output subject to demand, lingering at rest, rushing with physical exercise or whenever escapades and wild pranks are conjured by the bearer.

Electrotherapy to resuscitate stilled human hearts ferrying virtually dead ones across the agonal straits of no-return back to life has been a well-guarded secret for centuries; a prairie where saints, sorcerers, magicians, and physicians roamed. We played back testimonials of some of those miracles when we discussed cardiopulmonary resuscitation on earlier pages. To read or hear more, you know where to go. I don't have to tell. And, way before any animal molestation, electric current was applied to arrested hearts of Homo sapiens, restarting many.

Before pacemaker units were made available for implantation in patients on a regular basis, the whole thing had to serve time behind the bars of the animal laboratory. No one would dare act otherwise, regardless of the irrefutable evidence. Even if some dare, the FDA (Food and Drug Administration) would get on their case. The unholy sacrament of animal killing must be affected and completed first to confer grace and bequeath legitimacy onto the black box, the components of which we already know.

Dear patient, that silly, slim wire anchored to your heart, with its dainty generator (battery or pulse generator) brooding over your bosom safeguards your life. Even when you rest in the arms of Morpheus, it watches over you. And, you do not owe it to animal research.

LIGHTHEARTED, I'LL SAIL THE OCEANS, ROLL WITH THE RIVERS AND STROLL THE MEADOWS. AND WITH A NEW KIDNEY ON BOARD, A NEW MARROW IN MY BONES, A NEW LIVER BENEATH MY BELLOWS AND A NEW HEART INSIDE MY RIB CAGE, WILL I ACHIEVE IMMORTALITY? OR, SHALL I BIDE MY TIME AND DALLY WITH THE NEW GENETICS?

—ORGAN TRANSPLANTATION. HEART, KIDNEY, LUNGS, LIVER, MARROW, AND OTHERS—

First, we owe it to one another to have a clear understanding that organ transplantation, splendid, enigmatic and helpful as it may be, is not a panacea or an offering for anyone who needs it. Under current circumstances it can only prop a tiny fraction of patients who could benefit from it; abundant demand, short supply. And, the short supply is mostly our own doing. The whole attitude in hospitals and health care facilities—doctors, nurses and others—toward organ donation is one of ambivalence; a take it or leave it. Worthy organs are wasted; organ donation is seldom discussed; patients, accident victims and their families are rarely told about the shortage and what they can do to help shore up the meager supply. After Belgium introduced an "opt-out" scheme (organs are considered available after death unless otherwise stated), the number of donors substantially increased. Something to think about! Yet, the amazing fact is: most diseases that end up needing organ transplantation are largely preventable in the first place and comprehensively manageable by other means in many individuals. To a substantial degree the lavish demand is our own making. It takes knowledge, insight, planning and discipline to think and practice prevention. Attributes known to wither and tumble away in the rush, diversion and increasing shallowness of our lives. We earn some fun, but forfeit health, agility, joy and calm contentment.

Firstly, when you hear of the exalted heart or liver transplant and its triumph, don't forsake the many ingredients that made such a feat possible: anesthesia, X-ray, CT scan, magnetic resonance, blood transfusion, heart catheterization, antibiotics and several others. None of these breakthroughs were reaped in the animal laboratory; the chilling, forbidding quarters has hindered and delayed; a morass and a quagmire.

Secondly, with almost every organ transplant, be it kidney, heart, liver or otherwise, animals manifested much more serious reactions than humans did. Failure and rejection were the rule rather than the exception. It was dismal. Very few long-term animal survivors. Nothing to boast or brag about. When some surgeons moved on to human implementation, several dramatic successes were reported. Human successes were achieved before solutions to the problems ravaging the transplanted animals were found. Think of it for a moment. How can a report card tainted with so many poor grades extend credit or proffer high esteem to the mediocre experiment and the frivolous experimenter?

Cross species transplants have always failed. Recently in the U.S., at least three experiments to transplant baboon organs into humans were carried out. Absurd and sickly as it is, it happened; and every one failed. Now a squadron of knights errant are wandering about; adventurous, mischievous, and loathsome; well-equipped and heavily financed. To design animal organs that will resist rejection by prospective human recipients, the mercenaries of genetic engineering are breeding animals with human genes. From pigs to people, livers, hearts, lungs and other parts—we are told—are only a few years away. Spend your organs, lavish and ravish and just before you poop out call our toll-free number, user friendly; a hardy spleen, an inured liver, a brave colon and a lion's heart will be installed to replace the rotted out gear. Technology restituting temerity and prowess to the decaying corpse.

For a testimony they grafted the heart of a genetically-engineered pig into a baboon. Guess what? The poor baboon survived for a mere 19 hours, yet the pack claimed success, celebrated and broadcast the news. Of course we all know what happened to the pig after they snatched its heart. Truly, truly, I am terrified. They are aiming their machinery and high gear at the molecular basis of life. In the works are dreaded prospects: a genetic human underclass, a genetic human super-race, designer babies; genetic lines of animals and plants that will play havoc with genetic diversity and genetic balance within the species, and an assortment of genetically-engineered organisms to be tossed everywhere. The genetically altered animal organs will certainly trigger new problems and could transmit deadly viruses and bacteria, known and unknown. Even the introduction of so-called "specific pathogen-free" animals cannot eliminate this risk. "It only takes one transmission from one baboon to a human to start an epidemic. There's no way you can make it safe," cautioned Jonathan Allan in a recent *Time Magazine* article. Allan, a virologist at the Southwest

Foundation for Biomedical Research in San Antonio, Texas.* Many virologists voiced grave concern that new, perhaps more lethal viruses may evolve when nonhuman primate viruses exchange genetic material with human DNA or if primate and human viruses were to combine.** And don't count on human prudence, compassion or foresight; besides, can we entrust ownership and control of the planet's gene pool to major multinational corporations? What is going on fellows? In the crucible of genetic engineering our probity is being tried. Shall I hold my breath, pray, despair or eat my dairy-free pudding?

Thirdly, early techniques allegedly worked out in the animal laboratory for the purpose of human organ transplantation, all had to be drastically altered when human cadavers were researched for answers to problems and when human transplants were begun.

Fourthly, a cornerstone of organ transplantation is cellular and tissue typing. Blood group compatibility between donor and recipient is a must. At the turn of the century without animal research, Landsteiner discovered the human blood groups. Furthermore, in humans, white blood cells play the dominant role in transplant rejection. Such a make or break role was not seriously studied in the course of the mutilation and dismemberment of animals.

Fifthly, in organ transplantation, blood thinners (anticoagulants), heparin in particular, are frequently a pass to victory. It was McLean who discovered the blood thinning properties of heparin, a natural secretion of special cells called the mast cells. We all have those.

---

*Allan, J.S., "Xenograft Transplantation and the Infectious Disease Conundrum." *ILAR Journal*, 37 (1), 1995, pp. 37–48.
**Garrett, L. *The Coming Plague*, New York: Farrar, Straus and Giroux, 1994, pp. 572–575.

Sixthly, the various drugs administered to prevent rejection of transplanted organs—almost all of them—were already known for their suppression of the immune response in human beings way before their use in transplantation. Examples are: corticosteroids (naturally secreted by the adrenal gland), mustard gas and its derivatives (alkylating agents such as cyclophosphamide), and antimetabolites (e.g. azathioprine). Cyclosporins have something to do with animal experiments, but, it is a small coin in the basket that could have been gathered otherwise. Effects of radiation on white blood cells and bone marrow were appreciated before the era of transplantation.

Seventhly, even the artificial kidney used to dialyse (filter and purify blood) many patients with irreparably damaged kidneys is not a product of animal experimentation. The concept is built on simple physical laws of osmosis and migration of substances of high concentration through a semipermeable membrane to areas of low concentration. Dialysis wouldn't be a reality without blood thinners (anticoagulants). Also the vascular surgery techniques needed to gain access to blood vessels in order to dialyse were not developed in the animal laboratory. Kolff's artificial kidney was made of cellophane tubing and he carried his first dialysis in a tub of water, proving that an artificial kidney can work. No animals, no humans were used to illustrate the machine's merit. Dialysis is an important component in preparing patients for kidney transplantation and in treating some of the complications they encounter after surgery. So, when the impetuous crew seethe and soar, zealously telling you that animal experimentation gave us transplantation, let it go in one ear and out of the other. But, if you are eager to respond, retort with Bernard Shaw's classic definition of the vivisector. "These poor little dullards," said Shaw, "with their retinue of two-penny Torquemadas, wallowing in the infamies of the vivisector's laboratory and solemnly offering us as epoch-making discoveries their demonstrations that dogs get weaker and die if you give them no food; that intense pain will make mice sweat; that if you cut off a dog's leg, the three-legged dog will have a four-legged puppy. I ask myself what spell has fallen upon intelligent and humane men that they allow themselves to be imposed upon by this rabble of dolts, blackguards, impostors, quacks, liars and worst of all credulous fools.''

THE DISCOVERY OF INSULIN

Diabetes mellitus, the third or fourth cause of death in the U.S., afflicts approximately 11 million Americans. It doubles the risk of heart attacks and strokes; it is the leading cause of blindness under age 65, and everywhere in the body it accelerates blood vessel damage causing serious problems such as kidney failure and gangrene of the lower extremities. Insulin is not a cure for diabetes, it merely regulates blood sugar (glucose) level and helps prevent some acute complications triggered by high blood sugar levels and changes in blood's normally alkaline state. Insulin administration does not protect blood vessels, kidneys or eyes of diabetics. It is not a panacea or a magic shot.

Insulin is a hormone naturally secreted by the pancreas. An abdominal organ situated behind the stomach it secretes certain digestive juices as well. Contrary to vivisector's claim, association between diabetes mellitus and pancreatic disease was not established through animal research. It was known for a long time; matter of fact, it was settled by Thomas Crawley as early as 1788.*

In the course of an autopsy on a diabetic patient Crawley found a damaged pancreas with multiple calculi (stones).

---

*Opie, E. *Diseases of the Pancreas*, Philadelphia, 1910.

Many autopsies followed by several others establishing the connection between damage to the pancreas and diabetes mellitus. This was a cornerstone solving the puzzle and correcting the long-held misconception that diabetes was caused by damage to the liver, an erroneous conclusion based on Claude Bernard's animal research.* One more proof of animal experimentation's inherent deficiency as a tool to probe and explore human diseases. Ironically, Claude Bernard is revered as the "father of experimental physiology." In fairness to Claude, though, he was not the first, won't be the last, father to mislead his daughters and sons.

With the connection between the onset of diabetes and pancreatic damage firmly established by human observations and autopsy studies, various investigators reflexly began their quest to test these confirmed findings on animals. Bad habits again! Among the early risers who made the wrong turn to the animal laboratory were von Mering and Minkowski in 1889. Researchers worldwide tried to extract that substance from the pancreas which controls blood sugar: insulin. The Toronto team won. In the autumn of 1920, Frederick Banting, a young surgeon in London, Ontario, Canada, happened to be reading an article entitled, "The Relation of the Islets of Langerhans to Diabetes with the Special Reference to Cases of Pancreatic Lithiasis" by Dr. M. Barron, an American pathologist.**

Barron carefully studied the human pancreas and concluded that damage to the Islets of Langerhans must cause diabetes in humans. Barron concluded that an extract of these cells would yield insulin. In Toronto, Banting with his collaborators, Best and MacLeod pursued Barron's conclu-

---

*Bliss, M. *Discovery of Insulin*. Chicago: University of Chicago Press, 1982, p. 25.
**Barron, M. "Relations of the Islets of Langerhans to Diabetes with a special reference to cases of pancreatic lithiasis." *Surgery, Gynecology, and Obstetrics*, xxxi, 5, November, 1920, pp. 437–438.

sions in the animal laboratory and succeeded in preparing a pancreatic extract containing insulin. And, following Darwin's maxim of credit going to the man who convinces the world, the Toronto three did the convincing and received credit and the Nobel Prize. And the chorus sang Hallelujah. Praise be upon the animal executioners. Alas, the faulty refrain still plays and echoes.

VACCINATION, A MIXED BLESSING. THE TRUE STORY

Vaccination, a term coined by Louis Pasteur in 1881, means prophylactic inoculation. For a fruitful discussion of the subject, we need to move on to immunology and the immune system. A mandate of survival, the immune system recognizes harmful substances and responds by rendering them ineffective, a normal physiologic function. The invaders are called antigens, the body's response to them is production of antibodies; further, the body matches an antigen with an antibody allowing the two to interlock, almost like a lock-and-key system. Antigen is thus neutralized. Such a potential is almost inifinte, but—and it is a big but— there is a time delay. In this case time is a malady. For the body to garner its defense mechanism an interval is needed; in the interim, an offending agent, bacterial, viral or otherwise, can cause diseases; some are serious, some end in death. It is within this timelag that help is summoned. In 1796, a surgeon named Edward Jenner discovered that inoculation with matter drawn from cowpox lesions could prevent a human from contracting smallpox. A tremendous observation. Other vaccines followed and vaccination against smallpox became universally acceptable. It wasn't all honeyberries and roses though. Smallpox vaccines—as with many other vaccines—had several complications; a lurid example was the horrendous fatalities and morbidities that followed when ten million in the Philippines were vaccinated with smallpox.

In 1900, Walter Reed recognzied that a particular mosquito carried the yellow fever virus. Edward Hindle used rhesus monkeys to produce yellow fever virus vaccine. The animals were inoculated with the virus to produce the vaccine. This was in 1928. But thanks to Max Theiler in the United States who succeeded in developing an effective vaccine in tissue cultures in 1936, thus making possible vaccine synthesis in large quantites without killing animals. 1936 was a good year. Another auspicious year was 1949. Enders, Weller and Robins published a landmark paper on the cultivation of the virus causing poliomyelitis in human tissue cultures. Thus, a polio vaccine came on board, and a new venue became available for virologists to tender better products. The three good fellows were awarded the Nobel Prize in 1954. Around this year Salk, and three years later Sabin, put forth polio vaccines and large-scale clinical trials were begun. Unfortunately—despite clear evidence of already existing better alternatives—they used monkeys to produce their vaccines. What shall I say? The lush growth of the virus in cultures of minced kidneys of monkeys must have engaged their eyes. In addition to the work of Enders, Weller and Robins in the 1940s, it's now firmly established that polio virus can be grown on tissue cultures and cells that continuously propagate themselves (continuous cell lines). Thus replacing monkey kidney cells as the growth medium for the virus is entirely feasible.

Whether the polio vaccine has lived up to its high promise and dandy expectations or not, it is debatable still. Pretty serious complications have been encountered and many scholars believe that the reported decline in the incidence and ferocity of poliomyelitis were but natural occurrences in virulence and morphology, a phenomenon not infrequently noted with viruses. The downside of it all as Albert Sabin himself admitted was that work on poliomyelitis prevention was delayed by an erroneous conception of the nature of the human disease based on misleading experimental models of the disease in monkeys. "Erroneous conception," and "misleading experimental models": foul and pestilent attributes of animal experimentation. Please, read Sabin's statement one more time, slowly, in total concentration. A confession of sorts, unsolicited.

Another very good year was 1962. There, in test tubes (in vitro), the virus causing rubella was successfully isolated in tissue cultures. A vaccine in sufficient quantities, of high quality, was produced. No animals were put to death or tortured.

At this juncture, let's not arrogantly or hastily brush aside the possibility raised by some respected investigators that the use of live vaccines could have something to do with the onset of auto-immune deficiency syndrome (AIDS). Smallpox vaccine has been suspected; it is a live vaccine. The *New England Journal of Medicine* on March 12, 1987 referred to a report by a team of physicians from Walter Reed Army Hospital who examined a 19-year-old recruit who developed a number of AIDS-like symptoms in 1985, shortly after a battery of inoculations, including smallpox. The recruit died in 1986. And I am not hereby endorsing the theory of vaccine contaminants as a possible cause of AIDS, but I cannot in clear conscience flatly spurn or ignore.

Some physicians and scientists view vaccines as a time bomb. In 1976 swine flu vaccine caused paralysis in a number of individuals; subsequently it was discontinued. President Gerald Ford, an ardent advocate of the vaccine, was embarrassed, politically hurt as well. I guess, to a politician, the second is more relevant. Most politicians are vaccinated against embarrassment; their countenance and body parts rarely ever react to it, cool and indifferent to suffering as long as their political fortunes are secure.

Robert Koch, one of the founders of the science of bacteriology, identified the tubercle bacillus in 1882. Subsequently in 1890 he extracted tuberculin from the tuberculosis-causing bacillus. Based on his successful testing of tuberculin on guinea pigs Koch thought he had a wonderful cure for tuberculosis. The scientist was mistaken. Moving from guinea pigs to humans, he fell in the extrapolation gap: tuberculin, rather than immunizing and preventing, gave the disease to humans. Yet, cycloserine, a drug successfully used to treat tuberculosis, was almost tossed away because it did not work on laboratory animals.

Tissue cultures have reached a great degree of sophistication. Viral vaccines can now be developed in human embryonic lung cell cultures harvested from aborted fetuses. Don't tell past President George Bush. It was he who blocked the use of tissues from aborted fetuses in medical research. I thought that was political pandering and short-sighted on his part. Fetal cells have the distinct privilege of growing in culture media without becoming malignant. Furthermore, these cultures—known as ''diploid cells''—are free from viruses that may naturally occur in animal-derived cell cultures. Some of these unwanted viruses can cause cancer. An example are monkey kidney cells which are frequently populated by SF 40, a cancer-causing virus. Viral vaccines produced in conventional cell culture are not totally free of the potential risk of causing cancers. Human fetal cell lines are clear winners in this regard.

Now a new era has dawned: artificial vaccines, a thrilling technology that should eliminate the flawed practice of using animals in vaccine production and testing, besides remarkably reducing some of the serious complications such as paralysis and cancer. Artificial vaccines can be specifically targeted for a particular disease. Recent computer-imaging techniques and recombinant DNA technology made this advance possible.

Successes reported with this technique aroused hopes for eventually controlling viral diseases—AIDS included—cancer as well. But don't hold your breath, it could be a long wait. In the interim, stick to the basics: regular physical exercise, good nutrition—vegetarian diet highly recommended—abstain from smoking, don't use alcohol and other drugs, become an environmentalist, abstain from or practice safe (safer) sex, and don't let the stress and strain of modern times get you down.

Let's acknowledge the fact that the greatest advances made in health, disease control and longevity are the direct result of better hygiene, in particular, safety of the water supply, proper disposal of waste and general improvement in sanitation.

TEN MORE BREAKTHROUGHS WITHOUT ANIMAL RESEARCH

1. Discovery of the relationship between cholesterol and heart disease, the number one cause of death for Americans.
2. Discovery of the relationships between smoking and cancer and nutrition and cancer, the number two cause of death for Americans.
3. Discovery of the relationship between hypertension and stroke, the number three cause of death for Americans.
4. Isolation of the AIDS virus.
5. Discovery of the mechanism of AIDS transmission.
6. Discovery of the relationship between chemical exposure and birth defects.

7. Development of hormonal treatments for cancer of the prostate and breast.
8. Interpretation of the genetic code and its function in protein synthesis.
9. Production of humulin, a synthetic copy of human insulin which causes few allergic reactions. Humulin is available for insulin-dependent diabetics.
10. Understanding of human anatomy and physiology.

CHAPTER SIX

Reliable Alternatives to Vivisection Are Available

Alternatives to animal experimentation are many, versatile, available, ethical and reliable, scientific, not pseudoscientific like vivisection is. Vivisection has no reason to be.

Vivisection is the use of live animals in research and testing. In the previous pages we have identified the widespread harm caused by animal experimentation. Both humans and animals have been victimized by the cruel, unethical, unscientific practice. We haven't yet explored how committing or condoning cruelty or remaining silent can corrupt and impair the whole lot: the doer, the cheering and the apathetic. Vivisectionists often refer to vivisection as a "necessary evil." It isn't necessary, it is just "evil," pure evil. It has gone far and beyond and there is no end in sight. Even the most ardent of vivisectionists if they pause a little, just a little, think and reconsider, many will be hard pressed or unable to justify their animal experiments. In their fenced conditioned sphere, whenever their minds are lured or challenged, their quest is dissection and probing of animals. A journey in search of answers; destination, illusive; road, vexing, pitiless, degrading. What good can come out of dog-

133

head-bashing, paralyzing cats by breaking their spines or shooting at monkeys? Knights in pursuit of the Golden Fleece! What are we going to learn from studying the sexual behavior of cats? Is it to abstain, emulate or excel? Why don't we observe ours? Plenty of it. What advance could be made by getting primates drunk? Pubs, alleys, broken homes, broken hearts, broken bones, traffic toll, hospital wards teach and tell. Right where the problem is lies its solution. Why wander? Genetically engineering animal diseases won't decipher the mystery of ours. Errantry upon the entrancing seas of new-age technology; and we launch unworthy ships and tottering rafts. Technology is replacing humanity. The shrew must be tamed, to be had only as needed. We have been infatuated, habituated, indoctrinated. Why instill caustics and cosmetics into rabbits' eyes? Why car crash dogs, bulls, even rabbits? What about the many thousands of crashes, collisions, injuries and fatalities that taunt our roads day and night? Why go for the modeled, the contrived and the designed? The natural is plentiful! In military research they aim their weapons at monkeys, cats and goats; wherefore? Since WW II, 23 million humans have died in wars, and more, way more were wounded, not to mention a total of 71 million who perished in both global wars. Our military has done its share: anointed reverence, insignia and grand parades. The dead, the dismembered, the mutilated have all the answers we seek, revealed, genuine, shocking. And, let me tell you, if we do, we will see how monstrous we are. Our collective conscience might awaken and war might become obsolete. Not an impossibility. Not an impossibility. You can't imagine what can happen after rending the veil. Why carry out asphyxiation experiments on animals? Why starve those innocent, beautiful creations in order to study the decay, the wasting away and the utter devastation of starvation? Millions of humans all over the earth are undernourished, millions are starving, withering and dying in droves, in packs, by the thousands every single hour. Why suffocate animals to study the unbearable horror of suffocation? Why produce stomach ulcers in cats? Why immerse guinea pigs in boiling water? All these sizzling scenes of human-made horror and more, and more are executed in our animal laboratories nationwide, all in accordance with a brutal sentence imposed by the scholars. Hah, the scholars! In the pool of contemplation, shackles break loose, eye of the mind in witness; icons tumble and drown. And I cannot escape the sense of utter shame, anger and agony I have experienced, still do whenever I recall that dismal encounter in a well-known U.S. university medical school. On one of the floors of an animal research lab, a physician in his white coat remorselessly pounding a dog's rib cage with a huge stone made to swing at regular intervals. Its object, the dog, was wide awake, fastened in place to be smashed right in its bosom every few seconds. The animal's fright, excruciating pain, heart-rending cries, pleading and lament meant nothing to its tormentor. It was all part of a taxpayers' funded research project to study the effect of acceleration/deceleration injuries in humans, not infrequent injuries on our motorways.

The above is extreme, notoriously cruel, absolutely meritless. Without the least doubt, the vast majority of people in the U.S. or anywhere would readily condemn. But even animal experiemnts that sound reasonable and seem necessary, such as studying the effects of trauma, testing drugs and chemicals, teaching medical students and surgeons, research on cancer and other diseases, all, repeating all, are unnecessary, unreasonable, illogical, inherently cruel and evil. They don't solve our enigmas and riddles. A victim's expressed suffering may focus attention, may acquit and absolve, but the real measure of our stewardship, intelligence, decency and compassion is what we do to preserve life in all its forms, prevent harm, stop hurt, and realizing that in the natural order of things, our own good cannot actualize on the heels of detriment to others. Friends, most cries are silent, and the saddest tears are invisible. Still, a painless death is a complete death, and unendurable suffering is often unexpressed. And, there are no evil spirits, save for the ones we rear. Animal experimentation is not the answer to human health problems as we shall discuss in a separate chapter.

Vivisection is not the only way; there are alternatives—many, better, more reliable and scientific, boosters to human health and well-being. Vivisectors try to convince us that vivisection is imperative. It isn't. At best, and with ample acquiescence on my part, vivisection is a choice. A bad choice though. Grievous. Wicked. Unforgivable.

Martin Luther King said, "Cowardice asks is it safe? Expedience asks is it political? Vanity asks it is popular? But the conscience asks is it right?" Cowardice, expediency, and vanity aside, good conscience presiding, let's discuss alternatives to the use of live animals in research, testing, teaching and training. But never lose sight of a fundamental fact, one that I will never grow tired or bored of repeating and restating: heart and blood vessel diseases (heart attacks, strokes, gangrene of the extremities) plus cancer and accidents together account for at least 75 percent of all deaths annually, yet are largely preventable, principally through proper nutrition, exercise, not smoking and not drinking alcohol. Eighty percent of cancers are preventable and it is rare to encounter heart attacks in individuals whose blood cholesterol is less than 150 milligrams and who exercise moderately and do not smoke. The whole thing, vivisection, is a gimmick, diverting our attention and resources away from the real stuff, all while being harmed, impoverished and impounded in a labyrinth of misconception, lured into a yarn of splendored illusion. The information we garner from vivisection is misinformation. In liberating animals from the horror chamber (animal laboratory), we are restoring our sapiency and redeeming ourselves. Animal liberation is human liberation. Immanuel Kant said, "Out of the crooked timber of humanity, no straight thing was ever made." Well! Kant's statement is true, but I won't take it for a verdict. Together let's make one straight thing, just one, for a start. Begin with this one: Alternatives to vivisection.

1. CELL CULTURE

There, within individual body cells, action is. Make or break at cellular level. There we live or die, thrive or shrivel, rise or collapse. My cell in culture unveils more of me, the real me than a dog, a monkey or a rabbit would. My genes, my nucleus, my protoplasm, are all there, telling and foretelling. Science is more and more heading in the direction of cells and cellular components such as genes and mitochondria. And, hopefully the "crooked timber of humanity" won't make mess and advance grief, and monstrosity out of this. Cells, separated and given appropriate nutrients, temperature and abode (a test tube or a petrie dish) will multiply forming tissues similar to their parent kind. Numerous cell lines can be cultured time and again through many generations to produce specific cell types. Even pathologic cell lines such as cancer cells can be grown in cultures.

Quoting from *Coping and Beyond*,* "Aging is the hallmark of individuality. Organisms merging in colonial forms without a separate existence do not age. Individual entities that we are, we cannot escape the phenomenon of aging, yet we can delay its mandated arrival, slow its progress and with it keep a graceful company. While the human organism as

---

*Fadali, M.: *Coping and Beyond: A Surgeon's Reflections on Medicine, Science, Art and a Life Worth Living*, DeVorss & Company, 1990, 2nd ed., 1992, p. 112.

a whole is mortal, under exceptional circumstances, a colony of human cells may live seemingly forever. Henrietta Lacks, a young black woman, died of cervical cancer on October 4, 1951. A few cells taken from her fatal growth miraculously continue to thrive to this day in a laboratory dish at Johns Hopkins Hospital School of Medicine in Baltimore. Further, the vigorous 'He-La cells,' named after Henrietta Lacks managed to find their way to scientific laboratories worldwide, where they dwell, live and multiply forty plus years after Henrietta died.'' In 1966 to 1968 while at Johns Hopkins, I had the opportunity to witness and see with my own eyes the amazing feat. On multiple occasions I discussed cancer, cell cultures and future possibilities for such research with Dr. Guy and his wife, who initiated, cultured and nurtured this perky cell line. A breakthrough indeed. In this known environment (cell cultures) the unknowns and many variables brought on by using animals are eliminated. Better work can be performed and more reliable results obtained in several fields such as:

1. Cancer research
2. Immunity research, suppression and enhancement
3. Toxicology and toxicity testing
4. Vaccines production
5. Drug development, evaluation and screening
6. Inherited diseases and disorders
7. Earlier diagnosis of disease before the onset of symptoms
8. Infectious diseases, bacterial, viral and others
9. Developing, assessing and quantitating medical therapies

Cell culture as an alternative should be easy to sell to vivisectionists and could help weaning them off animal experimentation.

2. TISSUE CULTURE

Specific tissues can be cultured in vitro (test tubes and dishes) for more specialized testing depending on the procedure or agent being tested. The human fetal tissues from aborted fetuses is a prime example, very useful in developing viral vaccines and showing some promise in Alzheimer's disease research and some other incurable disease conditions.

The National Disease Research Interchange, a non-profit clearinghouse, provides more than 130 kinds of human tissue to scientists investigating diabetes, cancer, cystic fibrosis, muscular dystrophy, glaucoma and more than 50 other diseases. Certainly, there is no excuse to murder any of those innocent four-legged creatures. They all long to live. All are beautiful and loving. Some are naughty though, but none is wicked or wayward. Shepherd, befriend and protect them all. Will you? We must.

Replaying in my mind at this time "Song of Myself" by Walt Whitman, together let us share an offering in praise of animals:

> I stand and look at them long and long.
> They do not sweat and whine
>   about their condition.
> They do not lie awake in the dark
>   and weep for their sins.
> They do not make me sick
>   discussing their duty to God.
> Not one is dissatisfied
>   not one is demented with
>   the mania of owning things.

3. ORGAN CULTURE

The human placenta offers an excellent venue; it has a short and well defined lifespan, readily available—discarded after delivery—has established, thoroughly studied functions such as transferring nutrients, exchanging gases and producing hormones. Its cells are young and sensitive, thus highly susceptible to the side effects of drugs and chemicals. Study of birth defects and the aging process appear to be quite suited for the organ culture medium of the placenta.

Microsurgery whereby minute vessels such as those supplying the fingers can be connected together by elaborate techniques may be practiced for on the placenta. Artificial circulation can be designed in the placental model, a simulation of real-life situations.

4. EPIDEMIOLOGIC STUDIES

Comparative studies of human populations—of different segments, diverse and non-diverse—have provided critical and valid information about the causation of many diseases. Such studies are the backbone of tracing infections, detecting methods of transfer, planning isolation when necessary and preventing spread. Several breakthrough discoveries were the outcome of epidemiologic studies, to mention just a few: the relationship between smoking and cancer (tobacco alone causes 30 percent of all cancers), cholesterol and heart disease (the two are very much related and epidemiologic studies involving thousands of people demonstrated that below a certain level of blood cholesterol, heart attacks are extremely rare), high fat diets and common cancers (high fat intake increases the chances of contracting colon cancer 10 times, breast cancer 5 times and prostate cancer 3.5 times) and chemical exposures and birth defects (animal research frequently gives a false sense of security in this regard, such as the thalidomide tragedy where 10,000 major birth defects resulted from using a drug that was considered safe on the basis of animal research, also tegretol which causes facial, eye and nasal defects) and alcohol, even in mild consumption, by pregnant women can cause "fetal alcohol syndrome," a state of mental retardation of different degrees coupled with other abnormalities. Some epidemiologic studies have shown that alcohol is the commonest cause of fetal abnormalities. The mechanism of transmission of AIDS was also discovered through epidemiologic studies. None of this considerable information came out of animal research.

5. CLINICAL RESEARCH AND AUTOPSY STUDIES

Using sophisticated new scanning technology (CATscans, PETscans and MRIs) has inaugurated a fascinating era in the study of human patients. Largely non-invasive, so far it has identified certain abnormalities in the brains of patients with Alzheimer's disease, epilepsy and autism. Dietary studies of patients with multiple sclerosis demonstrated the benefit of a low-fat diet, reduction of death rates and rate of disease progression resulted. Autopsy studies have been crucial all along from the time Ibn Al Nafis discovered the route circulating blood takes rectifying Galen's flawed vivisection maps and charts. Many disease processes were discovered during autopsy: tumors, cancers, infections and diseases of the endocrine glands causing gigantism, acromegaly, Cushing disease, diabetes and many others.

6. COMPUTERS: MAKING VACCINES, MANUFACTURING AND SCREENING NEW DRUGS AND PROBING THE HUMAN CONDITION

Production of synthetic vaccines: The three-dimensional structure of a chemical can be fed into a computer. Along similar lines, computer-aided modeling of a virus protein structure has been successfully used in a number of laboratories to produce specific vaccines against specific viruses. The Scribbs Clinic's Research Institute has been a leader in the relatively new field. The first synthetic vaccine developed at Scribbs was for foot-and-mouth disease, an animal plague prevalent everywhere, except in North America and Australia. Computer imaging techniques and recombinant DNA technology can eliminate the use of animals in this regard, and promise to deliver vaccines without pathologic contamination and with less side effects.

Computers can remarkably predict the biological reactions caused by untested drugs based on knowledge of their three-dimensional structure. A significant contribution in this area would be the elimination of a brutal, despicable test known as LD-50. The test is used to evaluate acute toxicity of chemicals by determining the dosage needed to kill half of the animals tested. Rats and mice have been favorite subjects for the LD-50 massacre. Recent studies at Health Design, Inc., Rochester, New York, showed that the computer-estimated LD-50 values of tested chemicals were reliable. You see, we are getting in there. Our sincere effort will complete the job. Vivisection will then become history and there we will look back in disbelief and dread at what some of us had done.

Making New Drugs: The average new drug takes approximately $250 million and twelve years to develop, animals being the main test site for new drugs. Many complications, some fatal, have occurred when researchers moved from animal to clinical trial. Besides, for every drug that makes it to the market place, many would-be medicines are shafted away. Even the safety of the few which make it remains illusive. The process takes too long, is very expensive and dismally unreliable. Computers can do better, save money, time, health and lives.

To understand how most drugs work, think of a lock and a key. For example, the anti-anxiety drug Valium, like a key fits a receptor—a lock—on nerve cells. Now the Valium/receptor linkup slows the firing emanating from the nerve cells and relaxes the restless, tense patient. The same goes for many drugs, such as antibiotics. Using the lock-and-key concept, there are a few steps to go through: First, to determine the shape of the lock—in real life, the target receptor—by biotechniques, namely, recombinant DNA, X-ray crystallography and nuclear magnetic resonance. Secondly, comes the role of the computer, which is used to design a key that fits in the lock; in other words, design a new drug molecule. Thirdly, thousands of possible candidates are put on a silicon chip, a fraction of an inch across. The chip also holds the receptors. Now, let's find out which keys locked into which receptors; pick them out. This is done by a laser beam, which scans the surface of the chip, checking each sample. When a possible drug has locked into a receptor, a fluorescent dye lights up. Within minutes, thousands of candidates are screened and several promising compounds are identified. Agouron Pharmaceuticals in San Diego and Affymax Research Institute in Palo Alto, California, are on the leading edge of this technology. As a result, some new drugs are entering human trials. Agouron put forth some anticancer and AIDS drugs and Vertex of Cambridge, Massachusetts, has developed an AIDS drug and an anti-flammatory agent that shows some promise for victims of rheumatoid arthritis; toxic-shock syndrome patients may benefit as well. A new anti-anxiety drug with minimal side effects is being provided by Neurogen Corp. of Branford, Connecticut.

As we can see, these fascinating nerds, "computers," are capable of reasoninig logically and solving abstract problems. They can help determine the three dimensional structure of a biologically active molecule; this can lead to its synthesis.

Computers can also correlate the chemical structure of a chemical compound or drug with its biological activity. This one has far reaching implications, promising breakthroughs as well.

At its infancy yet the approach is fascinating, makes good sense, its broods are eager to fly: humans to beget safer remedies, and animal lives to be restored. Still, the safest remedy is prevention. Never forget nor overlook the well-established fact that most of our fatal and debilitating maladies are "Diseases of Civilization" invited by our meat-centered diet, consumption of eggs and dairy products, excessive fat intake, tobacco, alcohol and thousands of chemicals denaturing our air, water and soil, as well as a stressful lifestyle engendered by our confused, restless mind and lazy body parts.

Probing the Human Condition: mathematical models of different human systems, such as the cardiovascular system or the endocrines (hormone-producing glands), can be programmed with various data from patients and can project insights into the human realm. Artificial intelligence has come a long way. In American education, computer simulations are steadily replacing live animals.

7. BACTERIAL AND PROTOZOAL CULTURES

Bacteria and protozoa are single-cell organisms which can be used to assay vitamin levels in pharmacological and toxicological studies also in screening antibiotics. Being very sensitive to mutagens (genetic-altering agents), they can identify cancer-causing agents (carcinogens). The Ames Test, which utilizes a strain of salmonella bacteria—that causes typhoid—has confirmed the remarkable correlation between mutagenicity and carcinogenicity. It is an effective and economic alternative to the use of animals in carcinogenicity testing. Dividing every 20 to 30 minutes, many generations of bacteria can be monitored within relatively short time intervals while under standardized, experimentally controlled reproducible conditions. No animal model is capable of providing these wide spectra and dynamic sequences of carefully monitored events.

8. GROWING CELLS TO PRODUCE SPECIFIC ANTIBODIES—MONOCLONAL ANTIBODIES, THE AMAZING HYBRIDOMA

This is a line of cells that can be grown in vitro (not in a live animal or human) and is capable of producing a single specific antibody. These specific antibodies when made available can be prescribed as precise, specific remedies for a variety of infections, allergic reactions, hormonal disorders and cancers. Many therapies such as radiation or chemotherapy for cancer are sort of a blanket approach or shotgun therapy, incapable of sorting out normal from abnormal cells; the medicine knocks about at random. Reactions to such therapies can be quite nasty, such as hair loss and nausea, or devastating through incessant vomiting, profuse diarrhea, wasting, shortness of breath, weakness, bleeding, susceptibility to serious infections and eventual death caused by the remedy itself, not by the original ailment. A specific antibody will not do that, it will zero in on the abnormal cells, a dual benefit, that of detecting the culprits and selectively eliminating them. Interestingly, the term hybridoma is derived from the manner in which these V.I.P. cells were orginated. Two cells with desirable qualities could be united together into a single cell. Let us illustrate by example, lymphocytes (one kind of white blood cell we all have, constantly circulating and multiplying in many places such as the spleen) are adept at synthesizing antibodies in response to infections. Adaptable, lymphocytes can be programmed to manufacture antibodies to a specific agent (antigen). Kohler and Milstein successfully fused lymphocytes to myeloma cells. Myeloma cells are cancerous; the emerging hybrid cell took off, growing continuously, all the while producing the same specific antibody. Marvelous! Isn't it? In vitro, hybridomas can grow indefinitely and made to provide specific antibodies to cure specific diseases.

Early detection of disease and effective remedy. A great prospect. A bonanza. And the big boon is elimination of the use of animals, entirely. Animal experimentation is an anathema and a curse. A shameless sham, dooming animals and damning humans. Acquitting the first and exonerating the latter are long overdue.

9. THE CHEMICAL LANGUAGE. DNA SPEAKS: RECOMBINANT DNA TECHNOLOGY

We owe it all to our genes. Instructions to be or not to be and what will be are coded in minute particles in every single body cell. The mighty miniatures, the genes. The expression of this code is us: Our dreams, ambitions and passions, beauty, grace and ugliness, moods, sexual attitudes and behavior, tongue, lung and cheek, liver, heart and spleen. But, don't forget or ignore our potential. It isn't all cast in hard concrete; it isn't all games of chance; roles interplayed, plenty of room; a bag of tools, chips, cards, toys and rules. Knowledge is limitless, time flows, experience grows, memory endures, learning is vast.

There comes replicating DNA (deoxyribonucleic acid), the genes' substance. DNA speaks "chemical language." And, the lesson it does teach is that "life is more than language." Dialect is a set of instructions for the synthesis (manufacture) of proteins, specific ones. Nothing is haphazard: Perfect. Almost! Ever so rarely genes err and goof, mutations result; but, not all mutations distort and deter, some boost and promote.

The all mighty recombinant DNA technology is at hand. A momentous, know-how. Omnipotent! Given our mind-set and a heart pointing the other way, I am afraid this most formidable tool is quite likely to play havoc with the web of existence: its fiber, matrix and basic building blocks. With a little bit of wit, an ounce of insight, a pound of humility, it can fix many of our maladies and disabilities. Five steps to go through:

1. The instructions for specific protein synthesis are decoded (translated, deciphered, expressed) in chemical terms (the proper language, the chemical language).
2. Using these instructions an artificial gene can be grown —synthesized—in the laboratory bearing exactly the same set of instructions it has received.
3. With this precious artificial gene, it isn't hard at all to find a bacterium to implant it in its nucleus. Escherichia coli (E. coli), a bacterium normally inhabiting our intestinal tract—many other bacteria would do—is an appropriate host for the artificially created gene.

4. These bacteria grow and multiply at fantastic speed, producing trillions upon trillions of their duplicates, or clones.
5. The specific protein hidden (coded) in the artificial gene is produced by the bacterial growth in large amounts. It is a high output factory.

Substituting healthy genes for defective ones has not yet lived up to expectation. A promise still unfulfilled. Approximately 3,200 mutations in human genes can cause disease. As of this moment, gene therapy has not cured any disease be it cystic fibrosis, muscular dystrophy, familiar hypercholesterolemia, severe combined immunodeficiency or any kind of the many cancers that ravish our lot. Even if gene therapy succeeds it won't render a permanent cure, for the cells carrying the new healthy gene do not transfer it to their progeny.

EVEN THE TIMID EYE OF THE RABBIT, THEY BURN AND SCORCH. WHAT A SHAME! ALTERNATIVES TO A GHASTLY TEST CALLED DRAIZE

Their soft, silky fur, long, diaphanous ears, bobbed, comely tail, large, affectionate eyes and diffident nature didn't help rabbits win their plea for mercy in the lynch court of Homo sapiens. In a pack of six, frightened, unfortunate rabbits are put to the Draize test. John H. Draize, a toxicologist working for the Food and Drug Administration (FDA) introduced the test in 1944. A drop of the chemical compound to be examined—from shampoo to skin tone cream to toothpaste to floor wax to mascara and lipstick—is instilled into the eyes of conscious rabbits. The rabbit's eyelids are held together to distribute the material evenly. Periodic observations are made at intervals of 1, 24, 48, and 72 hours, up to 21 days. Injuries are graded on a scale of 1–6. Severe damage to the conjunctiva, corneal ulceration, blindness or even death may happen to the tested animal.

And now let me tell you something that will shock you and make you spurn and scorn government and its wasteful, fatuous agencies. The consortium that drew the specific standards and guidelines for the Draize test, the Interagency Regulatory Liaison Group (IRLG), was comprised of no less than the U.S. Consumer Product Safety Commission, U.S. Environmental Protection Agency, Food and Drug Administration (U.S. Department of Health and Human Services), Food Safety and Quality Service (U.S. Department of Agriculture) and the Occupational Safety and Health Administration (U.S. Department of Labor). The big wheels. Shame on them all; ignominy and contempt they duly deserve. Don't they have better things to do? But they gorge on the worthless and the frivolous, ever inclined to misappropriating public funds. Adding insult to injury: the fact that the test has proven unreliable; several substances that passed muster caused human damage; some that flunked were passed on to the faithful consumer; several of the failures were found safe. It's a joke, cruel though. Doltish and asinine. The eye of the rabbit isn't the eye of the human; it differs in many important aspects: pH, texture and extent of cornea, presence of a "third lid" and rate of blinking and tearing. For more detail see Chapter two, page 43.

Why is the Draize Test done at all? A logical question. And, the answer is: Legal liability. Not science. Not consumer safety. However, whether you get burned or bruised, your hurt is highly unlikely to win you a lawsuit. The crafty manufacturers insert a warning label telling the consumer that the product is potentially damaging for some users; here you are, "potentially damaging for some users." "Potentially" and "some" covers almost all possible mishaps and bad outcomes. Atra Skin Tone Cream promised a "lighter, lovelier skin beauty for you . . . a complexion fresh and bright as springtime." Wow! Promotion in motion, splendid: choice words, poetic-sounding metaphors. The plaintiff was a black woman who used the skin-lightening cream. Unfortunately, the gentle, loving enhancer burned and scarred her skin. She sued for damages, Harris v. Belton, and lost her case. The court ruled that the law does not prohibit the manufacture and sale of dangerous products, but simply provides that the customer be warned of potential adverse effects. Unlike in the case of drugs, when it comes to household items, such as shampoo, mascara and floor polish, etc. the FDA does not mandate prior animal testing. But they do it anyway. The whole thing is sour and foul, devious and malicious.

Carroll S. Weil, and Robert A. Scala (1971) of Carnegi–Mellon University and Esso Research and Engineering Company conducted a survey of intra- and inter-laboratory variability of the Draize Irritancy Test concluding that "the rabbit eye and skin procedures currently recommended by several agencies for use in the delineation of irritancy of materials should not be recommended as standard procedures in any new regulations. Without careful reeducation, this test results in unreliable results."*

Strange how all these horrible things go on and on while several alternatives are available: more reliable, less costly and cruelty free.

Here are some alternatives:

1. In-vitro cultures of excised human corneal tissue proved very successful in observing the effect of chem-

---

*Weil, C.S., Scala, R.A.: "Study of Intra- and Inter-laboratory Variability in the Results of Rabbits RIE and Skin Irritation Test." *Toxicology and Applied Pharmacology* 19276-360 1971.

ical irritants. Many human tissues of all kind are removed during surgical procedures, samples of which are frequently examined by pathologists; the rest is treated as waste and discarded. The extrapolation gap, from various animal species to humans is thereby eliminated, a gap in which we fall and get hurt. Let's close the gap. Clonetics Corporation has its Epi-Packs containing cultured human cells ready for use.

2. Computer model for toxicity: In February 1987 *Toxicology Newsletter*, Health Design, Inc. (HDI) announced a new computer model for toxicity prediction. TOPO-KAT, a softwear package for the prediction of toxicity endpoints from the structure of chemicals. It can predict the following endpoints:

   LD-50;
   Probability of mutagenicity (AMES);
   Probability of carcinogenicity (2-year essays);
   Teratogenicity (Franc malformation);
   Rabbit skin irritation;
   Rabbit eye irritation. (Draize)

3. The CAM Test developed by Dr. Joseph Leighton of the Medical College of Pennsylvania uses a chicken egg. A drop of the substance to be tested is placed on the egg membrane through a small window cut in the shell. Later the membrane is checked for changes in color, texture, blood vessel configuration and other variables.

4. The Agrose Diffusion Method: In this case a thin layer of cells is placed at the bottom of a flask. Small amounts of the material to be tested are placed on top of the cell layer. A thin cushion of agrose, a derivative of the sea plant agar, allows the test material to be held close to the cell without crushing them. If the test material is an irritant, a zone of killed cells will be seen around it.

At this juncture, a question begging for an answer is: Given all that has been already available for some time in terms of more trustworthy tests not performed on live animals while providing humans more protection, why in the world is an atrocity such as the Draize test still being committed, tolerated and permitted? Applying agreed upon measures and precepts of human logic, reason, intellect and presumed decency, why does the mayhem continue? Violence for its own sake, is it? An addiction that defies amends? Outmatched in its recklessness, madness and cruelty by a slug of other animal experiments, yet somehow the Draize strikes a raw nerve unveiling the true nature of vivisection. A practice that ordains testing lipstick, deodorants, mascara, shampoo and floor wax in the very eyes of live creatures is inherently evil and absolutely repugnant. Its fountainhead, its hatchery from the very beginning, is the violent-prone regions of the human mind.

10. GAS CHROMATOGRAPHY

This method separates and identifies components of, say, a drug, blood samples or urine down to their smallest constituents. It can easily pick up extrinsic or strange chemicals and be very helpful in scrutinizing different compounds and substances.

11. MASS SPECTROMETRY

Using radioactive chemicals analogous to those in the human body to analyze chemical substances, also to accurately find out location, ascertain reaction, and measure concentration. It is applicable and practical. Not daubed with blood or gore. One more implement to fill the void which vivisectionists profess will reign and prevail if animals were liberated from their iron fist.

12. ALTERNATIVES TO THE LD-50 ACUTE TOXICITY TEST

LD-50, "a ritual mass execution of animals," observed Gerhard Zbinden, a respected toxicologist from the Swiss Federal Institute of Toxicology and University of Zurich in 1973.*

Here's how the mass murder goes: A standard LD-50 Test involves a minimum of three groups of ten or more animals each; for each dose level, one group is branded. Each tested animal is given the substance by mouth, by stomach tube, inhalation as spray, powder or vapor, skin application or by injection under the skin, intramuscular, intravenous or intraperitoneal (abdominal). All fair game. They are mere animals! And, we got to use them. A dose is figured that will kill half of a test group of animals. During the period of observation, the victims of pseudoscience suffer some or more of these ills: vomiting, diarrhea, tears, unusual vocalization, bleeding from the eyes or mouth and convulsions. All survivors are killed and autopsied. Lethal Dose 50 is the dose that will kill half of the condemned class. Three major flaws render the LD-50 utterly invalid, of no force, with no reason to be:

1. It does not determine the safe dose of substances tested. To sound brains, this is what really matters. The vociferous Reaper pronounces but a vague estimate of the fatal dose.

---

*Zbinden, G., *Progress in Toxicology*, Berlin: Springer-Verlag, 1973.

2. The test cannot, never could, identify what side effects a test substance may cause in a human being. Doses administred to animals are at times so ridiculously high that its equivalence to human situations is far fetched. No wonder, with this test as a guide, many false assumptions have been made.

3. As was mentioned in chapter two, there are basic differences between different species which make this game of analogy and extrapolation a perilous gamble. At stake are our lives and theirs. And mass murdering them won't secure or improve ours. Wherefore? Can any sane soul tell me?

The test does not provide any information on the long-term effects of exposure to the substance assessed. In real life, what kills and causes disease in humans is generally the repetitive exposure or consumption of a certain article. Acute toxicity isn't the main question, even on this one. The test lies and misleads. It is fabrication.

Why then the LD-50 Test? As early as 1927, it was developed for the biological standardization of drugs and vaccines, then it became part of the government guidelines for toxicological testing and evaluation of chemical compounds in the U.S. The Food and Drug Administration (FDA), Environmental Protection Agency (EPA), Consumer Product Safety Commission (CPSC) and the Department of Transportation (DOT), refusing to acknowledge facts, still explicitly or implicitly require LD—50 determination. Authority imposing the hocus and bogus. What about the alternatives? Are there any? Yes, there are; here are some:

1. Computer models: Highly efficient in this regard, they analyze structure and activity models of chemicals. They match and outmatch the LD-50 in dose ranging,

selection of least toxic compounds, environmental evaluation and acute toxicity information.
2. Specific cell cultures.
3. Specific tissue cultures.
4. Organ cultures.

Keep in mind, this useless, illogical test kills 2 to 4 million animals every year; most if not all suffer before they die. Wherefore? Sheer madness, isn't it? Or is it arrogance? Callousness? Rancidity? Gold digging? All? Perhaps! I may sound hopeless; I am not, otherwise I wouldn't have written this book.

ALTERNATIVES TO THE USE OF ANIMALS IN VACCINE PRODUCTION AND STANDARDIZATION

We went through this earlier when we discussed vaccines; please refer to this part. Here are some, restated.

1. Cell cultures.
2. Tissue cultures.
3. Gene-splicing techniques.
4. Recombinant DNA technology.

Safer, more accurate, versatile, less expensive, help save lives—human and animal. Please tell it to your dogs and hogs, to the cats and bats; I'll let the frogs in the pond know, and my good neighbor will broadcast the good news to the gentle rabbits, the dainty guinea pigs, the suckling calves and the lovely little lambs. Open all the cages, let 'em all be free. Let 'em all be free.

CHAPTER SEVEN

Teaching Surgery in Animal Labs Is a Sham

Learning surgical technique by practicing on live animals is a sham, unnecessary, imprudent and cruel. It has never produced a great surgeon. There are decent means to acquire surgical skill and dexterity.

Learning surgical techniques by practicing on live animals is absurd, imprudent and cruel. It has never produced a great surgeon. The shameful practice was banned in Britain in 1876, yet thrives still in the U.S., consuming at least 2–3 million animals every eyar. Witless saga manifesting little sense and over-abundance of foolishness.

TEACHING

Annually, during the International Science and Engineering Fair, over one million animals are used. Of such a fair, the muster is callous and mediocre. It is administered by Science Service in Washington, D.C. Without question, on this one, the Washington agency is rendering neither service nor science; a fair; that is about it, dark and tragic.

New guidelines to regulate and hopefully discourage this

157

practice are under consideration. Being pursued, I am told. The whole terror show must be banned altogether, concessions, amenities, proceedings and protocols. Animals punished and annihilated in the fair are mostly frogs, mice, rats, hamsters, guinea pigs and cats, dogs and others are not spared the torment and rigors of the carnival. Plutarch observed, "Boys may kill frogs for fun, but the frogs die in earnest." Bad boys make very bad grown ups. Why crack a dog's rib cage to see the heart beating, injecting a drug to halt its beat, then another drug or an electric jolt to restart it? Why maim and bring to naught a frog merely to witness its muscle twitch whenever struck by an electric current? These mutilating rituals do not teach the student anything new; mere fragments of information already known from multitudes of previous human observations, followed by innumerable uncalled-for animal experiments. The experimental method must not be applied indiscriminately. Unfortunately when it comes to biology, the science of life, other lives become humankind's test site, a hellish domain where atrocious crimes are committed on a massive scale under the tempera of science. A stratagem that doesn't help or enhance. Corrupting? Yes. Desensitizing? Of course! Those who dispense misery and death don't have to endure or even remotely feel the debilitating pain and loss they inflict. The predicaments are not theirs to bear. Keen observation is a wise, pliable tool; besides, exquisite inanimate models of all sorts are available, so are audiovisual methods and several other means. Stop the wanton killing in our schools. It is a disgrace.

THE TRAINING OF SURGEONS

A question frequently arises: How can we train would-be surgeons to insure their dexterity and skill before letting them launch their scalpels and sharps into human entrails and flesh? Well! Anyone telling you that the animal laboratory is the venue to harness surgical aptitude either doesn't know the ropes, is misled or misleading. Sir Frederick Treves, a surgeon's surgeon, was director of the London Hospital and King Edward VII's choice for a surgeon. Renouncing his sojourn in the animal laboratory, Treves wrote, "Many years ago I carried out on the Continent sundry operations upon the intestines of dogs, but such are the differences between the human and canine bowel, that when I came to operate on man, I found I was much hampered by my new experience, that I had everything to unlearn, and that my experiments had done little but unfit me to deal with the human intestine."* A candid renunciation.

Crossing the Channel, cruising more recent times, let us hear from Abel Desjardins, then-President of the Society of Surgeons of Paris, "I have never known a good surgeon who learned anything from animal experiments."**

This has been my own experience as a cardiovascular and thoracic surgeon for many years; still am. I have not learned anything ingenuous or humanly applicable from the animal laboratory despite the fact that ill-fate, and a measure of ill disposition on my part, unrecognized, unseen at that time, put me there during my training years at a foremost—if not the foremost—School of Medicine in the U.S. Like Sir Frederick Treves, I had to unlearn what I have learned in the animal laboratory and in accord with Dr. Abel Desjardins, I have never known a good surgeon who learned anything from animal experiments; and, my whole being echoes the sentiment of Charles Mayo, one of the finest surgeons the world has known, "I abhor vivisection. I abhor vivisection."

---

*Treves, *British Medical Journal*, November 5, 1989, p. 1–9.
**Desjardins, A.: *Intransigent* 25-81925. Quoted by H. Ruesch in *Venditori di malanni e fabricanti di focomelie.* Edizioni CIVIS (Rome 1977).

The heinous, abominable court, though, has opened the eye of my mind. I often wonder, did I have to suffer the throes of hell before enduring purgatory's remorse? And, I dare not jest about the balm of paradise. Alighieri Dante and, three centuries before him, the immortal Syrian poet and seer, Al Maarri, narrated their personal experience as they journeyed the latitudes, longitudes, and arc of the ecliptic on the venerable stage of the "Divine Comedy." A seer once informed me that every man and woman experience a "Divine Comedy." Am I narrating mine? Divulging? My stage is not venerable though! And, I am not a Dante or an Al Maarri. Oh! Reader, please do not forbear, desist not, continue, continue. Mere renunciation does not wash the slate. Vivisection is an atrocious crime; thus I resolved to go further: recant and make amends. The scroll of my vow reads:

1. Never practice vivisection.
2. My contemplation, spoken and written word shall always condemn and convict vivisection.
3. Be a vegetarian, a vegan who does not consume any animal products as well.*
4. Never to wear animal parts.
5. Continue the pacifist path I have followed from my adolescence on. Wars kill all forms of life; none of them is just; all are fatal and the only cure is prevention. I believe war is a preventable disease. All humankind's wars, past, present—daresay future ones as well—are merely a chain reaction; the products of each war activate additional reactants, triggering new wars. A million sparks to light the fire. And, in a frenzy, we fools

---

*The primary consumer of plants are farm animals raised to feed humans. Becoming a vegetarian saves plants, forests included, wild life and other species.

move to the rhythm of the pyrrhic dance, a dance of death, skeletons leading the living to their graves.

At the symposium of Thoracic Surgery, 14–16 February, 1980, in Florence, Italy, training of surgeons was discussed by Professor R.J. Belcher, ". . . the aim should be to train the surgeon using human patients by moving gradually from stage to stage of difficulty and explicitly rejecting the acquisition of skill by practicing on animals . . . which is useless and dangerous in the training of a thoracic surgeon."* Amen.

The quintessential mark of a good surgeon is the polite, tame handling of live tissues, stealthily, reverently, ever so subtly, surreptitiously, yet affectionate and buoyant guided by a mind in a state of heightened alertness, yet serene, deliberate and resolute. None of these artful delicacies can be acquired by pillaging the entrails of a live dog or deflowering the bellows of a guiltless pig.

So, what should a conscientious, scrupulous surgeon do to achieve dexterity and harness the art and poise of his profession?

1. The most crucial attribute is one of character. He or she must be a kind person, with a compassionate disposition and honest mind, yet brave and decisive. Not to waver or hesitate to take the right course of action to salvage, mend or alleviate. Within the hallowed citadel of humans' interior abode, cutting, excising, trimming, grafting, replacing, rerouting and stitching should not be carried out unless absolutely necessary. Pride makes a surgeon fall. Many a time make or break depends on a surgeon knowing when to stop. Vainglory more often

---

*Quoted from Pietro Croce, M.D.: *Vivisection or Science, A Choice to Make*, Switzerland: Buchverlag CIVIS Publications, 1991, p. 72.

than ignorance lures the surgeon into venturing and continuing a specific course of action even though he or she sees that a patient's life or welfare is likely to be jeopardized as a result. Physicians, surgeons and other professionals are humans like the rest of us, subject to the entrapment of wantonness, extravagance, greed and conceit. Some are incompetent; arrogant, they don't know it. In all fairness, I hasten to add that a number of surgeons minister their healing art in the orbit of the divine. Qualities such as these can never be cultivated in the untidy mess of the animal laboratory.

2. Entering a training program with competent senior surgeons who will see to it that the trainee is given gradual (very gradual) surgical assignments under their close tutoring and scrutiny. If we are really serious about surgeons' competence, this is the best and most appropriate way to learn. It is how great surgeons are made. Equipped in the operating room under the tutelage of the master, not in the vivisection room.

3. Practicing techniques on human cadavers is valid and essential to learn human anatomy. Anatomy is a surgeon's road map directing and guiding while he or she explores the ailing terrain beneath the surface. Cadavers are the appropriate vehicle to learn not only normal human anatomy, but also pathological anatomy—that is, the abnormal manifestations caused by disease. Hence the great importance of autopsy studies.

4. Another tool is to practice on models. Nowadays we have organs and complete human simulations made of synthetic materials such as silicone, dacron, teflon and prolene. These models proved worthy for training and surgical exercise. They may complement the above methods, but should not replace them. When it comes to new methods their role becomes significant. Trying new techniques on animals has become a new fad over

the past few years, thanks to manufacturers of medical equipment and surgical tools who finance these absurd, contemptuous exploits. Stapling the lung, a major blood vessel, or intestine of a dog, sheep, pig or calf is gruesome and unkind, besides being utterly unnecessary. I didn't have to practice on animals to acquire skill in using these devices. Rubber or silicone will do for me. It did. Pressed, I go to the morgue, consult the cadaver.

5. Woe to those surgeons who practice micro-surgical techniques on animals. Using the microscope, what about exercising on the human placenta? Its minute, delicate vessels qualify for the honor. To be discarded after birth, why waste it? What about artificial vascular models? Plenty. There is no excuse to molest and mutilate live animals in pursuit of skill or information; both can be summoned through other means. Knowledge acquired by cruel, ignominious means, debases and diminishes the recipient.

The new technique of endosurgery, whereby certain surgical procedures are performed through small incisions (keyholes) with the help of endoscopes and special instruments, is expanding. All such techniques, as well as the most formidable of surgical feats, can be mastered without resorting to live animals.

Finally, don't let a surgeon who practices vivisection or received his or her surgical training in the animal laboratory operate on you, your family or friends. They are likely to be rough, lacking refinements, messy and sloppy.

I am heartened to report that the following medical schools have stopped using animals to train their medical students: Yale, Stanford, Georgetown, Jefferson in Philadelphia, Wayne State in Michigan, Northwestern in Illinois, University of Hawaii, West Virginia University, University of Oklahoma, University of Nevada-Reno, Ohio State and many others. The rest have optional labs only. At the time of this writing, the University of Colorado is the only civilian medical school in the United States which forces students to participate in animal experiments. Only two years after the American Medical Association's Council on Scientific Affairs declared animal labs "essential" to medical education, more than 30—including Harvard Medical School and Columbia University—have dropped them completely.* Trapped in a web of inertia, the august body spins its big wheels, carriage not moving though, and, wherever it goes into motion, present track guides the wheels. Out of touch the giant AMA remains, basking in the oblivious calm of intransigence.

And, I am told by Physicians Committee for Responsible Medicine, that thousands of physicians and surgeons have signed affidavits condemning the promotional practice of many companies which sponsor symposia, workshops and seminars to train their technicians and doctors on live animals. To them all, I say, "Be ashamed."

---

*Physicians Committee for Responsible Medicine, 5100 Wisconsin Ave. N.W., Suite 404, Washington, D.C. 20016 (202) 686-2210.

CHAPTER EIGHT

Animal Experimentation Is Unscientific and Cruel

Animal experimentation is inherently cruel and unscientific, useless and harmful to us as well; therefore, continuing it is senseless, heartless, mindless. Unforgivable. It must be out- lawed. Banned.

A saga of terror those who bore witness must tell; agony upon agony, pain ending in pain, loss embracing ruin, in- sight deluding sight and obliterating foresight, life degraded and death expunged of dignity. Narrated with hope rekin- dled that the telling will help end vivisection, the very word "viviseciton" being its own condemnation.

Bear with me, together let us go beyond suffering to: Ac- tion. Your empathy, compassion, seeing things as they are and your survival instinct will make what *seems* impossible, possible. Impossible and possible are states of mind, mere spectra of perception. Myself, I have experienced a sum of what I will be telling. I experimented on live animals and I ate meat. No more. No more. My days in the eclipse are over. A phantom named ego casting ignorance upon my being has withered. Died. I am not diabolical anymore. Stripped of drapery, I see what I am looking at.

In liberating animals, I have liberated myself. And, I won't call this conversion lest it be misconstrued and granted musk, ethereal oil and the zeal of religious conversion. Unfortunately, the word "conversion" is prone to summon the psychological aura of exchanging one faith for another. The "born," the "born again" and the convert have many a time faithfully unleashed their venom and wrath on "others." I won't call it reform either. Diminished and trivialized, reform brings change in forms and appearance, not in substance and essence. Throughout history, reformers have been—still are—launching their reform movements and revolts, yet the hell they are trying to reform is scalding more, refusing to die. Galloping! Reformers haven't promoted the human condition; their foremost achievers moved adherents from hell to purgatory, bypassing paradise, hearts left laden with remorse, driven by anger at those who stole their promised paradise.

I'd rather use the word transform for it connotes a genuine change, newness, deconditioning, dehabituation. Dare say unconditioning, for unless we erase the distortion and misconceptions that have been grafted on our minds, there will be no exit, only excursions within the prison cell, and reliving the past with all its horrors, dismal glory and injustice. For radical transformation, we must recover our freedom to observe and perceive "what is" "as is," not as handed to us by authority, secular or religious or whoever. What they hand us is ever mollified by their timbre, wrapped in obscurity, sanctified by myth and mystery and glorified by the awesome weight of history. That is why we are where we are, where we (humanity as a whole) have been, receiving suffering, bearing suffering, returning suffering; bartering a commodity that tears and annihilates. Believing the illusion that we are making progress, exterminating and dismantling "others" (human, animal, plant and planet) are readily taken for a mandatory payment for what we have achieved. Is it? Is it all worth it? Are we better off or worse? Vivisection is meritless, reckless, ruthless, mindless, heartless, yet for long has been permitted to thrive, again under the illusion of "progress."

Love is ink for this book. Sustained by its supreme energy, I reveal my station, cast away my burden and lose my inhibitions. Vivisection, its aura, rituals, mindset, enunciations and justification touch on and include religion, philosophy, psychology, anthropology, physics, metaphysics, mathematics, other sciences, art, ethics, medicine and every human interest topic. Thus, whatever spontaneously comes along or is deliberately gathered is relevant. After rending the veil, my offering for you is all that I have. In the court of love, sincere lovers hold naught. Animals do not use drugs, be it tobacco (the most lethal of all), alcohol (silver medal recipient, tobacco snatched the gold), cocaine, heroin, etc. They don't blow toxins in the air or dump them in the soil, sea, ocean and waterways; they don't slay the earth and botch the air with nuclear waste, the ingredients of which will remain active for thousands of years. They don't wear cosmetics; only in ludicrous human-made circuses, unworthy movies and distempered sickly commercials, all imposed on them by peddlers of triviality.

Can anyone with a working brain tell me why many experiments are still being carried out on live animals to determine the amount of fluid necessary to resuscitate and rehydrate human beings? We have known this already. Are we that moronic and asinine to figure it out this lurid way?

Radiation eye burn in monkeys. Wherefore? Fly those hard-hearted guys to Hiroshima or Nagasaki for a massive, jolting testimonial. Hopefully they'll experience the shock of recognition. For those afraid of flying very far, nuclear test sites in the U.S., Russia, France, Britain, and other countries is a field trip. Its reward is direct learning. Downwinders have higher death rates, more cancers, leukemias, lymphomas, anemia and cataracts. You don't need to cut, dismember, burn or poison pigs, monkeys, cats, dogs and other animals to know what causes those horrible things and to observe the stages of those human-inflicted maladies. Willing or pleased to torment? Some of us are.

Donald Barnes formerly with Brooks Air Force Base, San Antonio, Texas wrote, "In years past I was ordered to keep a death watch on these irradiated subjects, which meant simply to see what happened until they died of radiation injury. Do you have any idea how miserable it is to die from radiation injury? I do. I have seen so many monkeys go through it."*

Harvard Medical School, Masachusetts Eye and Ear Infirmary and Retina Foundation collaborated in a research protocol involving proton irradiation of the eyes of owl monkeys. After a follow-up period of 42 to 52 months, the project vivisectors stated, "It is difficult to extrapolate these data of proton beam irridation of monkey eyes . . . to the human eye which may have a different threshold of radiation damage."** Good grief! Are they disposed to inflict suffering?

In burn experiments, guinea pigs in large numbers were immersed for three seconds in 100-degree centigrade water (212 Fahrenheit). This produced full-thickness skin burns of 50% or 70% of their body surface.*** The charred bodies of millions of humans set ablaze, individually and collectively by their fellow humans, much less often accidentally or suicidally, starkly exhibit all that the animal research seeks to know. William Shakespeare testified, "Humanity must perforce prey on itself." Pyromania! Is this the reason why

---

*Pratt, D, *Alternatives to Pain in Experiments on Animals*, New York: Argus Archives, 1980, pp. 141–142.
**Gradoudas, E.S., et al, *Archives of Ophthalmology*, 1979, 97:2184.
***Robinson, K.M.; and Miller, H.I., *Circulatory Shock*, 1981, 7:457.

vivisectionists look the other way and set their own private boilery? Of a merciless dispostion, aren't they?

Everyone is fully aware that in the United States, other countries as well, hundreds of thousands of car accidents happen, injuring and killing passengers, drivers and pedestrians. Victims are medically examined, their injuries diagnosed, treated; and the deceased get autopsied. Voluminous information has been steadily piling up saturating hospital archives and medical school wards and libraries. Why then are simulated car crash studies using animals being done? The devil within choreographs the tragedy and we enact it live, so the gruesome routine is: Strap animals into special impact-sleds which propel them at high rates of speed into objects giving them severe injuries. Using less sophisticated methods some researchers abruptly, forcefully, drop down heavy loads on restrained animals. Of this notoriously cruel, lowly method, I have relayed my personal encounter earlier in this book, not as a perpetrator; ill-fated, I happened to be there. I was practicing cardiovascular surgery in a prestigious University Medical School on the U.S. East coast. My office was on campus, the evil-doer was a doctor in training smashing the dog's rib cage with a heavy rock, virtually committing murder in the first degree of an innocent dog. Surely, in this case killing was premeditated; as for malice, I couldn't attest to that. Lacking full knowledge of criminal law I am not certain whether malice is a necessry ingredient to convict on first degree for the loss of life witnessed. Our law has not yet encompased our fellow living creatures; still it limits itself to humankind. A slap on the wrist or a monetary fine is occasionally levied on transgressors who commit violence against animals. Penalties such as these are laughable. And, of course, behind the high walls of animal labs, the human pack is safely guarded. And, I am not an advocate of capital punishment; in itself a crime, it is absolutely cruel, pure vengeance. It doesn't deter, it is irreversible, it is heavily weighted against the penniless, the meager and meek. Can anyone tell me why in the history of the U.S., not a single rich person has ever been executed? Not one. Capital punishment is a state crime. All I am saying is: Crimes against animals should be dealt with as crimes. They are.

The despicable planned murder of that dog remained center-stage in my mind up to the presnt moment. Still, the ear of my mind hears the prey's grim lamentations. Like all dogs, that one was beautiful!

University of Michigan did utilize primates in head-impact studies, all at variance with their own report which reads, "although the primate geometry is the most similar to man's, it is significantly different in anatomic soft tissue distribution and skull morphology. This can present several problems when scaling the test results to human levels. Ultimately, these differences lead to complications in the very complex phenomena of head injury."* Can you believe that? Is this science? Not to be outdone, General Motors Research Laboratories, Warren, Michigan subjected anesthetized restrained rabbits, positioned supine on a platform to impact injuries from a pneumatic impactor. They concluded from these awkward, stinking, nauseating games that, "The spleen of the rabbits was not injured in the tests. . . . The spleen in man is a much more prominent organ, making it more vulnerable to injury."** Perhaps the number one car manufacturer is telling us that when their benevolent automobiles crash, our spleens will be out of harm's way. Any surgeon who has dealt with trauma cases can recount spleens smashed, livers busted, bowels riped apart, hearts

---

*Husholtz, G.S.; Melvin, J.W. and Alem, M.M. "Head Impact Response Comparisons of Human Surrogates." Presented at the 223rd Staff Car Crash Conference, San Diego, California, 1979.
**Lau, V. and Viano, D.C., *Journal of Trauma*, 1981, 21:115.

crushed, lungs contused, brains pulped; and don't forget the broken bones, spilled marrow and the dead. Alcohol was and still is the primary cause of more than half of those catastrophes. Tulane University, New Orleans and Oklahoma University and a score of others joined the race for Federal grants to torture and kill rhesus monkeys and pregnant baboons. Cruelty for its own sake, incomprehensible, inconsolable; vex and tantalize without pity or comprehension. Remorseless, they do it again. Their desire to harm is overwhelming.

The Veterans Administration Wadsworth Hospital, Los Angeles and the University of California School of Medicine, Los Angeles fitted cats with gastric fistulas (constructing a semi-permanent or permanent opening between the stomach and the outside). The fistula made for collection of gastric juice to assess acid secretion in cats under two conditions, a "harness" where the cat's movements were severely limited, and a wooden compartment in which the incarcerated, captured beauty could move freely within the slammer! Here is one of their highly intelligent observations: "It was observed that the cats strongly resisted while being put into the harness. After having been placed in the harness, they were meowing, urinating and trying to escape."* What a shame! What do sensible investigators expect an intelligent, defiant, betrayed, dignified, frightened lithe to do under this abject, degrading, painful condition? Purr for them! Lick their tormenting fingers! Caress and extend velvet paws! What is wrong with them? Why are they squandering time, energy and our money on trivial pursuits? Well! It is all wrong. And nothing right will ever come out of this tort.

To recover some respectability, they came up with the earth-shaking finding that emotional stress induced by re-

---

*Wyrwicka, Wanda and Garcia, Richard, *Pavlovian Journal of Biological Science*, 1979, 14 (4):249.

straining the cats in the harness led to an increase in gastric acid secretion. Fantastic! Shall we laugh or cry? Both! The absurd and dreadful often blend in animal labs. To elevate the sagging standard of their rhetoric, they invoked the name of a celebrity, Pavlov, while ruminating "an unconditioned stimulus which evoked a reflex of freedom."* Cat snatchers! What do you know about freedom? And, of good science and morally sound means you dare ramble, publish and preach? Fellows, this is too obtuse. Reconsider, will you?

Let us visit with the Ivy League at Yale University School of Medicine. The League is not doing well at all. Horrible things are happening down there. They designed impounders of different weights to break cats' backs in order to quantify variables associated with spinal cord injury. Imagine deliberately paralyzing the most graceful of creations. The body language of a cat is God's best composition. At Yale, the days of grace are over.

On the wings of adversity, the unmeritable affliction traveled to the University of Oregon. There, the group took to cutting the eye muscles of kittens, rotating some eyeballs while suture closing others. And they called their hideous throes a "visual orienting task." No. No. That task was nothing but horrible, lacking vision, devoid of orientation, steeped in all that makes humans God's most dangerous creature. In 1979, the Oregon league promised to publish more research papers.**

Have you heard of a drum named "Noble-Collip drum"? Apparently some vivisection bands include a drum and the drummer. Their percussion instrument is ferocious and pernicious. Viceroys of hell, their drumbeat proclaims a summary death sentence, violent, imminent, irrevocable,

---

*Ibid.
**Gordon, B; Moran, J. and Presson, J. *Brain Research*, 1979, 174, 167.

hanging over those condemned to its menacing ride. Circular and revolving, the drum has projections, or bumps which carry the animal up the side during a turn, then dropping it to be picked up by the following projection. During the ride—first and last—each unfortunate passenger is exposed to over 500 revolutions. Since the invention of the drum in 1942 by R.L. Noble and J.B. Collip, thousands and thousands of animals have been tossed and thrust about in this frightful, horrendous machine, crushing their bones, smashing their teeth and rupturing their internal organs. Toys are us. Their toys are them. That which lurks and moves about internally, projects externally. The inner creates the outer. Our toys, gadgets, songs, actions and theories are us. Some bequeath balm, others bestow wrath. Some sooth, others bruise. It's all in our coffers, and we hand out the pieces.

In search of a solution to crooked teeth in adults (human adults), vivisectors conducted studies using monkeys to test skeletal remodeling of the jaw. Monkeys underwent several surgical procedures, including applying force to the jaw using a "headgear appliance" anchored to their heads. Normally very active monkeys were kept in restraining chairs for 84 to 205 days. What do you say about that? It happened. It happened in the Department of Orthodontics, School of Dentistry and the Regional Primate Research Centers, University of Washington. Pathetic, isn't it? I see, to some, violence is seductive and haunting. Beware, the seeds of destruction are always tossed at us to sow discord and propagate monstrosity.

Ever romancing with guns, we have the audacity and demoniacal compulsion to shoot monkeys in order to know more about the grim and obvious. Investigators at the University of Chicago Hospital shot Rhesus monkeys in the head—right in the head—to create what they refer to as "clean wounds." Each animal was placed in a stereotaxic apparatus, which held the head firmly. Rifle attached to the stereotaxic frame—sooner or later—fatal multiple missiles were fired at very close range. Profiles in courage! Platitudes; sullen and disgusting. A puke.

Our own streets, alleys, parks, post offices, restaurants, subways, parking lots, homes, schools, hospitals and morgues are but an unending moribund exhibit of the escalating, bloody violence incurred by firearms. There, all valid medical and surgical lessons concerning human firearm injuries should be learned, the way they really are. Make-believe scenes of obscenity staged in the shadowy galleries of our medical institutions teach falsehood. The aphrodisiac appetites of some of our elite have turned its fury on the innocent. On Innocence. The acme of pornography; the climax where orgiastic rigors shudder one's being. Some quit, others indulge. Will they ever be satiated? Will they ever learn? Shall we hope for the glut of satiety or pray for the light of learning?

To investigate the inner ear, rabbits had their heads bolted to a stereotaxic frame, tracheostomized, skull penetrated to expose the exquisite nerves of the inner ear. Off anesthesia, tone pulses were sent through each rabbit's inner ear over a 4 to 5 hour experimental session. Conclusion: The inner ear of a rabbit closely resembles that of a cat. This came out of the lengthy torture sessions. What shall I say? Members of the pack, will they listen? Their inner ear hears its own tinitus and the ear of their mind perceives echoes of the tempest on the threshold.

Syphilis normally does not occur in animals, yet laboratory artificers and charlatans managed to infect chimpanzees with syphilis only to watch them die. Their papers were scribbled during the wake! Stages of syphilis in humans, their manifestations, disease transmission, prevention and treatment, all were already known. Why do they do those horrible things to chimpanzees? Aghast, I frown darkly, bosom, sore; anger, irrepressible. Their fall is precipitous, headlong. Are they redeemable? Are they?

Cruel starvation experiments are carried out on dogs, some entailing surgical mutilation. For what purpose? The hungry and starved number one billion and one. This is madness. Not stopping it—and we can—we permit it to continue. Each and everyone: Begin now. We will do it! And, I don't doubt it a bit. If I did, I wouldn't have written *Animal Experimentation: A Harvest of Shame*.

One of the arenas in which science gladiators chose to fight their so-called "War on drugs" is the animal lab. Can't fathom how in the world abusing, seducing, corrupting, menacing and killing animals will heal and solve our fatal attraction to drugs. After all, animals are not suicidal, they don't do drugs either. How can such a fabricated, totally contrived experimental sitution tell and inform? I have seen absurdity, I have known adversity, I have met effrontery. This one is all. Curtain aside, here it goes: At Harvard University, Georgetown, Duke, Vanderbilt, University of Chicago, Mississippi, Michigan and the National Institute of Mental Health, along with other fact-finding fountainheads of illumination, hundreds of animal studies have been conducted to crack the hard-to-crack heliospheres of cocaine. Animals used included Rhesus monkeys, squirrel monkeys, chimpanzees, baboons, pigtailed monkeys, patas monkeys, cynomolgus monkeys, dogs, cats, newborn rats, mice, hamsters, guinea pigs, rabbits, pigeons, and chickens. Even the South American electric eel was served slugs of cocaine. You see, in a madhouse, no one is spared the wrath.

Here are some conclusions drawn by the intelligentsia: "Cocaine is a drug of extremely high dependence potential."* Another dullard, silly gesture was widely reported in

---

*Johanson, C.D., "Assessment of the Dependence Potential of Cocaine in Animals," pp. 54–71; In *Cocaine Pharmacology: Effect and Treatment of Abuse* by J. Grabowski, ed. Rockville, Maryland: National Institute on Drug Abuse, 1984.

the media (including the July 5, 1985 edition of the *Boston Globe*) heralding that cocaine was discovered to be more deadly than heroin when given to rats for one month. Having had rudimentary wings the dodo couldn't fly. Closed up, the eye of the mind couldn't see; the first is now extinct, the second, threatened.

Not only cocaine, but also tobacco had to be sanctified and beatified by a research decree. Toward the lofty ideal, year after year, animals are forced to chain-smoke cigarettes to find out whether tobacco is harmful or not. Phillip Morris, the world's number one nicotine-dispensary maintained a secret animal lab to investigate nicotine's addictive properties. Victor DeNoble, a behavioral psychologist who ran the clandestine operation testified before the U.S. Congress in April 1994. There, Victor solemnly divulged the well-guarded secret—that has been common knowledge for centuries—revealing that Phillip Morris' rats repeatedly self-administered nicotine, a key property of an addictive substance. Even this tiny epistle was regarded as apocrypha, of doubtful validity, thus suppressed making room and media time for nicotine verse, "you came a long way, baby"; "we would rather fight than light" and the pompous parade of the horsemen and stallions of Marlboro.

Alcohol research on live animals is pious fraud practiced by deceiver and deceived. Since time immemorial, the goblet of sorrow has exchanged hands between the young and elderly, the rich and famous, the dispossessed and ill-disposed, the heart breakers and broken-hearted, harlots, harlequins, clowns and highbrow customers of happy hours and keepers of social graces. Human lost parts include runaway brains, brutal, withered minds, sagging hearts, hardening, vanishing liver pulp. Studying effects of alcohol on animals is a preposterous act of denial.

Battering, striking, crushing, piercing and electric shocks were applied—still are—to live animals to research pain.

There, the unending trail of human hurt is, spontaneous and inflicted; viscera, extremity, skin, marrow, muscle and bone, spirit and soul. Why pain animals for our travail? René Descartes, founder of modern Western philosophy, defended vivisection, believed that animals do not suffer and considered their cries meaningless. A mathematician as well, on this one his mental math went awry, his lopsided view must have skewed the lines of his thinking. Given René as founder, modern Western philosophy better examine itself. Psychological study is a big item on the rapacious menu. The captives and prey are subjected to: (a) studies on aggression induced by electric shock and other painful manipulations; (b) confinement; (c) mind altering; (d) sleep deprivation; (e) learned helplessness induced by electric shock. The construct, totally unreal, how can it yield credible conclusions? Diabolical rituals, defacing, tormenting. And, we inherit the four winds and the ill-tempered gale.

Their intransigence matches their senselessness. Studying learning and memory loss in animals is dull-witted. Society, home, school, market place, work place, infirmaries, convalescent facilities is where one should look, observe attentively, monitor, gauge, consult, advise, correct, help and follow-up. It's a lot of work commanding devotion, empathy, and real love for fellow humans, not to mention animals whose welfare is not on the agenda of many researchers.

Even human sexual behavior and misbehavior, forays and expeditions, prowess and impotence, function and dysfunction have been—still are—animal lab projects and adventures. Idiotic! This seminal nonsense goes on everywhere. Italy pitched in with a study alleging that, "disco music makes mice homosexual."* So what! Shall we dance?

Animals in countless numbers were electrically jolted, starved, stringed, mutilated, frozen, infected, maddened

---

*Giornale d'Italia, Edizione di Milano, anno '81, n. 44, 14 February 1981.

and killed to gain insight into human nature and conduct. By themselves, those awfully cruel experiments bear witness to humans' perverted nature and frenzied conduct. Anger, egocentricity and ferocity of core and countenance have inflamed our brain. Within and without an inflamed brain the inferno rages. Tongues of light; tongues of fire.

Even the less cruel experiments are notoriously silly and sickly, such as the "tail pinch" or forcing rats to eat hot chili pepper. Of course, any likeness between human and animal behavior will be biased and rendered irrelevant by the contrived leer of the experimental condition. Aren't there any other means? Means that are decent, trustworthy and sensible? Plenty. But they opt for lewdness and brutality. It is humans' boisterous, tempestuous, guileful terrain that begs to be pondered and explored; the terrain itself, without trespassing the domain of others.

For many years Dr. Roger Ulrich was inducing aggression in animals by causing them pain. Awakened—pained as well, I presume—he recanted and abdicated. In a candid letter to the *American Psychological Association Monitor*, March 1978, he confessed, "When I finished my dissertation on pain-produced aggression, my Mennonite mother asked me what it was about. When I told her, she repied, 'Well, we knew that. Dad always warned us to stay away from animals in pain because they are more likely to attack.' Today, I look back with love and respect on all my animal friends from rats to monkeys, who submitted to years of torture so that like my mother I can say, 'Well, we knew that.'" In many courts, the audacious odyssey still plays, self-perpetuating, feasting on itself, propelling carriage and crew. Unabashed, who will stop it? Us. We shall. It has no reason to be.

Armed at all points the military entered the fray on the proverbial plain of Megiddo. Armamentarium aimed at squads of live animals, snapshots of the gruesome scene tell and reveal: excreting rats, thirsty rats, vomiting dogs, vomiting monkeys, hypoglycemic dogs, whole body gamma radiation of dogs, rats and monkeys, exposure of sheep to high level blasts, bleeding pigs, shooting pigs with assault rifles, chemical warfare on guinea pigs and baboons, exposing Rhesus monkeys in utero to the dangers of polychlorinated biphenyls (PCBs) by feeding their mothers with chemicals; rats, mice, fish, quail and other birds were also exposed to PCBs, taste aversions and pain perception tests on rats, placing rats on hot plates, warm water and cold water swims as well as putting the sensitive, intelligent rats in hot incubators, high speed acceleration experiments with dogs and pigs, studying the effect of brain damage on learning in monkeys, the effects of neutron exposure on monkeys, diving experiments on dogs and crashing Rhesus monkeys. Military medical research facilities from San Antonio, to Colorado Springs, to Aberdeen, Maryland, Natick, Massachusetts, Dayton, Ohio, Brooks Air Force Base in Texas and Walter Reed in Washington D.C. all signed in, did what the higher authority ordered them to do. Comes to no good, though. Cruelty for its own sake: irreconcilable, unfathomable, grimly, sadistic. And, each is responsible for his or her actions.

In other chapters we spoke about the horrors of cosmetic testing on animals. A particularly dreadful example being the Draize test, whereby rabbits' eyes were bruised and torched with all sorts of chemicals. A foul blend of madness, stupidity and savagery.

Watch their syntax, terms and grammar: soft, affable, caring, yet, merely devotional mayhem. An animal model is nothing but a dog, cat, monkey or any other animal on its way to gross abuse, dismemberment and demise. Sacrifice sounds reverential echoing intonations of solemn supplication and the opening bars of the rhapsody of paradise thereafter. Of course, it all depends on who is being sacrificed. Animal sacrifice is animal killing. See it for what it is. Aversion stimulus, how neat! It is malicious arousal of antipathy, hatred and repugnance in animals. Our own dislikes and aggressions transmitted to them, just to watch them turning mean and unpleasant. The revised diction swarms with words; pitiful fig leaves covering the obscene horrors burrowing underneath. Remember "collateral damage," and "downsizing," metaphors for hordes of people losing their lives or their jobs. The new lingo points the other way, where things aren't.

Several institutions which indulge in animal experimentation have what they refer to as "Institutional Animal Care and Use Committee," a capricious ad hoc of sham and hypocrisy. These institutional ornamental pieces regulate, dose, set measures, priorities and illusive necessities in order to permit cruelty and contempt for animals to continue under a second skin, smooth, shiny, perspiring fragrance and small drops of dew. Licensing, regulating and inspecting cruelty will not end it. Stopping it will. The Animal Welfare Act is a whimsical farce. The only solution is an Act banning vivisection altogether. Such a magnanimous Act will promote human health and well being. Vivisection is falsehood; truth about ourselves and our ailments and infirmity will not come out of it. It won't restore nor cure. It is a harvest of shame. Addicted, we don't see many ways and means to seek and research good health and longevity. Addiction is reversible though.

A PERSPECTIVE ON GENETIC ENGINEERING

And now we come to the most serious of all: genetic engineering and patenting new forms of animal life; human genetic traits as well. We have journeyed through this amazing labyrinth earlier on in this book while discussing organ transplantation (pages 119–124). The whole venture is alarming and is giving cause for anxiety to responsible scientists, ethicists and to everyone with common sense, decency and basic knowledge of human conduct, past and present. And, I am not a pessimist or a retrogressive; I am a realist, with an optimistic disposition that keeps me going, instilling some joy and summoning the occasional laugh even while witnessing the absurd and the ridiculous. From the same well spring the laugh and the inconsolable cry. Ask the clowns, the gnostics and the seers.

As the global economy moves from industrial technologies to biotechnologies, the building blocks of life have become goods and wares. Genomes and chromosomes, genes, DNA's double helix along with junk bonds, stocks, commodity money; yen, dollars and marks are now legitimized currency for Wall Street, the stock market and megacorporations. Movables and articles to exchange, trade in, traffic, hoard, withhold and monopolize. With each seeking his or her own commodity, imagine what could happen! Laying human's self-centered mind and uneven hands on the nitty gritty, creation's bricks and mortar, fiddling, restructuring, redesigning, configuring, blending, mixing, transferring, downsizing, oversizing, demonizing, dedemonizing, merging and inventing new forms of life. A tempest in the cosmic web. The great tumult stirring up, rattling and unnerving four billion years of natural evolution, compressing millennia of wonderwork into seasons, trimesters and deadlines.

With genetic engineering for an epicenter, biotechnology stands to become a hefty $75–$100 billion industry within the next five to ten years (*The Kiplinger Washington Letter*, vol. 72, no. 31, p. 1, 1995). A lure and a bait not lost on the avaricious reckoning of a notorious powerhouse, the Pharmaceutical Manufacturers Association. It weighed in dangling inducements and waving enticements while threatening to go overseas if its wishes are not taken as commands. Ever susceptible to benefactors' largesse and bounty; always vincible to intimidation by patrons, corporate sponsors and body language of the new party bosses, the U.S. Congress did what it does best: heel and cave in to special interests. And the new hymn played in the hallowed chambers, an amendment to the ditty of pseudopatriotism. "The U.S. cannot afford to lose out in the genetic engineering race." While the band was playing, the fortune seekers sang, the tempo quickened and rapid deregulation followed. Genes in waiting, frightened, defenseless, a lucrative prey to be plundered and ravished at the discretion of the indiscrete. All dandy, all legalized, the ominous scroll has been tendered and handed down by the U.S. Supreme Court. 1980, a leap year, in Diamond vs. Chackrabarty, the venerable niners established patentability of any living thing "Under the sun made by man." Here we are, new gene combinations can be owned and the living vectors in which they are introduced can become private property. Transactions of the deadly kind. The Patent Office opted for an adlibitum interpretation of the Supreme Court landmine decision, including cells, microbes, plants and all animals on its newly revamped menu. Wonder and ponder. Discern your countenance. Blush, and, in contempt behold the new age and dare entertain the open-ended question. What about us? Ourselves? Well! Well! Lawyers already did their contemplation and research. And, here it is, a legal opinion, "Lawyer George Annas argues that there is nothing to prevent cloning enthusiasts from pursuing patents for genetically modified embryos."* Buddy, embryos are us. Remember? And you thought you were safe in your abode! Hah! Like "the house that Jack built," your progeny will be remodeled. And when you navigate the wilderness, you reminisce and you recall the rustic and bucolic; your heart aches and yearns and your vocals thunder, "Beware." Beware, but

---

*The Nation, March 11, 1996, p. 18.

they might not hear you. Wayfarer, the unthinkable has become lawful, acceptable, doable. So, where shall we go from here? And, what is on their agenda? Plenty, plenty, weird stuff, snafus, terrorism at the molecular level, piracy within the sacred walls of living cells. All genes are viewed as venues and vehicles for new products; the ecosystem is in for unprecedented savagery and abuse; cells and genes of indigenous people, the desesparados and descamizados are glittering diamonds and pearls to be had by the moguls of the new age supertechnology. The unholy flame has arrived and the race has begun to lay claims on cell lines and DNA patches, samples and patterns. The profiteers are now launching columns of well-paid gladiators armed with lethal microweapons aimed at other humans, other animals, plants, other lives, life itself, piercing, nipping, slaying womb and bosom.

Seated on the bleachers eyeing the depressing scene, gathering evidence, the Rural Advancement Fund International (RAFI) accuses some scientists and companies of certain industrialized nations of committing acts of "biopiracy." God! God! Imagine that! Biopiracy!? Pirates of our times do not have to brave the seven seas or even walk a mile. RAFI is planning to take this most serious matter to the International Court of Justice at the Hague. Does RAFI have the resources and the stamina? Will it get a fair hearing? And if the verdict is "Guilty," will governments of mighty nations and the CEOs of supermighty global corporations heed and listen? But, you can do something about it. Now. Don't sell your genes.

In my lifetime I have experienced some dreadful dreams. I have witnessed horror pressed into massive doses of shattering jolts. I have seen agony perfected and rained on others without remorse or lament. I pilgrimed to nuclearly holocausted Hiroshima, my leavings were verse and tears. I have learned with utmost distress of the genocide of the

American Indians, the Armenians, the European Jews and Gypsies. I have noted with utter despair the genocide of members of the Tutsi tribe in Rwanda and the Muslims in Bosnia. Other large-scale atrocities weigh heavily on my heart; grief-stricken, I mourn all, everyone. Equally. And, I have observed technology's train of gears spellbinding the human perception, blinding the eye of the mind, controlling thought, replacing memory, dictating action and stunting the restless creature to a pitiable, villainous lump of inertia. From arrow to dagger to musket to rifle to guns, tanks, aeroplanes, submarines, lasers, missiles and nuclear bombs, human's will and ambition couldn't resist the bait. He used them all, sparing none. None. What do you think is going to happen with this one? Do you think he will resist, desist or abstain? Thus talking about it we must. Warning against its horrendous potential we have to. Homicidal and suicidal, humankind might fall in the trap, and Homo sapiens might become history. Who said any species is immune from extinction? Oh boy!

Truly, truly, biotechnology—genetic engineering in particular—is the stroke that may splinter life's chemical code, rend asunder the double helix, disrupt the formula and spoil the primordial soup.

Here are some genetic engineering products: Genetic screening of individuals could disclose information about their lifespan and overall mental and physical potential, thus creating a "genetic underclass" that may be denied employment or insurance coverage. Oh! Yes! Habitually we stratify and categorize and many feel majestic and grand peering down across the Great Divide. Now, genetic screening will do it for us, finally confirming what many have believed all along, that some peoples' ingredients are inferior to theirs. A "Super-race" is in the cards; they talk about it; and when they do and get the means to do it, bet you, they will. "Designer babies" are being considered to fulfill dreams, expectations and ambitions of those who can pay the engineer. The dreaded Nazi regime toyed with the ghastly malignant idea. A fixation on genetic deficits causing and explaining all, from overweight to obesity to slimness, from anxiety to depression, from sexual prowess to orientation, gentle airs, charisma, poise, bad manners, crime, alcoholism, cancer, what have you. A risk-ridden trend diverting attention from environmental causes of illness, lifestyles, abuse practices and unhealthy diets, all notoriously contributing to serious physical and mental illness. So, let it all hang out, eat all you can eat, drink to satiety, stretch and slumber; and, we will facelift, tummytuck, liposuck, pinch your waistline, slip a balloon down your voracious stomach, and shorten your redundant bowels. You are addicted to food because you have the fattening gene of desire, and we will get the silly, nasty speck out of your system. Same goes for the rest of human foibles, failings and self-inflicted wounds.

Cross-species transplants through breeding animals with human genes to overcome rejection in human recipients are very likely to transmit fatal viruses and induce malignancies. Based on ontology, philology, morphology, metamorphosis, genesis of diseases and scientific history from ancient to present, I have no doubt that cross-species transplants will disfigure, disrupt and open unseen gates of new diseases for which we have no resistance nor ready remedies. The mad, wretched practice of inserting genes from one species into the embryos of another to create "transgenic animals" has already produced moribundly ill entities with new shapes and forms beset with terribly hideous diseases. Transgenic pigs suffered from gastric ulcers, heart problems, penumonias, kidney diseases, protruding eyes. Transgenic lambs have diabetes and die early. Transgenic mice develop cancer all over their bodies and miserable outcomes happen to every animal species that is subject to this sick science.

Genetically engineered organisms could create environmental chaos and may trigger new pandemics and major devastating epidemics; a real possibility based on epidemiology, bacteriology, virology and the basic scientific tenets of botany and zoology. Agricultural crops designed to grow big and resist infestations will eventually increase the use of complex chemicals. Pests will always find new ways to ensure their own survival and the highly toxic compounds will find their way to air, water and soil ending up in our organs and very tissues. Done—I presume—with good intentions, transfer of insects, other animals and vegetations from continent to continent, from environment to environment has frequently wreaked havoc on domestic and wild life. Shortsighted, we see the immediate gain, forfeiting the big loss on the threshold and beyond.

Genetic diversity and balance within and between the species are pillars in the venerable scheme of existence. Interdependence keeps life's flow, beat and munificence. Planet's genetic pool cannot be proffered to global corporations; life's stock, bricks and mortar cannot be exchanged on the stock market.

This very serious matter deserves ample contemplation and prompt action. Surely, if we see it for what it really is, we will act decisively. So, for right seeing, I shall ardently work and passionately entreat. Then and there genetic research may render help to all.

CHAPTER NINE

Animals Have a Fundamental Right to Life

Animals have rights, the most basic being their right to life.
They all long to live. In the land of compassion there is no
superior, there is no inferior and, unless we respect and sanc-
tify life in its TOTALITY, we are doomed.

"Animals have rights, the most basic being their right to life.
In the land of compassion there is no superior, there is no
inferior, and, unless we respect life in its TOTALITY, we are
doomed. Homo sapiens, live up to your name. . . . Homo
sapiens, wouldn't you rather be a shepherd than the executioner you are? You have killed your brothers and sisters.
You have organized and perfected mass slaughters and rationalized single, multiple and mass murders. Recover your
original face, opt for life and rise. All we are saying: Give
compassion a chance." (From the introduction, pages xxxi–
xxxii.)

"Recover your original face." What is that—the original
face of man? "Then God said, 'Let us make man in our
image, after our likeness; and let them have dominion over
the fish of the sea, and over the birds of the air, and over the
cattle, and over all the earth, and over every creeping thing
that creeps upon the earth.'" So, God created man in his

own image, in the image of God he created him; male and
female he created them. And God blessed them and God
said to them, 'Be fruitful and multiply, and fill the earth and
subdue it.' '' (Genesis 1:26,27,28.)

So, God was given an anthropomorphic image, in man's
likeness. What about woman? What about the tree, the
flower, the river and the sea? Where are the bears, the cat,
the bat, the butterfly, the penguin and the songbird? And
don't forget dawn, lofty mountains, wind, the sun, rain,
moon and Mars. What about galaxies beyond and the entire
unfathomable universe? Words are mere symbols. Truth,
meaning, essence lie between the words, between the lines.
Beyond symbols. And who will define God's Image? Even
within different conclaves and congregations of one religion
or the other, scholars, spiritual masters and pontiffs differ,
their difference ranging from the temperate to the intense,
from the unitary to the dualistic, from the monophysitic to
the polyphysitic. Their debates and dialogues weren't even
confined to the temple, the church or the monastery. The
fire set at the altar frequently spread to the brie underbrush
of the believers igniting hell and infernos that holocausted
the faithful and unfaithful. And that is always the way it is
whenever you restrict, divide and define, for flocks of the
excluded long to be included and many included yearn to
be excluded, with shadings in between eager to have it both
ways.

Most of us agree that God created the universe; thus the
universe inclusive of all animate and inanimate is the expression of God's prowess and power, reflecting His eternal Being, no gender, no species. All, repeating all, thus God's
image (manifestation) is the whole universe, the entire cosmos, every engendered creation. All are One: Oneness of
Being/Oneness of Perception (Seeing). This is the path to
end sorrow: universal sorrow, collective sorrow, personal
sorrow.

The biblical notion that God created man in his own image is not universally shared by other beliefs and religions. And, I often wonder whether conferring on man the image of God justifies bestowing on God the image of man? And, the image, the essence, the nature of God; are they all One and the same? God's attributes are manifest; God's Essence is nonmanifest, hidden, undisclosed. On the nature of God, religions differ. Even within the Christian faith the nature of God and Jesus still evokes lively, often contentious dialectics and debates, not to mention the many historical confrontations, bloody wars and wanton executions. Armageddon previews, ghastly rehearsals.

The image of God shall not be restrictive, it is omnimorphic, inclusive of all creations. God the Compassionate has created them all; therefore, He must love them all.

In God's image! What about the Fall? The Fall from grace, the sins, guilt and shame? Is it the pristine, primal image of man at the time of first creation before contamination and tarnish? The original nature being pure, benevolent and loving? Man's image and doings over the millennia isn't God's image. For sure.

What about man's dominion over all the earth and the other creatures? Dominion involves the exercise of power. In the exercise of power, there are the kind and the cruel, the gentle and the brute, the responsible and the reckless, the sensitive and the unfeeling, shepherds, executioners, stewards, robbers, trustees and plunderers. Choose. And your choice will bring about joy or sorrow, order or havoc, life or death. Choose. In reality, the provident and the compassionate have no choice—better put—transcend the choice; they see clearly the full spectrum and without procrastination, prejudice or pretense, they act. Their actions come out right. While the clock claims the hour and the day, we all reap the fruits of our actions. And, in the orchard we cultivated, bitter and malicious fruits are plenteous.

Quoting Genesis again, "and fill the earth and subdue it." Misunderstood or beguiled by many as a commandment, a divine permit to be licentious and unrestrained in relationships with other creatures. In this context, the word "subdue" is crucial. Using language, a word comes to signify several meanings and connotations. Choice of meaning depends on situation and circumstance, but is primarily the product of one's own interpretation, prefixed ideas, needs, wants, intentions and conditioning. Consulting *Webster's New Twentieth Century Dictionary* Unabridged Second Edition, the word "subdue" has eight meanings: (1) to conquer; (2) to tame; to make submissive as by training; as to subdue a stubborn child; (3) to reduce to mildness; to repress; as to subdue the temper or passions; (4) to overcome by persuasion or other mild means; as to subdue opposition by argument or entreaties; (5) to captivate, as by charms; (6) to make less intense or less harsh; to soften; (7) to destroy the force of; to lower; as medicines subdue a fever; (8) to till or cultivate. You may choose to conquer, tame or train; to reduce to mildness, subdue by entreaties, captivate, or charm; to soften, destroy the force of, till or cultivate. It is all within the palm of your hand: A whole array, a bouquet of dispositions.

And one must ask: Superiority or supremacy should it transcend morality? Morality. Oh, morality. Such a loaded word, charged, weighted on certain sides, so as to yield to temptation, collectively established tenets and designs. A priorly-asserted stratagem, historically worked out to ambush the meek, the daring and the different. Off the ornate snare I go, on to the egalitarian latitude of compassion. No ambiguity, no contrivance, no rites of passage, for the gate is gateless and everyone is a prince. Let me rephrase my interrogatory: Superiority or supremacy should it transcend compassion? The rationalists of ancient Greece, principally Plato and his disciple Aristotle, made things worse. The Platonic school of thought glorified intellect and the power of reason, placing it above all other human attributes. In the process, the physical side of human nature was disjoined from the whole, degraded as vile and corrupt. In Plato's opinion, the hallmark of human intelligence is knowing abstract rules and applying them to information. He believed that principles of mathematics are capable of organizing and streamlining a chaotic world. Astute observations on the workings of the human mind, artificial intelligence and brain research clearly demonstrate that reasoning and solving problems—considered by many to be human attributes—are not necessarily superior to or more reliable than knowing through seeing, hearing and remembering, tools we share with animals. Immanuel Kant, the eminent German philosopher who had strong influence on Einstein, reiterated what seers have been saying all along, for thousands of years, that the mind does not give us undifferentiated, uninterpreted knowledge of the world, but consistently instills bias, altering "what is" from its special point of view. Aware and knowing ourselves as we really are; conscious of the inherent limitations of our faculties tames our pride, makes us humble and compassionate. Seeing, observing and perceiving the limitless circle rather than remaining constrained to a particular pie at an imagined boundary. From his special point of view, Aristotle visualized the natural world order as an intellectual hierarchy, arranged in strata one upon another, humans perched on the very top with animals and plants at lowly levels, depending on their reasoning abilities; each created to toil, labor and satisfy the gastronomic appetites of the utilitarian doctrine of higher-ups. "In his metaphysics, Aristotle defended the princple of contradiction, condemining the doctrine of 'All things are one' as absurd."* Trapped in the mire of logic's induction and deduction, he stretched out the pecking order to include hu-

---

*Fadali, M., *Coping and Beyond: A Surgeon's Reflections on Science, Art and a Life Worth Living*. DeVorss & Co., p. 23.

manity condoning the despicable Grecian slave trade. In the order of rank, those considered savage and barbarous had lesser intellect; hence they were created to serve those on the higher rungs of the ladder of rationalism.

Aristotle's view of the Universe was erroneous. He considered the earth to be the center of a finite Universe. Copernicus published his treatise in 1543, giving life to the much older concept of ancient Egyptians, Greeks, Indians and Arabs that earth revolves around its star, the sun, not vice versa. Aristotle's geocentric, anthropocentric view of the Universe was a foible. Copernicus died before he had to face the grim fate of Giordano Bruno (?1548–1600), who stipulated the same opinions as Copernicus, further advocating that the Universe is infinite and our solar system is not the center of the cosmos inferring that many such systems might exist, some inhabited. Refusing to recant these heretical views, he was condemned by the Church to be burned at the stake. Ten years later Galileo reiterated the Copernican heliocentric theme. The Roman Inquisiton incarcerated him to be later released after he was obliged to recant. The influential Dominican, St. Thomas Aquinas (1225–75) espoused the Neoplatonist Aristotelian philosophy blending it into Christian theology. On animal rights Aquinas wrote, "God's purpose in recommending kind treatment of brute creation is to dispose men to pity and tenderness towards one another." Thus, according to him, humankind has no moral duty toward animals. Animals have no rights, but if it serves our own interest, then we ought to grant them a modicum of rights, be courteous and proffer kind sentiments to them. Outrageous! Egotistic! Isn't this exactly what most of us are guided by in dealing with one another? Mental schemes shape and dictate one's behavior. A scheme such as this one is defective and distorted. The bloody, savage medieval Inquisition was launched by Pope Innocent III on the heels of the publication of Thomas Aquinas's 12 volume *Summa*

Theologiae, and Pope Gregory IX subsequently assigned most of the task of the Inquisition to Aquinas's Dominican order of friars. A search and destroy mission to eradicate heresy, generally defined as any view or practice that denied or asserted the opposite of the Thomist view of human supremacy over the rest of creation. Millions perished. For alleged witchcraft, approximately three-quarters of a million individuals were tortured and burned by the Inquisition.

In the mid-19th century Pope Pius IX refused to permit the founding of a society for the prevention of Cruelty to Animals in Rome. Wherefore? According to the pontiff, it is a theological lapse to assume that humans have a moral duty toward animals. He assembled the First Vatican Council which in 1870 defined the dogma of his infallibility. Along with John XXIII and Pius XII, Pius IX were the only three popes who have been made saints in the last 900 years! The fourth apparently will be Pope Paul IV. Enrolled among the saints, Pope Pius IX is in heaven and capable of interceding for sinners. The concepts and teachings of Thomas Aquinas helped justify and propagate wanton cruelty that fell upon animals and nature. Plato, Aristotle, Aquinas and others to follow, chiefly Francis Bacon and René Descartes thought that animals have no intrinsic value; they are merely means to human ends, their relationship with humans is utilitarian based on how much worth they are to man's goals and wants.

Actually Plato and Aristotle were wrong on many counts:

1. As always has been the case: intellect is more likely to make errors than the senses are. Scientific knowledge and computer technology have reaffirmed the obvious; even Francis Bacon cautioned, ''For let men please themselves as they will in admiring and almost adoring the human mind, this is certain: that an uneven mirror distorts the rays of objects according to its own

figure and section, so the mind, when it receives impressions of objects through the senses, cannot be trusted to report them truly, but in forming its notions mixes up its own nature with the nature of things."* More than 750 years ago Ibn al-Arabi (1165–1240) the foremost Sufi seer wrote, "There are six things which perceive: hearing, sight, smell, touch, taste, and reason. Each of them—except reason—perceives things incontrovertibly. They are never mistaken in the things which normally become related to them. A group of rational thinkers have erred on this point by attributing error to sensation. That is not the case; the error belongs only to that which passes judgment."**

2. Thinking is shaped by the information fed into the brain. Information and knowledge are not one and the same. Mistaking information for knowledge, we act on the basis of incomplete knowledge. All actions founded on incomplete knowledge are inclined and deficient. To affirm this, one need not go very far. Look around, witness outcomes and results.

3. The human brain is not a logic machine, it is a knowledge medium impregnated, frequently inundated, with information items. Logic being the science of correct reasoning.

4. For logic to be exercised, it needs a system of perfect information. To be perfect, information must be complete. And, better admit it: we do not have complete information about almost anything: the humming bird, the rat, bats, dolphins, galaxies, what have you. As

---

*Francis Bacon, "The Great Instauration" (1620), in Jeremy Campbell, *The Improbable Machine*, New York: Simon & Schuster Inc., 1989, p. 123.
**Ibn-al Arabi, translated and quoted from "The Futuhat al-Makkkiya" by William C. Chittick, *The Sufi Path of Knowledge*, Albany, NY: State University of New York Press, 1989, p. 160.

time goes on, what we have taken for absolute, undeniable facts, prove to have holes and serious flaws. Modern physics shook the foundations of Newtonian physics and recently, Stephen Hawking and others have pointed to certain weaknesses and deficiencies in the hallowed relativity theory of Einstein. In Hawking's "black holes" Einstein's theories and premises are undergoing critical cross-examination.

5. Astute observations and a plethora of research in cognitive psychology clearly show that Homo sapiens is logic only at the superficial levels; at the core, deep down there, biased, prepossessed and illogical. Our routine daily reasoning is primarily dictated by what we know, how it is stacked in memory and what triggers it. Common sense is not a road map, not even a charted labyrinth; it is a boisterous, illusive terrain, defying logic.

Francis Bacon (1561–1626), father of the empirical method of science, recommended "torturing nature out of its secrets." One of his egotistical statements: "Man, if we look for final causes, may be regarded as the center of the world, insomuch that if man were taken away from the world, the rest would seem to be all astray, without aim or purpose."*

Mr. Bacon, I beg and dare to differ with you. From what I have seen, heard and read, it is man who has led the rest of the world astray, not the other way around.

Then came the prince, the most influential, haughty, prepossessed, self-assertive and biased. Pompous, René Descartes got entrapped by the intricate web of thought which interprets the world according to its own climate and terrain. He regarded animals as complex machines, like clocks, capa-

---

*Quoted in Thomas, K., *Man and the Natural World: Changing Attitudes in England, 1500–1800*, London: Allen Lane, 1983, pp. 17–22.

ble of automatic functions, incapable of conscious thought or sensation, soulless automata, mindless, they don't even suffer. Wow! What an indictment! Sore and sour, ill-conceived. Wrong. A Descartes seventeenth century contemporary eyewitness described how they "administered beatings to dogs with perfect indifference and made fun of those that pitied the creatures as if they felt pain. They said the animals were clocks, that the cries they emitted when struck were only the noise of a little spring that had been touched, but that the whole body was without feeling. They nailed poor animals up on boards by their four paws to vivisect them and see the circulation of blood which was a great subject of conversation."*

They inflict pain, yet deny their victims the right to experience, feel or tell of their own pain. It isn't mere cruelty. Ignorance and arrogance added shield cruelty from being recognized for what it is by its perpetrator. While they agonize at every pore, while they writhe with extreme anguish, the tormentors, the torturers and executioners enact their grisly exhibit. Reruns, morbid, dreadful. Of pride, ascendency and ultimate supremacy, spiritual authority has satiated the vainglorious ego of man. Of fragmentary information, idle thought and shadowy tenets, earthly authority —the icons and high priests of science—has glutted the slumbering, conditioned mind of man. Mesmerized by the two powerful magnets, Homo sapiens lost universal intelligence, innate innocence, primal beauty and natural freedom. Left with the lesser attributes: skill, linear conventional knowledge and a notoriously self-destructive selfishness, it wanders astray, aimlessly aiming, obsessed by its wants, overlooking its needs.

---

*Quoted in Singer, P., *Animal Liberation*, Northants: Thorson's Publishers, 1984, pp. 217–223.

Not all Christian theologians preached giving man a free reign over the universe. St. Francis of Assisi (?1181–1226) urged love of nature and a compassionate relationship with other creatures. But the brute carried the day. Still does.

The publication in 1859 of *The Origin of Species* by Charles Darwin dealt a severe blow to literal doctrines asserting that all creations, plants and animals alike are custom-designed to fulfill specific missions in life with humans specifically built to rule and govern the universe. According to the Darwin/Wallace theory of evolution, plants, animals—humans included—are not custom-designed, but all in the same boat, propelled by the inexorable force of natural selection, essentially a cumulative process, fundamentally nonrandom. Despite opposition by the religious establishment, the theory is being taught worldwide, though it has its own shortcomings. The Anglican Church attempted an amiable synthesis by maintaining that the biblical account of creation was allegorical, and God had set the relentless wheels of evolution in motion.

Islam acknowledged animal rights and emphasized human's responsibility for their welfare. The Koran, Islam's Holy Book, stipulated that all species of animals are "communities" like the human community, their rights are intrinsic, innate, not subject to the human community's needs, wants and designs. "There is not an animal on earth, nor a bird that flies on its wings—but they are communities like you" (Koran 6:38).

According to the Koran, animals' consciousness transcends mere instinct and intuition. Animals have a cognizance of the creator and pay their obeisance to Him through worship and adoration, "seest thou not that it is Allah whose praises are celebrated, by all beings in the heavens and on earth, and by the birds with extended wings. Each one knows its own mode of prayer and psalm. And Allah

(God) is aware of what they do" (Koran 24:41). "The seven heavens and the earth and all things therein, declare His glory. There is not a thing but celebrates His praise, and yet ye mankind! ye understand not, how do they declare His glory" (Koran 17:44). When the deluge came, Noah was issued the following divine command, "Load in the Ark two of *all species*, one male and one female of each pair" (Koran 11:40). No species is dispensable. Not one. All must be saved. ALL.

The Creator provides for them all, "There is no moving creature on earth, but Allah provides for its sustenance" (Koran 11:6). Yet, we, the created deprive them of their natural habitat, raid their self-sustaining communities, blowing away nest and retreat, bulldozing den and lair, ransacking hive, hill and burrow. We drain their drinking water, rob them of nutriments they have prepared for their unweaned pupas and broods, denature their food supply with fertilizers, pesticides and nuclear waste. Mindless and heartless we kill them for their furs and feathers, tusks and musks, horns and hoofs, fat and flesh, gonads and marrow. Ignorant and arrogant we vivisect them in order to learn about ourselves, to discover cures for diseases self-induced and handicaps self-imposed. We plunder and redesign their genes in pursuit of longevity, remedy, good looks; prowess and profit. As our kids would say, "Give me a break!" "And the earth, He has assigned to all living creatures" (Koran 55:10).

The prophet Mohammad's compassion, actions and instructions on the treatment of animals are illustrated in the Hadith. In Islamic jurisprudence, the Hadith is an explanatory appendix of Koranic law based on the deeds and pronouncements of the prophet. "The Holy Prophet told of a prostitute who, on a hot summer day, saw a thirsty dog hovering around a well, lolling its tongue. She lowered her socks down the well and watered the dog. Allah forgave all her sins (for this one act of kindness)."* "The Holy Prophet narrated a vision in which he saw a woman being chastized after death because she had confined a cat during her life on earth without feeding and watering it, or even letting it free so that it could feed itself." (Muslim). "The Holy Prophet forbade the beating, or the branding of animals. Once he saw a donkey branded on its face, and said: 'May God condemn the one who branded it.' " (Muslim). "The Holy Prophet passed a camel who was so emaciated that his back had shrunk to his belly, and said: 'Fear God in these beasts, ride them in good health and free them from work while they are still in good health' " (Abu Dawud). Caging animals is against the tradition of Islam, "The Holy Prophet stated: 'It is a great sin for man to imprison those animals which are in his power.' " (Muslim).

On vivisection, the prophet expressed condemnation and there are numerous Islamic proclamations forbidding vivisection. Ibn Umar reported the Holy Prophet as having condemned those who mutilate any part of an animal's body while it is alive. (Ahmad and other authorities). "The Holy Prophet forbade the setting up of animals to fight each other." (Tirmidhi and Abu Dawud).

In past times, human sacrifices were ordained and enacted. Animal sacrifice is preislamic. It was the prophet Abraham who instituted animal sacrifice to take the place of human sacrifice. Abraham was commanded by God to substitute a ram for his son as a sacrifice to the deity, a sacred ritual of surrender and atonement. The prophets of Israel continued the practice which was also incorporated in Islam, but many fail or decline to interpret the command within the context of the Koran which states, "It is not their meat, nor their blood that reaches Allah. It is your piety that reaches

---

*Source: Muslim, one of the two most respected sources of Hadith; the other is Bukhari.

Him'' (Koran 22:37). In Christian theology, the essence of the Passion and death of Jesus is to bring about the reconciliation of God to humankind. The symbolism is quite obvious.

The Jewish and Muslim practice of slaughtering animals rather than stunning them was installed for health reasons. To me, whether you stun them, gas them or slaughter them, it is killing them; thus abstaining from eating animals or consuming their products, I have elected and strictly adhered to. Actually, humans separated from the chimpanzee seven million years ago. For most of that period, we were vegetarians. Only lately, we invented hunting and trapping tools, discovered fire and used it domestically; thus our feasting on other animals was intiated. Lusting after their flesh and products followed. Lascivious orgies to gratify unrestrained appetites. Yet, as we indicated in Chapter One, page 5, our genes and the chimpanzee's genes differ by a mere 1.5 percent and our metabolic pathways fail to handle our meat-centered banquet. Their dismal failure is manifested as ''diseases of civilization'' such as heart attacks, strokes, cancer, diabetes, arthritis, and obesity. All largely preventable by a vegetarian diet that does not include eggs and dairy products. Matter of fact, being a vegetarian helps to save the plant kingdom. The primary consumer of plants being the livestock we raise, ordained to doom in the course—I should say courses—of our obscene gluttonous feasts, the three-plus daily meals. The principal reason for erasing the rain forests is to provide vast pastures to supply flesh for flesh-eaters, the human carnivores who have forgotten or failed to acknowledge that humankind is omnivorous, thus perfectly capable of subsisting on animal or vegetable nourishment. You don't have to eat 'em to survive or thrive. Without 'em one's survival and thrivingness are better served. Much better indeed. A vegetarian diet generally consists of portions or products of a plant rather than the whole. This does not apply though to certain food articles such as potatoes and lettuce; of eating the latter some vegetarians refrain. Guided by the compassion of your own heart and the wisdom of your own mind, you draw the line; you can do it all in one stride or in several steps; the enterprise is omnipresent, heart's beat sets the pace, passion plays the music, spins the verse. Proceed. Move. We will revisit this admittedly-complex issue later on in the book.

In the holy books, there exists an unmistakable trail clearly depicting animals' good nature, charm, spontaneity, and affectionate sincerity. Candor and absence of malice are a hallmark of animal behavior. Their love is meritless, limitless and true; their pain is real, expressed and experienced; their feelings are truthfully displayed, without guile or pretense. Animals, especially mammals, manifest individuality, perceive time and space; many recognize color, tunes and are keen at differentiating different things; able to make judgment on what they encounter, they recognize dangers on the road and think of ways to avoid them. They express likes and dislikes, loyalty, respect, hunger, tenderness, joy and sorrow. Many endanger their own lives for the sake of the rest of the pack with which they live; skillfully they communicate with one another, with others as well; they have memory and expectations. They court, propose and hold out inducements. Their hearts ache and rejoice. Holy books are replete with stories, allegories and anecdotes illustrating these qualities: It was the crow who bore witness to the very first homicide committed by Homo sapiens, Cain's murder of Abel, his younger brother. And, it was the crow who showed Cain how to entomb his slain brother. It was the hoopoe (Al Houdhoud) who was prophet Solomon's messenger and trusted ambassador to her Majesty, the Queen of Sheba. In exalted roles, in sublime characters, ants, spiders, cows, birds, cattle, dogs, and elephants paraded the transcendental platform of religions. Ahmad Bahgat wrote an elegant, heart-caressing treatise entitled, *Stories of Animals in the Koran.** Correspondent and concordant narrative is portrayed in the other sacred books. And, you don't have to take tales and memoirs literally. Essence is in the echo; beyond the word, on the further side of the books. And, all that counts is essence. Before the word, there was essence. In advance of the primordial soup, there was essence, then came rivers of existence, rolling, cascading. Before thought, ahead of perception, and conception, transcending all is essence. Reach out, your feeling dendrites will take you there. As for those who put their faith into the literal interpretation of holy books, do not exclude those tales and anecdotes in praise of animals. Contemplate the wonderwork of those amazing creations. Stand in awe. Bow!

J. Krishnamurti, the renowned 20th century spiritual teacher, wrote, "But if you have no relationship with the living things on this earth you may lose whatever relationship you have with humanity, with human beings. . . . If we could establish a deep abiding relationship with nature we would never kill an animal for our appetite, we would never harm, vivisect, a monkey, a dog, a guinea pig for our benefit. We would find other ways to heal our wounds, heal our bodies. But the healing of the mind is something totally different. That healing gradually takes place if you are with nature, with that orange on the tree and the blade of grass that pushes through the cement, and the hills covered, hidden, by the clouds. . . . Man has killed millions of whales and is still killing them. All that we derive from their slaughter can be had through other means. But apparently man loves to kill things, the fleeting deer, the marvelous gazelle and the great elephant. We love to kill each other. The killing of other human beings has never stopped throughout

*Bahgat, A., *Stories of Animals in the Koran*. Beirut & Cairo: Dar Al Shrouk, 1983. Translated into German and French; English translation in progress.

the history of man's life on this earth. If we could, and we must, establish a deep, long abiding relationship with nature, with the actual trees, the bushes, the flowers, the grass, and the fast moving clouds, then we would never slaughter another human being for any reason, whatsoever. Organized murder is war, and though we demonstrate against a particular war, the nuclear, or any other kind of war, we have never demonstrated against war. We have never said that to kill another human being is the greatest sin on earth.''*

In Hinduism there is animal sacrifice in the ritual. The Vedas give great weight to sacrificial rituals condoning sacrifice of goats, horses, oxen, and other animals. The sacrificial animal is not looked upon as an animal per se, it is a symbol of the higher powers for whom the sacrificial rites stand. In the Vedas and other scriptures as well, there are passages alluding to the origination of the universe through sacrifice of a cosmic animal such as a cow or a horse or a cosmic purusa signifying man. On rare and very special occasions even a human being is sacrificed. But this has now practically become a thing of the past such as the old religious practice of Sati, whereby the widow is burned on the funeral pyre of her husband. In India, though, the killing of a cow is considered sin and it is difficult to determine when the cow has become sacred, the most sacred animal. Its dung so pure that in addition to using it for fuel and as disinfectant, floors, walls, and temples are washed with it. Most scholars believe that the emphasis on non-violence which was later incorporated in Hindu culture is the influence of Jainism and Buddhism.**

---

*Krishnamurti, J. (1895–1986), *Krishnamurti to Himself: His Last Journal*. San Francisco, Harper and Row, 1987, pp. 9–10.
**My primary source for the Hindu perspective is: Lal, B.K., ''Hindu Perspectives on the Use of Animals in Science.'' In *Animal Sacrifices*, ed. by Tom Regan. Philadelphia: Temple University Press, 1986, pp. 199–212.

In Jainism, "All beings are fond of life; they like pleasure and hate pain, shun destruction and like to live, they long to live, to all, life is dear." (Jain Sutras, 1.2.3.) Jains, though a small minority in India—comprising less than one percent of the total, have actively protested against the Hindu practice of animal sacrifice; and, primarily because of their efforts, vegetarianism is common in India and animal sacrifice has been banned in most Indian states. Jainism attributes a thinking faculty (manas) to animals. The religious creed originated in India approximately 900 years or so B.C., predating Buddhism, which also started in India approximately 540 B.C. Both Jainism and Buddhism prohibit animal sacrifice. Gautama Buddha left his palace, bearing witness to the immense suffering of humans and animals alike. He would not turn back. Never returned to his palace. The "Awakened" Gautama sought enlightenment and proclaimed the precepts of Buddhism. The first Buddhist precept being: Not to harm or injure living things. According to the first of the six perfections (paramita), the Buddhist is not allowed to give anything that may be used to inflict injury on other living beings "nor is he allowed to give poisons, weapons, intoxicating liquors, and nets for the capture of animals." "He should not bestow upon others a piece of land on which the animals may be hunted or killed."* Emperor Asoka of India (ca. 274–232 B.C.) converted from Hinduism to Buddhism and legislated laws to protect animals. In earnest, he tried to propagate the Buddhist dharma (principles of right life). In the eighth year of his reign he renounced military conquest and embraced what he referred to as "conquest by dharma." Vegetarianism is not a Buddhist precept but some sects stress the virtue of not eating meat. My research leads

---

*The Bodhisattva Doctrine quoted by C. Christopher in "Noninjury to Animals: Jainism and Buddhist Perspectives." In *Animal Sacrifices*, ed. by Tom Regan. Philadelphia: Temple University Press, 1986, pp. 213–235.

me to conclude that Jainism is totally opposed to animal experimentation while Buddhism frowns on it, almost against it.

Classical Confucianism and Neo-Confucianism: Lun Yu, Confucian analects are considered the primary source of the teachings of Confucius (511–479 B.C.). Neo-Confucianism refers to Confucianism that started during the reign of the Sung Dynasty (960–1126) and thrives until our time. Both did not reject meat-eating and did not ban animal sacrifices, culpability being restricted to the methods utilized to capture them. Mencius (372–289 B.C.) is regarded as the principal interpreter of Confucius and his views are held in great esteem by the Neo-Confucian movement. Neo-Confucians consider humans superior to animals. Chu Hsi, viewed as the orthodox Neo-Confucian interpreter of the relationship of humans and animals, taught that the nature of humans and the nature of things are similar in certain aspects, different in some others. Many researchers regard the basic Confucian moral vision as follows: The man of moral insight cannot bear to see the suffering of others, and it is their inability to bear the suffering of others that culminates in moral action. And, if this perception can be developed, then according to the Neo-Confucians, man will experience a true sense of "one body" with all things.*

I end this chapter by saying that animals have intrinsic value in themselves. We have not created them, they have a right to life, they do not exist for our usage and consumption. The utilitarian concept applied to animate and inanimate creations is faulty and has gone very far, destroying others, ourselves as well, for we are an integral part of others, though most do not see it this way. Once we begin

---

*A primary reference on the Confucian perspective is: Taylor, R.L., "Of Animals and Man: The Confucian Perspective." In *Animal Sacrifices*. Ed. Tom Regan. Philadelphia: Temple University Press, 1986, pp. 237–263.

categorizing, unity of being is ruptured. Set in a relation of opposition, the different factions will continue to wrestle and fight. What comes out of it all: abuser and abused, oppressor and oppressed, tormentor and tormented. And, sorrow will never end. Animal sacrifices and human sacrifices go hand in hand. Inseparable. Witness wars, domestic violence, meat-eating, vivisection and all forms of human and animal subjugation and servitude. The root is one, the solution is one. And the religious better be concerned with sanctification of life rather than salvation of souls and recreation by grace rather than justification by faith, for in so doing both soul and faith will be redeemed. And, no compulsion in religion.

EIGHT MILLION PETS IN ANIMAL SHELTERS CAN THEY BE SAVED? THEY MUST

Mostly lost or abandoned, their numbers are staggering, estimated to be at least eight million annually across the United States—pets, mostly dogs and cats. Opportunisitic, rationalistic to a degree, in a certain sense pragmatic, vivisectionists argue that since the dejected, forlorn pets are destined for annihilation, why not make use of them in the marketplace, the animal lab? This logic is faulty. Abandoning pets is awfully wrong. Immoral. Using them for animal experimentation is terribly erroneous. Appalling. Immoral and appalling horrify the stoutest heart. Two wrongs do not make a right. Error does not rectify error. Abuse and mutilation do not redeem nor rescue the condemned. What about abandoned kids? In some countries they are being used as donors of organs for transplantation to recipients in rich countries or for those who can afford the hefty price in their own native land. Useless, why not make use of them? Advocates and participants will tell you. The same logic and justification go for the undercover practice of coercing or seducing poor and homeless people; good for nothing, so let us sell their organs to the wealthy. Shall we set aside this analogy and focus on the very problem itself? The evidence has proven beyond doubt that animal experimentation misleads and does not promote the human condition, nor solves our problems; matter of fact, it harms human health, thwarts longevity and hinders well-being. Besides, its very nature is evil, cruel, filthy.

As we view and contemplate the universe, the utilitarian concept must be discarded. It is dangerous, corrupting, ultimately self-defeating. All along it has debased our being, brutalized life's ground substance and anguished the web of existence. When it comes to abandoned or lost pets, the right inquiry is: How can we save them, not how can we use them? Posing the right question, the right answer emerges. Tendering absurd, self-serving, perverted questions summons answers of the same mettle. So, what to do with the millions of abandoned and lost animals overpopulating animal shelters? The vast majority of these animals will not reunite with their previous owners (I should say their human family rather than owners) and are unlikely to find a new home. So, after a short waiting period in the so-called animal shelter, they are done with and tossed in trash bins. Our animal shelters are not places of refuge; they do not afford protection, nor render safety.

Neutering pets to control their population is a must. It is an individual and societal responsibility. In some parts of the country, certain community organizations, even some city municipalities, encourage such a policy and issue coupons to have pets spayed at discount prices; many veterinarians accept those vouchers in full payment.

As a physician, time and again I have witnessed the good that pets bestow on people. A cure for loneliness, a remedy for stress and anxiety, a stimulus for the recumbent to get up, feed and care for the pet; taking the dog for a walk is a good exercise for both. All helpful activities. But, to my dismay, I have seen dogs waiting all day to be taken for a walk, and it is not unknown for "owners" to forget to feed their pets; other forms of neglect and maltreatment occasionally arise. And I am not hereby endorsing the use of animals to fulfill humans' needs and desires. A mutually loving relationship is what I have in mind.

The real tragedy is: the whole calamitous sequence of events is preventable, shouldn't have existed in the first place. Still remediable and controllable, though. Its fountainhead is our fragmented, self-centered mind which condones and rationalizes using the lesser, exploiting the weaker, ruining the different, all while deliriously adoring how tall we have become, all while sowing our deadly refuse, nuclear, chemical and otherwsie in the valley, the meadow, the mountain, the air, the river and the vast seas. In natural law, self-centered is self-destructive. Evidence is all around; past tells the story; present lives it. Befriending earth, befriending us it will; loving others, loving us they will. Earth's shepherds and caretakers, where are you?

CHAPTER TEN

Mere Strength Frequently Dooms

Survival of the fittest not the strongest. Let's take charge of ourselves, stay healthy, live better and longer. Fitness is survival's magic tool. Mere strength frequently dooms.

Charles Darwin stated, "Animals, whom we have made our slaves, we do not like to consider our equal." In Darwinian terms, survival is for the fittest, it isn't always for the strongest. Species most fit to survive are those who adapt and maintain harmony with their environment; interacting rather than wrathfully acting and vehemently reacting. Interdependency is key.

Throughout man's wanderings and forays in the minefields and forbidding lands he has created and nurtured, he has been notoriously adept at shifting the blame and distancing himself from the ugly, deadly exploits committed by his own brutal hands. Tools of guile, implements of disguise researchers refer to as "distancing devices." Hyam Maccoby's book, *The Sacred Executioner** is an insightful expedition into the darkest, shady terrain of cunning and artifice. Human sacrifices, animal sacrifices, environmental treach-

---

*Maccoby, H., *The Sacred Executioner*, London: Thames & Hudson, 1982.

ery, breach of life's covenant, yet, through manufactured "distancing devices," the bipedal monster slips away with a cleared conscience, mind disburdened, mind desensitized. Separated and distanced from guilt, yet, ever haunted, ever ambushed between opposing mirrors, eventually lost to the darkness behind the mirror. Basically, the four pernicious devices are: detachment, concealment, misrepresentation and shifting the blame. All sound familiar! Too familiar, isn't it? How much can the wounded bosom of humanity bear? When will the mask of cold indifference drop? Will they sigh? Will their eyes blink? Can they weep?

Detachment: is a time honored—dishonored I should say, or at least hope for—embroidery designed by humans to distance themselves from the opponents and would-be-victims. Enemies are ridiculed, demonized, dehumanized, depersonalized in order to extinguish them with abandon; forsaken in the lump. Distancing ourselves from animals we kill or inflict agony upon is a routine stratagem, daily practiced. And it gets the job done. "Today for breakfast, I ate some fried bread and sausage. Both the sausage and the lard that the bread was fried in came from a pig that I used to know as a dear little piglet. Once that stage was over, to save my conscience from conflict, I meticulously avoided any further acquaintance with that pig," Nobel Prize Laureate, ethiologist, Konrad Lorenz wrote in his book, *Man Meets Dog.**

Aristotle's concept of a natural hierarchy with Homo sapiens seated at the pinnacle of all existence disdainfully looking down on the other species helped foster and enforce detachment. Réne Descartes's notion that animals are mere machines, devoid of feelings, incapable of experiencing pain or enduring suffering strengthened Aristotle's concept and

---

*Lorenz, K., *Man Meets Dog*. London: Methuen, 1954, p. vii.

legitimized the abuse and mutilation of live animals. Detachment by way of barrier, impenetrable, absolute. Animal sacrifices to placate and appease God, thus shifting the blame for killing from the actual killer to a supernatural entity. Blame shifted, distance traveled, barrier erected, one's own responsibility for one's own action is abrogated. Nullified. Cheers! And, the walls keep rising.

Animal farming is a relatively recent distancing scheme keeping animal flesh eaters from seeing, hearing, touching or even smelling a cow, bull, ox, steer, heifer or calf. Same goes for pig, fowl and fish farming. Just taste is permitted. Relish! Enjoy! Enjoy! In those farms—relatively recently called plants—day-to-day care of animals is done by machines. Keepers are separated from livestock; distanced.

Detachment can be selective. Many hunters, whale killers, and animal experimenters keep pets and display remarkable affection toward them. Is it to absolve oneself from guilt? Is it to prove to others that their reservoir of kindness is not empty? Or is it merely cold-blooded detachment? Their inner milieu is selective and compartmentalized. Pathetic.

Concealment: Another invention the guileful executioner summons consciously and unconsiously to create a void between himself and his victims. Physical concealment seems convenient and opportune. A play perfected. Slaughterhouses and animal laboratories are usually kept out of sight to tone down public outcry. Out of sight, out of mind, goes the refrain. Recently, we have heard, read or seen on television examples of mass outrage in Britain, France and some other countries, when some of their ethnic minorities ritually slaughtered one or more animals. Stone throwers were largely ruddy, plethoric and chubby; meat-eaters, I bet you. Many of them had bacon and eggs for breakfast, a hotdog, hamburger or a barbecued chicken leg for lunch, and were eagerly fancying a roasted leg of lamb or a zesty, bloody prime rib for their dinner. The pig, the steer, the cow, the lamb and the chicken were concealed, locked out of the perimeter of their discovery—short-sighted. See naught, hear naught, feel naught. Loathsome! They know, though! Shift the blame, and go for it; after the righteous tumult, comes the feast, a culinary orgy in waiting.

In large-scale production facilities, animals are crammed together in the thousands, numbered, branded, tagged, ear-notched and tattooed. Impersonalized, deindividualized, inanimated. Concealment through numbers.

Verbal concealment is another gadget. "Slaughterhouse" is referred to as a meat plant or a meat factory. "Pork," "veal," "beef" and the "harvest of the seas," rather than pig-meat, calf-meat, bull-meat, or fish and shellfish. Same euphemisms are vocabulary in the profane temples of vivisection. An incarcerated, spurned, bruised dog or cat is referred to as a model. The word punishment is banned, "aversive stimulus" instead; many do not even know what aversive means; pain and harshness disguised some. "Deprivation" not starvation, "phonate" not scream, "agitate," not struggle. And the most fradulent of all, "sacrifice," which stands for the ultimte sin: Killing. Varnish guilt, polish up cruelty, brush ugliness, pomp the ungainly. A cursory look won't behold nor rend the flimsiest of veils; close attention does.

Misrepresentation: Another wicked scheme of distancing victim from villain. Mercilessly practiced, willfully deployed when contending with our perceived enemies and in dealing with other species. An irresponsible fictitious example is our decharacterization of the wolf as a pitiless, malevolent, sly beast bent on kidnapping little girls and snatching limbs off people's torsos. Far from it, the wolf has a gentle disposition and an affectionate demeanor. The ancestor of man's best friend, the dog, can't be all that bad. We have cultivated the vast wilderness and erased the lush forest; the wolf's natural prey dwindled or vanished altogether. Driven by the survival instinct, the wolf had no option but to feed on domestic livestock. We sack and plunder and the wolf eats humble pie. Dirty dog, filthy swine are but some other unconscionable misrepresentations. Dogs are not dirty, and pigs are not filthy. In stinking piggeries we jam pigs in overcrowded, overheated rotten quarters; they sleep on metal or concrete floors awash with their excrement, and when feeding time comes, it is a frenzy. We have transmitted to them some of our bad manners and we did not spare them the abominable ways by which we treat a large contingent of our fellow humans.

Shifting the Blame: ''Once a year at the great Bouphonia or bull-slaying feast in Athens, a bull symbolizing Zeus, the father of the gods, used to be sacrificed on the temple altar. Immediately after the sacrifice, the priests who were responsible for the killing fled from the altar in mock panic, crying out a formula that absolved them of guilt. Later a trial was held in which the blame for slaying was attributed to the sacrificial knife, which having been found guilty, was then punished by being destroyed.''* In ancient civilizations sacrifices were believed essential to satiate the voracious appetites of supernatural forces and capricious gods that mandate the destiny of man. Legends portrayed sacrificial animals favorably disposed, voluntarily tendering their hearts, livers and lives for immolation. Shaking the head was the beleagured animal's signature of consent to its own extinction. Devious spirits. Sly, with habitual inkling to hurt and deceive. Between the devil and the deep, animals along

---

*Serpell, J., *In the Company of Animals*. Oxford, U.K.: Basil Blackwell, 1988, pp. 163–164. Serpell's reference for the bull-slaying feast is Maccoby, H., *The Sacred Executioner*.

with others endure the excruciating alternatives. Who is the devil? Ponder the story. Discern the legend. Misbegotten? Nay! The Tempter of man and woman is home-made. A native. And, I am not advocating for the devil; I am merely pointing where the demon resides.

The mock panic scene of Athens still plays, in theaters, worldwide. A throw of dice, avalanche of misfortune, plots, designs, supreme sacrifice of life, while it bubbles and throbs in others. The scent of prey isn't lost to the human hounds. And, on curtain call, all invoke God's name and blight the blasphemous devil. Roles interplayed between cast and spectators. Action is real!

Homo sapiens is a predatory species. The most dangerous of all, "Frontiersmen acutely sense that they battled wild country not only for personal survival but in the name of nation, race, and God. Civilizing the New World meant enlightening darkness, ordering chaos, and changing evil into good. In the morality play of westward expansion, wilderness was the villain, and the pioneer, as hero, relished its destruction. The transformation of wilderness into civilization was the reward for his sacrifices, the definition of his achievement, and the source of his pride."* Wolf bounty laws were enacted, and within a century, the magnificent, gentle being was virtually eradicated from the U.S. The North American bison or buffalo suffered the worst fate of all; mass murder in the first degree. Between 1850 and 1880, no less than 75 million bisons were massacred by brutish murderers euphemistically called hunters; disposed to kill; delighted in inflicting pain. The North American bison is sacred to the American Indians but in pursuit of Manifest Destiny, the settlers from Europe were determined to do away with anything that stood in their ordained path. Their

---

*Nash, R., *Wilderness and the American Mind*, New Haven: Yale University Press, 1982, p. 24.

ferment of desire was sweat, blood and tears. Through an-
them and oath, the intoxicating brew passed on to their
brood. And, deliriously they march on, Manifest Destiny
tempestuously reaching beyond the Western Hemisphere
menacing the other hemisphere as well. A morality play of
global dimension. On the wings of technology—its invisible
planes, illusive submarines, not so smart bombs, misguided
missiles, laser spears and nuclear incinerators—neofrontiers-
men ride. In his momentous work, *The Triumph of the West*,
historian John Roberts concluded that along with confidence
and self-centeredness, the West has ''passed to the rest of
the world a bias towards self-destruction.''*

Cruelty to animals is a state of mind surreptitiously
shaping relationships with others, humans, other species,
environment; the entire spectrum. Consciously and uncon-
sciously its tort and foment favor the different and ones
viewed as inferior. Doctor Michael Giannelli wrote, ''In my
judgment, vivisection is a grave social evil because it fosters
the worst in human nature; our arrogance, aggressiveness,
selfishness, callousness, and our sense of alienation from the
rest of nature. It is all the more problematic because it is
promoted by the intellectual elite, professional scientists pursuing their craft for the presumed welfare of humanity,
leaders who are in a position to shape the society of our children and the world of their children's children. Even if one
does not accept this assessment, it is clear that the essence
of ethical behavior is a system of self-restraints in the pursuit of one's perceived self-interests.''

''We must remind ourselves that scientific progress is not
invariably human progress. The continued expansion of human knowledge at the cost of human character is a pathetic
trade-off which, if continued, will eventually destroy the

---

*Roberts, J., *The Triumph of the West*, London: BBC Publications, 1985, 427.

civilization we glorify. At present, there appears to be decreasing prospects that humanity will ever make peace with itself. Many say, this being the case, how can you expect humanity ever to make peace with the rest of the animal kingdom? There is hope for animal liberation because it also represents human liberation, freeing ourselves from the ages-old dependence on animal sacrifice. There is also hope for animal liberation because other animals do not represent the threat to us which we do to each other. As a species, with good reason, we distrust and fear each other far more than we distrust and fear other animals. The only animal which threatens to push us away from the dinner table is man himself. Perhaps, just perhaps, there is hope for facilitating the peace process by first de-escalating our aggression against the other, less warlike, species which inhabit this fragile earth."*

Unless we retrain our mind not to bear the suffering of others, we are doomed. A true sense of one body with all things is the only worthy prescription to provide remedy for the primary threat to life—including our own—which is ourselves. Superiority of humans over all others is a myth, reared and ripened in our fictitious ego. And, superiority does not necessarily mean exploitation, plundering and savagery, and, must not do away with responsibility, grace, decency and compassion.

---

*Giannelli, M.A., "Three Blind Mice, See How They Run: A Critique of Behavioral Research with Animals." In *Advances in Animal Welfare Science*, ed. M.W. Fox & L.D. Mickley. Washington, D.C.: The Humane Society of the United States, 1985, p. 159.

EATING: MORAL ISSUES OF RELEVANCE WITH A WORD ON THE HEALTH, SOCIAL AND ECOLOGIC PROBLEMS LINKED TO A MEAT-CENTERED DIET*

It would be hypocritical, ill advised, and cowardly on my part not to mention the slaughter-vivisection of sort-of seven billion animals yearly in the U.S. for food. After all, animals have rights, the most basic being their right to life. And here is how the vicious circle goes: we raise animals for food—animal farming being the most sinister of all—this entails killing wild animals to protect domestic animals and erasing forests to give them grazing land, then billions of the domestic animals are killed to eat, then many millions of animals of different species are killed to eat, then many millions of animals of different species are killed in the course of experimentation to find cures for diseases primarily caused by consuming animals and their products, and millions of people are harmed as a result of such unscientific, hocus, bogus research. It is a pity! The Surgeon General had stated that sixty-eight percent (68%) of all diseases in the U.S. are diet related, but he failed to confess that his government—our government—subsidizes the meat and dairy industries with our tax dollars, not to mention the hefty bounty for growing tobacco. The cost of health care will continue to escalate as long as we focus on search for cures and seek amelioration rather than setting prevention as our primary goal. As of this moment, preventive medicine is largely ignored.

Eating animals causes illness and death; experimenting on

---

*Mostly quoted, with permission, from: Fadali, M. *Coping and Beyond: A Surgeon's Reflections on Science, Art and Medicine and a Life Worth Living*, Marina del Rey, CA: DeVorss & Company, Publishers, 1990, pp. 134–140.

animals also causes illness and death, yet 95 percent of people eat meat and a majority approve vivisection. I am puzzled how a manifest danger such as this escapes attention by many, is ignored by a whole lot, forgotten by most. Despair not, become an activist. Mission not impossible. Matter of fact, for most of our existence on earth we were vegetarians. Meat eating followed the invention of hunting tools and the discovery of fire—both were late developments. Please revisit this important fact in Chapter One, page 5 and Chapter Nine, page 200.

STOPPING FOR REFLECTION: EATING POSES A MORAL DILEMMA OF SORTS. I see the bird eating the worm and devouring the grain, the spider entangling and feasting on the fly, the lizard gulping the moth, the cat chasing and ravenously eating the mouse, big fish feeding on small fish, and certain plants attracting and trapping insects. I see humans consuming animals and plants to satisfy hunger or satiate appetite. A mutual eating society, isn't it? As though our very survival couldn't survive without terminating another's survival. Painfully true! In my humble opinion: this is the "Universal Sin"—a mandate of necessity! Or so it seems.

Obligatory and innate; then does it constitute a sin? If it qualifies as one, is it pardonable? Can we atone and make up for it? Is there an alternative? Is there a way out of this transgression short of inanition and death? Starving one's self to death is a prima facie act of suicide. We're told that suicide is a form of homicide, strictly forbidden, a sin—ungodly, unpardonable.

At every crossroad, the human conscience is being tested and challenged. The crowd—caring less—looks the other way, bypassing the burden of personal responsibility. Certain religions command the faithful to abstain from what is meat. Distressed by animals' suffering and the guilt of taking their lives, many opt for vegetarianism. Some ethicists reach the same decision through philosophical thinking and diligent soul-searching.

Vegetarianism has clear benefits and gain. Many fail to notice that the primary consumers of plants are the domestic animals raised for the sole purpose of human consumption. The rain forest in Central and South America is being erased at an alarming rate of 6 acres per minute (27 million acres every year) to furnish pasture for cattle that will be shipped north to feed the hungry tigers of the U.S. Eighty percent of corn grown in the U.S. goes to feed livestock. Vegetarianism not only spares animal lives, but also greatly lessens the magnitude of harm and destruction incurred on the plant kingdom through the bad habit of meat-eating. A road of lesser harm to abate, ". . . the primordial guilt of life that lives on life."* For humans to survive and thrive meat-eating is not only unnecessary but also an impediment. An obstacle; unseen, unrecognized, denied. At this juncture certain research data on the heatlh, social, and ecologic problems linked to a meat-centered diet ought to be told.**

WORLD HUNGER

Number of humans who will starve to death
this year: 60,000,000
Number of humans who could be adequately fed
by grain saved if Americans reduced their intake
of meat by 10%: 60,000,000
Pounds of grain and soybeans needed to produce
1 pound of feedlot beef: 16

---

*Campbell, J. *The Way of the Animal Powers*, London: Times Books, 1984, pp. 53–56.
**The following data are from John Robbins, *Diet for a New America*. Walpole, N.H.: Stillpoint Publishing, 1987.

Percentage of corn grown in United States eaten by
human beings: 20
Percentage of corn grown in United States eaten by
livestock: 80
Pounds of potatoes that can be grown on 1 acre of land: 2000
Pounds of beef that can be produced on 1 acre of land: 165

HEALTH CARE

Most common cause of death in U.S.: heart attack
Risk of death from heart attack by average
American man: 50%
Risk of heart attack by average American
pure vegetarian man: 4%
Increased risk of breast cancer for women who
eat meat daily compared to pure
vegetarian women: 5 times higher
Increased risk of prostate cancer for men who consume
meat and dairy products compared to pure
vegetarian men: 3.6 times higher
Increased risk of colon cancer for people who
eat meat and dairy products as compared to pure
vegetarians: 10 times higher

NATURAL RESOURCES:
CONSUMPTION AND POLLUTION

More than half the water consumed in the U.S. is for:
livestock production
Water needed to produce 1 pound of wheat: 25 gallons
Water needed to produce 1 pound of meat: 2500 gallons
Percentage of water pollution due to organic waste
from U.S. humans: 10
Percentage of water pollution due to organic waste
from U.S. livestock: 90

CONSUMPTION OF PESTICIDES

Source of pesticide residues in the U.S. diet:
meat—55%; dairy products—23%; vegetables—6%;
fruits—4%; grains—1%
Percentage of male college students sterile in 1950: 0.5
Percentage of male college students sterile in 1978: 25
Principal reason for sterility and sperm count reduction
in U.S. males: pesticide residues
Percentage of U.S. mother's milk containing
dangerous levels of DDT: 99

RAIN FOREST AND SPECIES SURVIVAL

Driving force behind the 6 acre/minute destruction
of the life supporting, oxygen-producing
Central American rain forests: creation of
grazing land to grow beef for export
Current rate of species extinction due to
destruction of Central American rain forests
and related habitats: 1000/year
Amount of trees spared per year by each individual
who switches to a pure vegetarian diet: 1 acre

POLITICAL TENSIONS

Barrels of oil imported daily by U.S.: 6,800,000
Principal reason for U.S. military intervention in the
Persian Gulf: dependence on foreign oil
Amount of imported oil U.S. needs to meet present demand
if 10% of population became fully vegetarian: none

For our very existence, bodily nutrition is, of course, imperative. No matter which way we choose to look at it, our existence is not a free enterprise, it is not self-sustaining; it subsists at a tremendous expense: that of other lives. Maintained at a dreadfully high cost, our life must have a purpose, a meaning, some value, a certain promise. Wouldn't it be a shame and a pity to waste it? Certainly ungrateful and unworthy to use it to harm, diminish, or destroy one's own self or others. In life's covenant, "others" reads: humans, animals, plants, and environment. In the well-guarded covenant, all are included as one. Such a wasteful destructive course of action stares humankind right in the face as cowardly and abominable. A moral sin. Live, let live; love, let love; gain, let gain; heal, let heal; wander, let wander; be free, let be free; worship, let worship. Our personal pursuit of happiness will be consummated only by giving happiness to others. Matter of fact, happiness is a state of mind, a state of heart, a state of being; unpursued, it dawns and blooms where the air, the core is clear.

Every action has a reaction that bounces back on the doer. Pain and grief repay pain and grief; kindness and caring return as kindness and caring. The form of the rendering might differ, but in effect and essence it matches the original act that triggered it in the first place. The happy tune is ours, if we play it. This is the way to make amends and expiate for the sin of taking other lives to nurture our own. It is a "Deed of Trust." Without our carrying our part, the Universal Sin will not wash out, will stick to us, tarnishing our psyche and clouding our intellect.

The "mark of Cain" is acquired, individual, delible, curable. Human wrongdoings ever yearn to be righted. If this basic understanding is affirmed by realization and crowned by fulfilling our obligation in the "Deed of Trust," the habit of eating is then purified of its moral repercussions. Living to eat is reprehensible, immoral and wasteful. It is unkind, unhealthy, ultimately self-destructive.

Laying no claim to originality, and without condescending or patronizing, I'd like to share with you some practical guidelines. Following them, I found solution to several of my own serious trepidations about eating. A measure of comfort and internal serenity followed, better digestion as well.

1. I have adhered to a vegan vegetarian diet.
2. For the sake of our senses of taste and smell, food ought to be palatable and agreeable; this helps its digestion. Modest, yes; exquisite and consummate, no; otherwise it is likely to stimulate desire for more and may unleash and open up appetite, thereby inviting gluttony. Gluttony perverts the human lot, corrupting body and spirit. Every religion and moral creed has opposed gluttony.
3. "Eat only when hungry, and never feed to the full."* "We should take only enough for our needs; otherwise the plants and the animals and the worms we have killed would turn against us and cause us disease and misfortune."** They do. They do.
4. Show gratitude for the favor received and always remember the hungry and the starving. This is the moral of invoking or quietly contemplating a blessing before and after eating; a gesture of gratitude and remembrance. A tradition of grace traceable to societies past and present.

---

*Hadith of the Prophet Muhammad.
**Castaneda, C., *A Separate Reality*, New York: Pocket Books, 1971, p. 226.

5. Back to earth I go when I die to feed worms and vege-
   tation. Ending in a compost heap is a just proposition.
   Recycled.
6. Given life against overwhelming odds and for sustenance, other creatures—plant or animal—pay dearly.
   Life must be precious and meant to be worthy and
   deserving of some praise. I will therefore honor the
   high promise, preserve life, and pay my dues to the
   captive creditors whose parts and sum perished so I can
   survive.

In conclusion, the very word vivisection is its own condemnation. It is a grave error to view it as necessary or imperative. Given this frame of mind, we will rationalize and
justify the detestable, cruel practice. Vivisection is not imperative, is absolutely unnecessary; it is a choice, a bad one,
unscientific, utterly malicious. Vivisection is wretched fraud,
counterproductive and damaging to human health and well-
being. Eating meat is not necessary, it is a choice, unhealthy,
harming our health and shortening our life span; whether
we know it or not, it debases our psyche. War is not necessary, is not imperative, is not inevitable; it is a fatal disease;
the only cure is prevention. And, the primary obstacle to
preventing war is our belief that war is not preventable.
Wars never stop war, a war always leads to another war.
Wars are mass murders of humans, animals, plant, environment and planet, spheres and realms beyond as well. You
do not justify what is just. Vivisection, meat-eating and war
being injust, must be justified; being unnecessary, they have
to be rationalized. Whatever seemingly good one attains
through evil, cruel means cannot be good; eventually it will
harm and degrade. Always does. Look back, discern the
tearful anguished history of humankind. The verdict is,

"You cannot do evil that good may result."* **ANIMAL EXPERIMENTATION IS A HARVEST OF SHAME**. And, the primary threat to our life is ourselves.

Finally, animal experimentation and animal exploitation in all forms have no scientific proof, no religious basis, no philosophical merit, no ethical vindication and no health reason; therefore they must be stopped. NOW. Persevere upright. The task is not impossible.

---

*The American Antivivisection Society, 1883–Present.

Index

About the Author

Dr. Moneim Fadali is a poet, writer, philosopher and surgeon. His book *Coping and Beyond*, published by DeVorss & Company, is due for a third printing—a book of essays and observations profound in their contemplation of life and living. A prescription to end sorrow and move beyond where the air is clear, where fear, stress and doubt come to an end and one's awesome potential is realized.

Dr. Fadali is also a renowned published poet. *Love, Passion & Solitude* is a selection of his poems. His poetry transcends convention and restriction of every sort, it encompasses life in all its manifestations. His verse is forceful and daring, yet rich and refined. A heroic passion for world peace, justice, freedom and preservation of the cosmic web is the vital force of his poetry. Oneness of being/Oneness of seeing is the essence of his verse.

Dr. Fadali is a frequent guest on radio and television where his poetry is read and his insightful, progressive views on the environment and the human condition are sought. His television series, ''Total Transformation. The Unconditioned Mind'' is shown on television nationwide. It probes the intimate and the nitty gritty pointing to the fountainhead of right seeing, unending energy, compassion, joy and inner peace.

A practicing Vascular and Cardiothoracic surgeon, Dr. Fadali has published extensively in his surgical specialty and is a member of several of the most distinguished national and international medical and surgical societies.